JavaScript
Programming

for the absolute beginner

THE FUN WAY TO LEARN PROGRAMMING

PRIMA TECH

ANDY HARRIS

A Division of Prima Publishing

Prima Publishing and colophon are registered trademarks of Prima Communications, Inc. PRIMA TECH is a trademark of Prima Communications, Inc., Roseville, California 95661.

Microsoft, Windows, Windows NT, and Internet Explorer are trademarks or registered trademarks of Microsoft Corporation in the U.S. and other countries.

Netscape, Netscape Navigator, and JavaScript are trademarks or registered trademarks of Netscape Communications Corporation in the U.S. and other countries.

All other trademarks are the property of their respective owners.

Important: Prima Publishing cannot provide software support. Please contact the appropriate software manufacturer's technical support line or Web site for assistance.

Prima Publishing and the author have attempted throughout this book to distinguish proprietary trademarks from descriptive terms by following the capitalization style used by the manufacturer.

Information contained in this book has been obtained by Prima Publishing from sources believed to be reliable. However, because of the possibility of human or mechanical error by our sources, Prima Publishing, or others, the Publisher does not guarantee the accuracy, adequacy, or completeness of any information and is not responsible for any errors or omissions or the results obtained from use of such information. Readers should be particularly aware of the fact that the Internet is an ever-changing entity. Some facts might have changed since this book went to press.

ISBN: 0-7615-3410-5

Library of Congress Catalog Card Number: 2001086

Printed in the United States of America

01 02 03 04 05 BB 10 9 8 7 6 5 4 3 2 1

Publisher:
Stacy L. Hiquet

Associate Marketing Manager:
Heather Buzzingham

Managing Editor:
Sandy Doell

Series Editor:
Andy Harris

Acquisitions Editor:
Melody Layne

Project Editors:
Melody Layne and Kim Spilker

Technical Reviewer:
Michael Vine

Copy Editor:
Andrew Saff

Proofreader:
Lorraine Gunter

Interior Layout:
Danielle Foster

Cover Design:
Prima Design Team

Indexer:
Sharon Hilgenberg

Send Us Your Comments:

To comment on this book or any other PRIMA TECH title, visit our reader response page on the Web at **http://www.prima-tech.com/comments**.

How to Order:

For information on quantity discounts, contact the publisher: Prima Publishing, P.O. Box 1260BK, Rocklin, CA 95677-1260; (916) 787-7000. On your letterhead, include information concerning the intended use of the books and the number of books you want to purchase.

To Heather, Elizabeth, and Matthew

Acknowledgments

I first acknowledge Him from whom all flows.

Thank you again, Heather, for listening to the keyboard clicking all those late nights. You are the sun and the stars to me.

Thanks to Melody Layne for being a good friend and a good editor (at the same time, even!).

Thank you to Kim Spilker for your encouragement on this project, and to all the folks at Prima for being nice people to work with.

A special thank you to Andy Saff for copyediting. If this book makes any sense at all, it's because of you.

Thank you also to Michael Vine for technical editing. I appreciate your efforts very much.

A very special thank you goes to Scott Porter for his excellent game development library. His clever programming and selfless generosity make JavaScript game programming much more accessible than it has ever been before.

I especially want to thank all my students, present and past. You have taught me so much more than I was ever able to teach you.

About the Author

Andy Harris began his teaching career as a high school special education teacher. During that time, he taught himself enough computing to do part-time computer consulting and database work. He began teaching computing at the university level in the late 1980s as a part-time job. Since 1995, he has been a full-time lecturer in the Computer Science Department of Indiana University/Purdue University—Indianapolis. He manages the IUPUI Streaming Media Lab for the department and teaches classes in several programming languages. His main interests are Java, Visual Basic, Perl, JavaScript/dynamic HTML, virtual reality, programming on portable devices, and streaming media.

Contents at a Glance

Contents

CHAPTER 4

The Basic Mad Lib Program and Object-Based Programming   63

CHAPTER 5

Advanced Mad Lib: Using the Other Form Elements   89

CHAPTER 6

Petals around the Rose: Dynamic Output   115

CHAPTER

Image Swapping and Lookup Tables: The Basketball Game   139

CHAPTER

Dynamic HTML: The Stealth Submarine   171

CHAPTER

Sprite Animation: The Racer   203

Using Other gameLib Features: The Dogfight Game 235

Cookies and the Mouse: The Jigsaw Puzzle 261

The Game Creation Process: The Brick Game 289

Introduction

I n the early 1980s, my brother and I bought a computer. My mom thought we were crazy, because it didn't do anything. She was right. There was very little software available. We spent many nights typing in programs (usually games). They almost never worked when we finished typing, so we always had to look back carefully over the code. Eventually, we were able to fix typographical mistakes and make the games work. Then, we found ourselves changing the code, so we could improve the games that we were typing in.

That was a great way to learn how to program. We were working in a simple language without too many confusing options. We were writing games that were even more fun to play because we had crafted them ourselves. We were able to combine both logical thinking and our creative drives. Game programming was especially rewarding, because the results were programs that we actually wanted to use. Our skills improved because game programming provided lots of challenges. We later found that the skills we learned by developing games were very useful in more "serious" applications as well.

Today it would appear difficult to learn programming in the same way that my brother and I did. Computers are much more complicated than that old machine that my brother and I used. Programming languages have become far more complex at the same time, and the programmer's toolbox of compilers, integrated environments, and debuggers seems expensive, complex, and forbidding to somebody who just wants to get started and play around a little bit.

Still, it is possible to learn to program in almost the same way. A new crop of beginner-friendly languages is popping up. Specifically, the JavaScript language has emerged as a new programming language perfect for beginners who want to see what programming is all about, and who want to learn in a non-threatening but real way. JavaScript is embedded into popular Web browsers, so the language costs nothing. It is available on nearly every major type of computer system. The language has a reasonably straightforward syntax that provides beginners a gentle introduction to some important modern concepts, such as object-oriented and event-based programming. It also does not have so many features that it requires a degree in computer science to understand.

The purpose of this book is to teach you the main principles of programming. You will learn the major concepts used in most programming languages, and you will apply them specifically in JavaScript. I will use the context of game programming to teach the concepts, but you will find that you can use the techniques for purposes far beyond game programming. If you already know JavaScript, you will still probably find some new ideas in the descriptions of game programming. If you have already done some game development, you might be surprised at the things that you can do with

JavaScript. If both areas are new to you, you're going to have a great time exploring some new things.

Although you will probably not immediately make a million dollars selling computer games, I think that you will find this book's approach reasonably friendly. You will also see that you can easily apply the skills that you learn more generally to other kinds of more serious programming. Besides, the addition of a game to a Web site can drastically improve its popularity, making game programming a very practical skill for any Webmaster.

I am not presuming that you have any programming experience at all. I do expect that you are comfortable with HTML and that you know how to build Web pages with a plain text editor. You should have a good text editor, a graphics editor, and a sound editor. The CD-ROM that accompanies this book has examples of all these programs. Of course, you will need access to a computer that can run these programs. You will be running your programs in a Web browser, so you should have access to recent versions of Netscape Navigator (4.0+) and Internet Explorer (5.0+). Some of the later examples in this book take advantage of gameLib, a special programming library. The CD-ROM includes a copy of gameLib. Finally, if you wish to publish your pages, you will need access to some sort of Web server.

How to Use This Book

To learn how to program a computer, you must acquire a complex progression of skills. If you have never done any programming at all, you will probably find it easiest to go through the chapters in order. Of course, if you are already an experienced programmer, it might not be necessary to do any more than skim the earliest chapters. In either case, programming is not a skill you can learn by reading. You'll have to write programs to learn. This book has been designed to make the process reasonably painless.

Each chapter begins with a complete program that demonstrates some key ideas for the chapter. Then, you'll look at a series of smaller programs that illustrate each of the major points of the chapter. Finally, you'll put these concepts together to build the larger program that you saw at the opening of the chapter. You'll be able to see important ideas in simple, straightforward code, and you'll also see more involved programs that put multiple ideas together. All the programs are short enough that you can type them in yourself (which is a great way to look closely at code), but they are also available on the CD-ROM.

Throughout the book, I'll throw in a few other tidbits, notably the following:

These are good ideas that experienced programmers like to pass on.

There are a few areas where it's easy to make a mistake. I'll point them out to you as you go.

IN THE REAL WORLD

As you examine the games in this book, I'll show you how the concepts are used for purposes beyond game development.

TRICK These will suggest techniques and shortcuts that will make your life as a programmer easier.

EXERCISES

At the end of each chapter, I'll suggest some programs that you can write with the skills you've learned so far. This should help you start writing your own programs.

CHAPTER 1

Variables, Input, and Output

Programming is nothing more than controlling in a more direct way what you want your computer to do. You probably already use a computer in a number of ways, and you control it to some extent by the programs you use and the way that you use them. Still, without programming, you are always at the mercy of the programs designed by others. In this chapter, you will look at how you can begin to influence the computer's behavior. Specifically, you will:

- Examine how you can put code inside a HyperText Markup Language (HTML) page

- Use dialog boxes to interact with the user

- Learn how computers store data in variables

- Learn how to get data from the user

- Perform basic operations on data

The Project: Name Game

In Figure 1.1, a special box pops up in a normal Web page that asks the user for his or her name. Then, a series of other boxes pop up, asking for a last name and then finding other ways to manipulate the name.

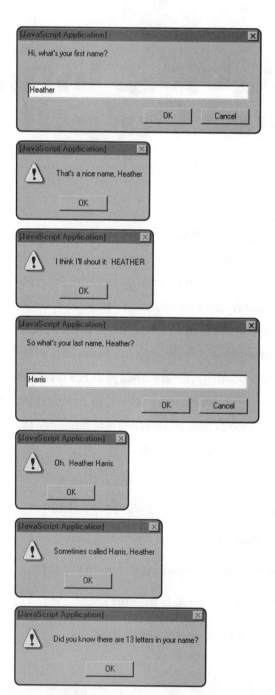

FIGURE 1.1

By the end of this chapter, you will be able to create this simple name game.

No game publishers will throw money at you after this effort, as the game itself is not exactly thrilling. However, even this mildly interesting game elevates your Web page far above the ordinary. Most Web pages do not enable the user to interact with them at all, so this page immediately stands out as something special, even though what it does is kind of pointless and silly. Don't underestimate the power of the Web page appearing to know your user. It can make the page seem much more personal to the visitor. You can add this functionality to any Web page you have, and your users will think you're really clever.

Adding Code to HTML

Web pages provide a rich background for programming. With the knowledge of HTML that you already have, you can generate pages that look pretty good. For example, you can control how text looks and add images. You might even have some experience with the finer-grained control of cascading style sheets. Still, plain HTML pages lack true interactivity. The only way that the user can really exert any control over the page is by clicking on links. This is interesting, but that fun takes the user only so far.

Creating the Hello, World! Application

It would be interesting to make the page a little more dynamic. Both of the major browsers, Netscape Navigator and Microsoft Internet Explorer, support JavaScript, a scripting language that is perfect for adding interactive features to a Web page. Take a look at the following snippet of code:

```
<html>
<script>
  //hello world
  //the classic first program
  alert("hello world");
</script>
</html>
```

If you save this code as a Web page, then load that page into a browser, it generates the screen shown in Figure 1.2.

This code snippet consists of normal (if very abbreviated) HTML, but it uses some features you might not have seen before. The `<script></script>` tag set specifies to the browser that any code between the tags is not written in HTML, but in a scripting language. Both the Netscape Navigator and Microsoft Internet Explorer browsers use JavaScript, their default language, unless you specify another language. (Technically, Microsoft Internet Explorer runs a variant called Jscript, but the code works the same as either JavaScript or Jscript.)

You can place script tags anywhere in an HTML document. All of the code between `<script>` and

> **IN THE REAL WORLD**
>
> Although users typically don't love things popping up and interrupting the flow of the program, alert boxes are useful for a number of reasons. First, they're very easy to program. Some of the more graceful ways of talking to the user require a little more effort. Second, they do succeed in getting the user's attention. Third, you will find them an important utility as you program. For example, you might often want the program to pause momentarily and send you a message about itself as you are testing it.

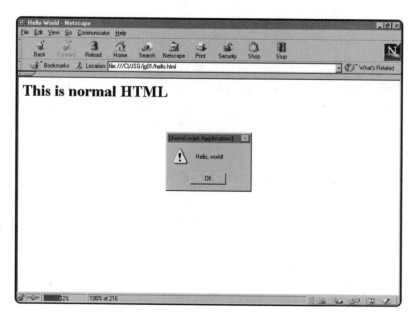

FIGURE 1.2

When the Web page
is loaded into the
browser, a special
box pops up.

</script> is written according to the rules of JavaScript. JavaScript is a different language than HTML, and its rules are different.

The // characters denote a comment. The interpreter ignores anything that follows on a line that begins with these characters. However, the information that programmers provide in comments is still critical. Comments are mainly for the benefit of the programmer. It's a great idea to add lots of comments to your programs, because good comments can make your code much easier to repair. This particular program has lots of comments. They explain what the program is intended to do. Such comments are always a good way to begin documenting your program. You'll look at some other useful places to put comments as the code becomes more complex later in this book.

Sending a Message to the User

Only one line of the code fragment does anything particularly interesting:

```
alert("hello world");
```

You use the alert statement to send a special kind of message. The message pops up in its own box, called a *dialog box*. The dialog box is pretty insistent. If you try to click on the page before you close the dialog box, it will ding at you with a sound, but it will refuse to do anything else. The box will not close, and the other programs on your desktop will not receive the focus. It will insist that you respond to it in some way before you go on to other things in the browser.

You might have noticed the semicolon character (;) at the end of the alert line. This character indicates the end of the alert statement. Most lines of JavaScript code end with the semicolon. The comments did not need a semicolon, because the compiler ignores them. You'll see some other places later where a semicolon is not needed at the end of a line, but for now it's fine simply to assume that most lines require this character at the end.

Using Variables

One of the most important aspects of programming to learn is how the computer uses data. *Data* is defined as the information that the computer collects and manipulates. In your first few programs, the data will be text, such as names or phrases. Later in this chapter, you will learn how to use other kinds of data, such as numbers. Programming languages use something called *variables* as a tool for managing data. In the next section, you will see how variables are used to store information.

Creating the Hello, Joe! Application

Take a look at the program shown in Figure 1.3. It shows an example of output with a new twist: This time, the computer generates a message already stored in the computer's memory.

This program's code looks like this:

```
<html>
<head>
<title>Hello Joe</title>
</head>

<body>
<h1>Hello, Joe</h1>
<script>
//hello Joe
//Demonstrate basic variable concepts
//Andy Harris, 09/00
var greeting;
greeting = "Hi there, Joe";
alert(greeting);
</script>
</body>
</html>
```

Essentially, this program stores the text "Hi there, Joe," then displays the message to the user as soon as the Web page is loaded into the browser. This program illustrates how the computer can store information for later retrieval. A special kind of element called a *variable* is the secret.

Computers essentially work with information. It's important to understand how computers store the information.

Think of it this way: If you carry a lunch to work or school, you probably don't just grab a handful of last night's leftovers and carry them around in your hands until lunchtime. Instead, you probably use some kind of container, such as a sack. You put the lunch in the container, which you then carry around until it's time to eat. You don't actually deal with the food until lunch, because it's easier to work with the container than the actual food (that is, you would rather carry the sack containing the food than carry the various items of your lunch individually). Variables fulfill a similar function for the computer. They hold information until the computer needs to work with it.

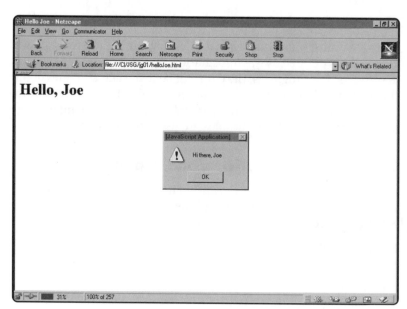

FIGURE 1.3

A greeting to Joe
pops up.

You'll learn a lot more about variables later. For now, you simply need to understand that whenever you want the computer to have some information, such as a user's name, a message, or a rate, you'll need to use a variable.

Using the var Statement

Every computer language provides some kind of support for variables. In JavaScript, programmers use the var statement to create a new variable. When you create a variable, you need to give it a name. This is just like putting labels on the food containers in your refrigerator. When you look at the label, you can see what is inside without having to open the container. Take another look at this statement, which occurs in the preceding Hello Joe program:

```
var greeting;
```

The term var indicates that the computer should create a variable. The word greeting is the name that I gave the variable. This line ends with a semicolon, as most lines do. After interpreting this line of code, the computer generates in memory a chunk of space named greeting. Thereafter, you can write code that writes new values to the memory chunk, and write code that reads the values from the chunk.

Guidelines for Naming Variables

Computer programmers get to name a lot of things. Experienced programmers have established a few naming conventions. You might want to keep these guidelines in mind:

Be careful about case. In many languages (including JavaScript), username, userName, and USERNAME are all completely different variable names.

Make names descriptive. You probably shouldn't use a name such as r or x, because later it will be hard to remember exactly what the variable is supposed to contain. Names such as taxRate or greeting will make your code much easier to follow.

Don't use spaces or punctuation. Most languages don't allow multiword variable names. Many programmers use capitalization (taxRate) or underscore characters (tax_rate) to make multiple word variable names easier to read. (I'll use the capitalization convention in this book.) Many of the punctuation characters have special meanings, so it's not a good idea to put these in a variable name.

Don't make your variable names so long that they are impossible to type correctly. Many programmers prefer variable names from 5 to 15 characters long.

Assigning a Value to a Variable

Take a look at this line from the Hello Joe program:

```
greeting = "Hi there, Joe";
```

Essentially, this line assigns the text "Hi there, Joe" to the variable `greeting`. Everything between the quotation marks is called a *string literal*. (Computer programmers love to give complicated names to simple ideas. Get used to it!) *String* is the term that computer programmers use for text, because computers handle text as a string of characters. *Literal* means that you are actually specifying the literal value `"Hi there, Joe"`.

The equals sign (=) indicates assignment. It might make more sense to read this statement as follows:

```
greeting gets the string literal "Hi there, Joe".
```

TRAP

It would not be exactly correct to say that `greeting` **equals** `"Hi there, Joe"`. **Equality is an entirely different issue, which I will deal with in the next chapter.**

Finally, the word `greeting` is the name of a variable that gets the string value `"Hi there, Joe"`.

If you want to give a variable a particular value, you can do so by using a similar assignment statement. Coding a variable assignment statement is like putting leftovers in a container.

Using the Contents of a Variable

You carry a lunch bag to keep all your food items neatly in one place. If you pull your lunch bag out of the refrigerator, you are in effect pulling out the entire lunch. In a similar way, you specify a variable's name to refer to a variable. Take another look at this line:

```
alert(greeting);
```

When the user runs this Web page, he or she does not see the term "greeting" pop up. Instead, he or she sees "Hi there, Joe," which is the content of the `greeting` variable. It doesn't matter what the value of `greeting` is, as long as it is some kind of text. This line of code can output any value stored in the variable `greeting`.

Getting Input from the User

In addition to sending information to the user, computers can also retrieve information from the user. This kind of exchange is called *input.*

Sometimes people get confused about whether something is input or output. For example, suppose that you are reading a text message on a computer screen. As you read the message, you input it to your brain; however, from the computer's perspective, that message is output to the screen. The convention in programming is that when you talk about either input or output, you are speaking from the point of view of the computer.

Creating the Hello User! Application

Take a look at this program, which illustrates a simple kind of input:

This time, the computer asks the user his or her name and uses that information in another statement.

Here's the code that made this happen:

```
<html>
<head>
<title>Hello User</title>
</head>

<body>
<h1>Hello, User</h1>
<script>
//hello user
//ask user for name
//Andy Harris, 09/00
var userName;
userName = prompt("What is your name?");
alert(userName);
</script>
</body>
</html>
```

This program has a variable, but this time a value embedded in the program does not determine the variable. Instead, the user gets an opportunity to enter a value into a special dialog box, and the program copies whatever the user types to the variable. Now that you can get values from the user, you can create programs that are much more flexible. For example, you can create a program that calls the user by name, even if you have no idea what that name will be when you write the program (see Figure 1.4).

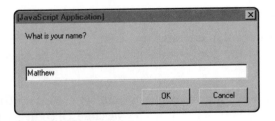

FIGURE 1.4

This program asks the user for his or her name, then returns that input in another dialog box.

Using the prompt Statement

The secret weapon that makes it possible to let the user enter data into a variable is the prompt statement. It is used in this line:

```
userName = prompt("What is your name?");
```

As you can see, the line starts out much like the assignment statement in the Joe program, but this time, the value that the program is sending to userName is not a literal value, but the result of some kind of operation.

The prompt statement causes a dialog box much like the alert box to pop up. This dialog box is different, however, because it not only sends a message to the user, it also provides a place for the user to type a response.

The primary purpose of a prompt statement is to get a value back. Every prompt statement includes some sort of variable, ready to catch the value.

Think of eating your lunch at a cafeteria. You have to get a tray to hold your lunch, but then you have some choices. You tell the person behind the counter what item of food you want, and he or she then places that selection on your tray. Much like a tray holds your food selection, your variable provides a place in which to input a value.

An input statement, such as the prompt statement you have seen in this example, is used when you are going to fill up a variable with the answer to some kind of question. In later chapters you will see some other forms of input.

The prompt statement calls up a dialog box that presents the user with a question and a place to type an answer. It is almost always used as part of an assignment statement to assign the user's answer to some variable.

TRICK

When you generate a prompt dialog box, you need to determine the question that you want to ask, and you also need to have a variable ready in which to store the answer.

Saying Hi to the User

Now that you have a variable that contains the user's name, it is a reasonably simple task to return that value to the user. The following line does the trick:

```
alert(userName);
```

Because `userName` is not in quotes, the computer interprets it as a variable name and displays to the user the contents of the `userName` variable. Of course, the contents provide a pretty limited greeting, but you'll fix that in the next section. If you did put quotes around userName, the actual value "userName" is what the user would see, rather than the value associated with the userName variable.

Building More Complicated Text

It would be much nicer if the greeting could be friendlier. If the user's name is Susan, maybe the program should say "Hi, Susan!!" Figure 1.5 shows the enhanced program's output.

Creating the Concatenation Program

To create the screen shown in Figure 1.5, you must combine string literals (the "Hi," part and the "!!" part) with the value of a variable. Specifically, you will create `userName` and give it a value just as you did in the previous example. The only difference is the output. The earlier program's only output was the value of the variable, without any other text around it. In this program, you'll figure out a way to include the value of a variable inside other text.

Concatenating Strings

Creating this program requires a process that is another instance in which programmers have given a simple idea a complicated name:

String Concatenation: The combination of two or more text strings. They can be string literals or string variables (or the values of string expressions, which you will learn about later). In JavaScript, you concatenate strings by using the plus sign (+).

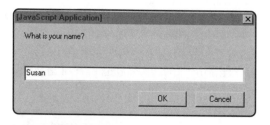

FIGURE 1.5

Now the greeting integrates the user's name into another string.

String concatenation is a lot simpler than it sounds. Here's how the code looks:

```
<html>
<head>
<title>concatenation</title>
</head>

<body>
<h1>Concatenation</h1>
<script>
//concatenation
//ask user for name
//Andy Harris, 09/00
var userName;
var greeting;
userName = prompt("What is your name?");
greeting = "Hi, " + userName + "!!";
alert(greeting);
</script>
</body>
</html>
```

 TRICK If you are testing a page and you want to see it again after it's finished, just click the browser's Refresh button.

Joining Variables and Literals

The concatenation program uses two variables: userName is meant to hold the user's name, and greeting contains the text that the program will output to the user. The program obtains userName from the user through a prompt statement, just as in the previous program. This is the only new line:

```
greeting = "Hi, " + userName + "!!";
```

By now you should recognize that the program assigns a value to greeting. To form that value, the program concatenates the string literal "Hi," with the contents of the userName variable and joins another string literal ("!!") to the end of that one. You can use string concatenation to make really long, complex text strings. The great thing is that the user won't ever know that you did any manipulations. He or she will just see that the program used his or her name.

Working with Numbers

Computers are pretty good at working with text values. They are even better at working with numbers. Deep inside the computer, text and numbers are stored the same way, but programmers use many schemes and conventions to encode data. (If you really want the details, consult your neighborhood computer scientist.) JavaScript is pretty good at hiding this complexity from users and even programmers. It generally guesses whether you are talking about numbers or text. Still, sometimes you'll need to do some special tricks to help JavaScript guess correctly.

Creating the Adder Application

The program shown in Figure 1.6 provides a handy service. It looks at the cost of a meal, adds a 15 percent tip, and calculates the total bill.

This program does its work with variables, as you can see from the code:

```html
<html>
<head>
<title>Adder</title>
</head>

<body>
<h1>The Adder</h1>
<script>
//Adder
//Demonstrates how a computer does math

var meal = 22.50;
var tip = meal * .15;
var total = meal + tip;
alert ("the meal is $" + meal);
alert ("the tip is $" + tip);
alert ("Total bill: $" + total);
</script>
</body>
</html>
```

FIGURE 1.6

The Adder program displays the cost of a meal, the tip amount, and the total cost.

Using Numeric Variables

The Adder program has variables, but their values are not text. In this program, you want the computer to do mathematical computations on the data, so the variables must be numeric. Notice that there are no quotation marks around the value 22.50.

Also, you can combine the var statement with an assignment statement, so the variable immediately has some kind of value.

The following line calculates the value of the variable tip by multiplying meal by .15 (or 15 percent):

```
var tip = meal * .15;
```

In computing, the asterisk (*) usually means multiplication.

The following line creates the total variable:

```
var total = meal + tip;
```

This statement adds up the contents of meal and tip, then places the sum in the total variable.

The alert statements work just as you would expect. The program automatically converts all the numbers to text when generating the output.

Diagnosing the Bad Adder Application

This program would be more useful if it allowed the user to enter the cost of the meal. Look at this variant of the Adder code:

```
<html>
<head>
<title>BadAdd</title>
</head>

<body>
<h1>The BadAdd</h1>
<script>
//BadAdd
//Demonstrates a potential pitfall
//Andy Harris, 09/00

var meal;
var tip = meal * .15;
var total = meal + tip;

//get the cost of the meal from the user
```

```
meal = prompt("How much was the meal?");

var tip = meal * .15;
var total = meal + tip;

alert ("the meal is $" + meal);
alert ("the tip is $" + tip);
alert ("Total bill: $" + total);
</script>
</body>
</html>
```

The program looks reasonable, but the results, as shown in Figure 1.7, are definitely not what you wanted. Something went wrong somewhere. Before reading on, see whether you can figure out the problem.

Interpreting Numbers and Text

Here's what happened: The `prompt` statement returns a string value. The computer stores this value as text, which is no problem until you try to do math on it. In the following line, meal gets a string value, because that's what the `prompt` statement returns:

```
meal = prompt("How much was the meal?");
```

The following line multiplies the value of `meal` by .15:

```
var tip = meal * .15;
```

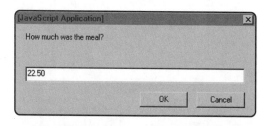

FIGURE 1.7

This time the user gets to enter the cost of the meal, but the program's calculations are incorrect.

It doesn't make sense to multiply by a string value, so JavaScript simply converts the string `meal` to a number, and the multiplication works. The next line is where the problems begin:

```
var total = meal + tip;
```

The computer still interprets `meal` as a string and `tip` as a number. The problem is the plus sign (+), which is an operator that tells the computer to add up numbers. If the plus sign is used in the context of string variables, it will concatenate the strings. In this statement, the plus sign has a number on one side and a string on the other, so it confuses the computer. In this case, the computer decides to treat both values as strings and concatenate them. So, the result of concatenating "22.50" and "3.375" is another string value, "22.503.375".

Creating the Good Adder Application

JavaScript provides a number of ways to solve this problem, but the easiest is the `eval()` function. Take a look at this version of the code:

```html
<html>
<head>
<title>GoodAdd</title>
</head>

<body>
<h1>The GoodAdd</h1>
<script>
//GoodAdd
//Demonstrates eval function
//Andy Harris, 09/00

var meal;

//get the cost of the meal from the user
meal = prompt("How much was the meal?");

//convert the value to a number
meal = eval(meal);

var tip = meal * .15;
var total = meal + tip;

alert ("the meal is $" + meal);
alert ("the tip is $" + tip);
alert ("Total bill: $" + total);
</script>
</body>
</html>
```

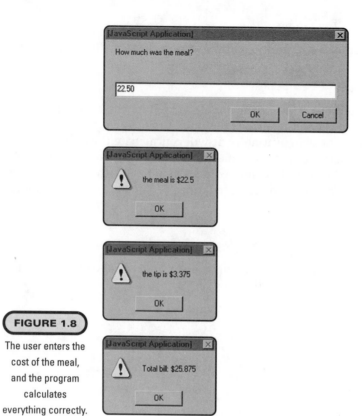

FIGURE 1.8

The user enters the cost of the meal, and the program calculates everything correctly.

There's only one new thing in the code. That is this line:

```
meal = eval(meal);
```

This statement simply evaluates the string value that the user entered. The program reassigns that result to the `meal` variable. In this case, the program returns a numeric value. Look at the results shown in Figure 1.8, and you'll see that the program now works correctly.

Using String Methods

In addition to enabling you to manipulate numbers, most programming languages allow you to manipulate text inside string variables. Most languages have features that you can use to change a variable to uppercase or lowercase, commands that allow you to determine the length of a string, and techniques for concatenating strings. You can combine all these feature, commands, and techniques, along with input and output, to generate your old friend, the Name Game program, from the beginning of the chapter. First, however, Table 1.1 reviews the new syntax you've learned in this chapter.

TABLE 1.1 SYNTAX SUMMARY

Statement	Description	Example
`var varName`	Create a variable called `varName`.	`var userName;`
`var varName = value`	Create a variable called `varName` with a starting value of `value`.	`var userName = "";`
`alert(msg)`	Send the string `msg` to the user in a dialog box.	`alert("Hi there");`
`varName = prompt (question)`	Send a dialog box with the string `question` and a text box. Then return the value to `varName`.	`userName = prompt("What is your name");`
`eval(string)`	Evaluate the string expression. If it's a number, return the number.	`number = eval("3");`
`stringVar. toUpperCase()`	Convert `stringVar` to all uppercase letters.	`bigName = userName. toUpperCase()`
`stringVar.length`	Return the number of characters in the `stringVar` variable.	`nameSize = userName.length`

Returning to the Name Game

Remember the Name Game program that you learned about at the very beginning of the chapter? Take another look at that program. You should now recognize that the program's code demonstrates many of the concepts that you've learned in this chapter. You'll also spot a few new things.

```
<html>
<head>
<title>The Name Game</title>
</head>

<body>
<center>
<h1>The Name Game</h1>

<script>
//nameGame
//plays around with user's name
```

```
//uses string methods

var firstName = "";
var lastName = "";
var numLetters = 0;

firstName = prompt("Hi, what's your first name?", "");
alert ("That's a nice name, " + firstName);
alert ("I think I'll shout it:  " + firstName.toUpperCase());
lastName = prompt("So what's your last name, " + firstName + "?");
alert ("Oh. " + firstName + " " + lastName + ".");
alert ("Sometimes called " + lastName + ", " + firstName);
numLetters = firstName.length + lastName.length;
alert ("Did you know there are " + numLetters + " letters in your name?");

</script>
</body>
</html>
```

You have seen most of this code before. Basically it is nothing more than some input and output statements and a few new string manipulation tricks.

Writing the Variable Creation Lines

The first few lines simply create all the variables you will need:

```
var firstName = "";
var lastName = "";
var numLetters = 0;
```

Programs typically begin with some comments followed by statements that create the variables for your code. Most other statements depend on variables, so it's sensible to create them all first. It's also nice to place them somewhere easy to find. Then, when your code gets longer, it's easy to spot which variables you have working.

Note that when creating variables, I give them a default value. JavaScript doesn't require that you choose whether a variable will contain text or a number, but it still matters. I like to initialize those variables that I intend to be strings with the "" value, and if I expect a variable to be a number, I initialize it with 0.

Converting to Uppercase

After the program obtains the user's first name, it does some manipulation:

```
alert ("I think I'll shout it:  " + firstName.toUpperCase());
```

In JavaScript, sometimes variables have special powers. Strings have a bunch of things they can do, called *methods*. You'll spend much more time with them later, but for now it's fun to explore a few and see what they do. The command `firstName.toUpperCase()` converts the value of the `firstName` variable to all uppercase letters. The command then concatenates that value to the end of the string `"I think I'll shout it:  "`.

Concatenating Complex Strings in Input and Output

You can see in this code that complex string concatenation is common in input and output statements. The following prompt statement includes two literal values and a variable in the question:

```
lastName = prompt("So what's your last name, " + firstName + "?");
```

Such complex string concatenation is completely legal, and often a good idea.

Counting the Letters in Strings

The last `alert` statement tells how many letters are in the user's name. Here's how that works:

```
numLetters = firstName.length + lastName.length;
```

`numLetters` is a numeric variable. `firstName.length` returns the number of characters in the `firstName` variable. Likewise, `lastName.length` returns the number of characters in `lastName`. The program adds these values together and stores the total in the numeric variable `numLetters`.

HINT

You might be curious why `stringName.toUpperCase()` has parentheses at the end of the command whereas `stringName.length` does not. This is because length is technically not a method of string variables, but a property. The distinction will be much more important later in this book. For now, it's enough to just recognize the pattern.

Combining Numbers and Text

At this point, you might be very anxious about when something is a number and when it's a string. Don't panic. JavaScript is a very friendly language. It tries to guess what you mean, and it is often correct. Test your programs, and if you see a concatenation happen when you are expecting an addition, use the `eval` statement on the variables that JavaScript should interpret as numbers. If you have numbers that your program needs to concatenate to a string, that concatenation generally happens automatically, as in this line:

```
alert ("Did you know there are " + numLetters + " letters in your name?");
```

Summary

In just one chapter, you have learned a lot. You have seen how you can embed JavaScript programs inside Web pages. You've looked at output with the `alert` statement, and input with the `prompt` statement. You've learned about variables and literal values. You have begun to explore some of the operations you can do with numbers and strings.

In the next chapter, you'll begin to see how computers can make choices based on the value of variables. You will also look at how to generate random numbers. These skills, along with those you've already learned, form the foundation for all game programming.

EXERCISES

1. Write a JavaScript program that will ask the user for his or her first name, last name, and middle initial. Return them back in the order of last name, first name, and middle initial, then in first name, middle initial, and last name format.

2. Write a program that asks the user for two numbers, adds them up, and returns the result to the user.

3. Improve the preceding program so that it also does subtraction, multiplication, and division on the two numbers. (Hint: Division uses the / symbol, and multiplication uses *.)

4. Have a program ask the user his or her name and shoe size. Determine the user's "lucky number" by multiplying the number of letters in his or her name by the shoe size. Return the results.

5. Create a program that asks the user for the height and width of a rectangle and then returns the area (h * w) and perimeter (2*(h+w)).

The Fortune Teller: Random Numbers and the if Statement

In the last chapter, you learned how to get data from the user, how to manipulate that data, and how to send output back to the user. In this chapter, you'll learn how to do even more with data. Specifically, you'll learn how to:

- Generate random numbers

- Manipulate those numbers to be within a specific range

- Build a condition

- Use conditions to branch program logic

- Build more complex conditional structures

The Project: The Fortune Teller

Figure 2.1 shows the Fortune Teller program, which generates a random fortune for the user every time that the page is loaded.

Getting Random Numbers

Games are most interesting when they are not completely predictable. Game programmers frequently use random numbers to simulate the unpredictability of the real world. The ability to generate random numbers in any specified range is an important skill for game programmers.

Creating the Number Maker Program

The Number Maker program (see Figure 2.2) is very limited, yet it gives you the foundation of many games. Every time that you load the page, you will get a new random number between 0 and 1. Although such numbers aren't entirely useful by themselves,

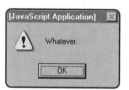

FIGURE 2.1

The Fortune Teller program generates a random fortune for the user each time that the page is loaded.

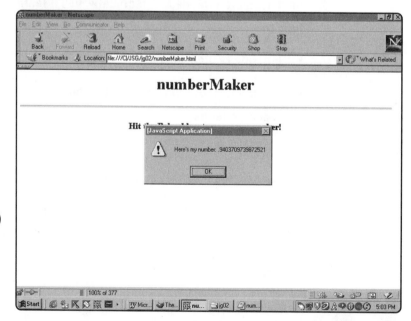

FIGURE 2.2

The Number Maker program generates a random number between zero and one.

they do turn out to be very flexible. As you'll see shortly, you can do some clever tricks to use random numbers for other, more practical applications, such as dice.

Take a look at the code for the Number Maker, to see how it works:

```
<html>
<head>
<title>numberMaker</title>
<script>
// numberMaker
// Andy Harris
// Demonstrates the random number generator

var number;

number = Math.random();
alert ("Here's my number: " + number);

</script>
</head>

<body>
<center><center>
<h1>numberMaker<br></h1>
</center>
<hr>
<h3>Hit the Reload key to see a new number!</h3>

</body>
</html>
```

As you can see, this code includes very little that is new, except for one line. Clearly, number is a variable that gets a value, but this value is neither acquired from the user nor directly coded by the programmer. The value of the number variable comes from the Math.random() line.

Using the Math Object

JavaScript is referred to as an *object-based language.* The exact implications of this will become far more important in later chapters, but you have already begun to see the importance of objects. Recall from the last chapter that string variables are objects that have methods attached to them. An *object* is some sort of entity, and a *method* is something that the object can do.

JavaScript supplies the Math object. This object just holds a bunch of interesting (if you like math) methods and properties. Any time you are looking for some kind of math function (such as calculating the cosine of an angle, or figuring out a logarithm or power), you might check in the Math object for a useful function. Table 2.1 describes many of these functions.

TABLE 2.1 USEFUL METHODS AND PROPERTIES OF THE MATH OBJECT

Method	Description	Example	Result
abs()	Calculates the absolute value.	Math.abs(-3)	3
ceil()	Returns the next higher integer.	Math.ceil(3.5)	4
cos()	Returns the cosine of an angle (in radians).	cos(Math.PI/2)	0
floor()	Returns the lower integer.	Math.floor(3.5)	3
max()	Returns the larger of two values.	Math.max(3,5)	5
min()	Returns the smaller of two values.	Math.min(3,5)	3
pow()	Returns the first number raised to power of second.	Math.pow(2,3)	8
random()	Returns a random value between 0 and 1.	Math.random()	0.348557233 (the result varies)
round()	Rounds to the nearest integer.	Math.round (3.2)	3
sin()	Returns the sine of an angle (in radians).	Math.sin (Math.PI/2)	1
sqrt()	Returns the square root of a number.	Math.sqrt(16)	4
tan()	Returns the tangent of an angle (in radians).	Math.tan (Math.PI/4)	1

Using the Math.random() Method

The Math.random() method is of particular interest to game developers, because it generates a random number. The number will be some value between 0 and 1. Most languages have some form of random number generation, and it is very common for such functions to return this kind of zero-to-one value. Specifically, the following line gets a random value and copies it to the number variable:

```
number = Math.random();
```

HINT

Technically, the values are only pseudorandom, because they are derived by a complex mathematical formula based on the current time. That's not usually a problem, because they are close enough to truly random for game development.

Making Specialized Random Numbers

Now you can generate a zero-to-one value, but such values aren't terribly interesting. Usually, you will need numbers to be within some other kind of range. If you are creating a dice game, for example, you might want the values to be between 1 and 6.

FIGURE 2.3

Two dialog boxes
generated by the
Die Roller program.

Creating the Die Roller

Take a gander at the Die Roller program, which simulates rolling one six-sided die.
Figure 2.3 shows a couple of runs of the program, just so you can see how it works.

The program generates a value between 0 and 1, then does various manipulations on
that value to turn it into an integer between 1 and 6. This particular program prints
the intermediate steps, although the user usually would not be concerned about how
the program generated the number.

The code for the Die Roller program is as follows:

```
<html>
<head>
<title>dieRoller</title>
<script>
// dieRoller
// Andy Harris
// converts random numbers to six-sided die

var rollRaw = 0;
var rollBigger = 0;
var rollInt = 0;
var rollFinal = 0;
var result = "";

rollRaw = Math.random();
rollBigger = rollRaw * 6;
rollInt = Math.floor(rollBigger);
rollFinal = rollInt + 1;

result = "rollRaw: " + rollRaw + "\n";
result += "rollBigger: " + rollBigger + "\n";
result += "rollInt: " + rollInt + "\n";
```

```
result += "rollFinal: " + rollFinal + "\n";

alert(result);

</script>
</head>

<body>
<center><center>
<h1>dieRoller<br></h1>
</center>
<hr>
</body>
</html>
```

The program starts, as usual, with a number of variable creation statements. I made a bunch of variables to handle the various steps of the number conversion process. Although having so many variables is not absolutely necessary, it does sometimes make the code a little more clear. The `result` variable is intended as a string, but all the other variables are numeric. Although JavaScript isn't fussy about variable types, my convention is to indicate at least what type of data I expect the variable to hold.

Getting the Raw Value

The first step in the process is to get the raw (zero-to-one real number) value. You saw this done in the last project, and you see in this code a now-familiar line:

```
rollRaw = Math.random();
```

This line of code generates a zero-to-one random value and assigns it to the variable `rollRaw`.

Making Larger Numbers

You now have a zero-to-one value with a lot of digits behind the decimal point stored in `rollRaw`. You're looking for a value between 1 and 6, with no decimal point, because that range includes the legal values of standard dice. You'll need to go through a few steps to get such a value. The first thing that you'll need to do is get a number in the zero-to-five range. (You'll see why I chose this range in just a moment.)

The following line performs the trick:

```
rollBigger = rollRaw * 6;
```

This command multiplies the value in `rollRaw` by 6. This results in a value larger than 0 and less than 6, but still with a huge number of decimal values. To prove this, run the program a few times and take a careful look at the relationship between `rollRaw` and `rollBigger`. Although you're getting closer to your goal, the decimal values are still a problem.

Converting to an Integer

You might remember from grade school math that positive and negative numbers without decimal values are commonly referred to as *integers*. Numbers with decimal values are frequently called *real numbers*. Specifically, computers use a form of real numbers called *floating point* notation.

Deep in the hardware of the computer, integers and floating point numbers are stored and manipulated in completely different ways. Although you might not care much about the difference, it's quite important to the computer. Most languages give you ways to translate numbers between the different types of variables. Going from a floating point number to an integer is reasonably easy. JavaScript actually gives you three different ways to do it. Take a look at this line of code, and you'll see how I did it in this program:

```
rollInt = Math.floor(rollBigger);
```

The Math object has a floor() method, which simply lops off the decimal value. The program takes rollBigger (a value with decimal points between 0 and 6) and just chops off everything after the decimal point. The program then copies the resulting integer value to the rollInt variable. rollInt is now an integer. Its value will be 0, 1, 2, 3, 4, or 5.

HINT

Earlier I mentioned that there are three ways to get an integer. The Math object also supplies the ceil() method and the round() method. You can use either of these alternatives, although they would give you slightly different results. ceil() always rounds up, and round() rounds according to normal conventions. Not every language supports these functions, but almost every programming language has some form of the floor method (although it might have a very different name, such as parseInt or intValue). If you learn how to generate random numbers with the floor() method, you'll have a strategy that you can easily transport to other programming languages.

It's a good idea to look again at the program running a few times. Examine the relationship between rollBigger and rollInt.

Getting Values Larger Than 0

The rollInt variable gets pretty close to what you're looking for, but it still has one big problem. Although it generates six different values, they are not in exactly the correct range. A typical die has values from 1 to 6, not 0 to 5. This line takes care of that problem:

```
rollFinal = rollInt + 1;
```

This line simply increases the value of rollInt by one. Now, every time the program runs, it generates a number in the range 1 through 6. Try the program a few times and see how it works. It's also instructive to look at the results of this program and examine the relationships between the variables, so you understand how this code works.

Developing an Algorithm for Random Numbers

Getting random numbers in a certain range is a very common problem in game programming. Here's a summary of my solution for making random integers between `low` and `high`:

1. Get a random floating point value.
2. Multiply the value by `high`.
3. Convert the value to an integer.
4. Add the value of `low`.

You will use this technique often when you write games. Even when you write programs in other languages, the same strategy will apply. Such generic strategies are called *algorithms*. Algorithms are proven strategies for solving specific problems. Once you have a good algorithm, it is generally pretty easy to implement it in code.

Making Decisions with the if Statement

So far, all of my programs have been *sequential*. They have simply been a list of instructions for the computer to carry out. This is a completely legitimate form of programming, but in other cases you might want the computer to perform different tasks in different situations. The way that you get computers to make decisions requires much the same process that you use when making decisions yourself, although a computer must rely on a much more formulated process.

When you got up this morning, you probably listened to the radio. Most people like to know what the weather will be like before they get dressed in the morning. They say to themselves something like "If it's cool out today, I'll wear a sweater." Although you probably did not have to concentrate very hard on this thought process, it more than likely did occur at some level.

This is an example of logic in action. It relies on a very important construct, called a *condition*. A condition is an expression that can be evaluated as true or false. In the weather problem, the condition is "It will be cool today." That statement will be either true or false. As you can see, in human terms, conditions are a lot like yes/no questions. When you are designing algorithms, you will often need to think about your logic so that you can turn it into this kind of yes/no question. You can usually turn such questions into conditions easily, then use those conditions in a number of interesting ways.

Creating the Low Temp Program

Figures 2.4, 2.5, and 2.6 show a few runs of the Low Temp program. This game generates a random number to indicate the current temperature, then recommends dress appropriate for the weather if the temperature is under a threshold temperature of 65 degrees.

FIGURE 2.4

The Low Temp program generates a random value for the temperature.

FIGURE 2.5

The program suggests attire appropriate for the current weather conditions.

FIGURE 2.6

This run of the program generates a random temperature that is above the threshold of 65 degrees. No "Wear a Sweater" message appears.

The code for this program is as follows:

```
<html>
<head>
<title>lowTemp</title>
<script>
// lowTemp
// Andy Harris
// Demonstrates the basic if statement

var temp = 0;
var perfectTemp = 65;


temp = Math.floor(Math.random() * 100) + 1;
alert ("It's " + temp + " degrees outside. ");

if (temp < perfectTemp){
  alert("Wear a sweater!!");
```

```
} // end if

</script>
</head>

<body>
<center><center>
<h1>lowTemp<br></h1>
</center>
<hr>
<h3>Hit Reload to see another temperature</h3>
</body>
</html>
```

Generating the Temperature

The temperature-generation line looks intimidating:

```
temp = Math.floor(Math.random() * 100) + 1;
```

If you look at the line closely, you will see that it is really just another way of stating the algorithm that you developed in the last section. The parentheses denote the order of operation, just as in math, so the program executes `Math.random()` first. The program then multiplies the resulting random value by 100. The computer then adds 1 to the floor of that value, resulting in a number between 1 and 100. This is a reasonable range for temperatures.

Making Decisions with Conditions

Of course, the computer is never as flexible as the human mind. Consider all these statements:

> It will be cool.
>
> It is cool.
>
> Today will be cool.
>
> It will be a little brisk today.
>
> Temperatures will be in the low 60s.
>
> Today will be a lot like yesterday.

Your mind is flexible enough that you might correctly interpret all these statements (and many more) as meaning the same thing. Humans are blessed with the ability to understand many different kinds of *syntax* (the basic structure of the statement) and determine the correct *semantics* (meaning). Computer languages do not handle subtleties well. Most of the time, there are very few ways to say something that the computer will understand. The art of programming is refining the expressive language of humans to a more restrictive computer language such as JavaScript without losing too much of the meaning.

TABLE 2.2 COMPARISON OPERATORS IN JAVASCRIPT	
Operator	**Meaning**
<	Less than
>	Greater than
==	Is equal to
!=	Is not equal to
<=	Less than or equal to
>=	Greater than or equal to

To express this kind of condition in JavaScript, you need a condition construct. Usually, a condition compares some variable to a value or another variable. For example, the weather statement might be as follows:

```
temperature < 65
```

Take a careful look at how this works: Temperature is a variable. The programmer has presumably already created it and given it a starting value. You can use any type of variable in a condition (usually) but you must be careful not to compare different types of values. (More on that later.) The less-than sign (<) is a comparison operator. Table 2.2 lists JavaScript's comparison operators.

Using the if Statement

Once you understand conditions, the if statement is simple to understand. Look again at this code from the Low Temp program:

```
if (temp < perfectTemp){
  alert("Wear a sweater!!");
} // end if
```

The if statement contains a condition in parentheses, and then a left bracket ({). This line tells the computer to analyze the condition. Any condition will evaluate to either true or false. The computer will execute the code between the left brace ({) and the right brace (})*only* if the condition evaluates to true. In this case, only one line of code is between the braces, but you can put as much code as you wish there.

> **IN THE REAL WORLD**
>
> The if statement is an example of a logic structure. Logic structures are the programming elements that allow you to write flexible programs. Most of the logic structures you will learn are based on conditions, so it is vital that you understand how conditions work. This is true in any kind of programming.

The if statement is incredibly powerful, because it allows you to write code that will execute only in certain circumstances, as long as you can write a condition to describe those circumstances. In this program, the message "Wear a sweater" should pop up only when the value of the temp variable is less than the value of the perfectTemp variable. If temp is greater than or equal to perfectTemp, nothing at all happens, and the next line of code after the right brace (}) executes. In this program, the brace is on the last line, so program execution simply stops.

Indenting Lines and Using the Semicolon

You might have noticed some things about the structure of the if statement. First, the alert line is indented from the margin. JavaScript is not very picky about spaces, indentation, or carriage returns, but clever programmers have learned to adopt some conventions that improve the readability of their code. You should indent any code inside a pair of braces. I indent two spaces, but it doesn't matter that much as long as you are consistent. The right brace aligns vertically under the beginning of the line containing the left brace. This helps me see the beginning and end of the structure plainly. In this case, I am indenting an if statement, but you will see other structures that require indentation. You will be learning some other kinds of structure statements soon, and you can nest them inside each other. It can be really tricky to know exactly where you are, so indenting is a great idea. As you look at other books or source code, you will run across many other conventions. Programmers often develop their own personal styles, but this style of indentation is reasonably common.

You might have also noticed that the brace lines do not have semicolons at the end. Semicolons are not needed on any lines that end with a left or right brace.

Using the else Structure

The if statement is used to deal with logic that should execute only when a condition is true. Sometimes you will want one set of statements to execute when a condition is true, and another set of statements to execute if the condition is false. For example, you might wish to wear a sweater or a bathing suit. If the weather is cold, you'll wear the sweater. If it is not cold, you'll want the bathing suit. The following section describes a program that simulates exactly that situation.

Creating the High or Low Program

Figures 2.7 and 2.8 show the High or Low program's output. Once again, the program generates a temperature randomly, then presents a message related to the temperature. This time, however, that message varies depending on the temperature.

FIGURE 2.7

If the temperature is high, the program presents the message "It's hot!!"

FIGURE 2.8

If the temperature is low, the program presents the message "It's cold!!"

The High or Low program starts out much like the last program, but it has one new feature. See whether you can spot this feature in the code:

```
<html>
<head>
<title>highOrLow</title>
<script>
// highOrLow
// Andy Harris
// Demonstrates the if-/-else structure

var temp = 0;
var perfectTemp = 77;


temp = Math.floor(Math.random() * 100) + 1;
alert ("It's " + temp + " degrees outside. ");

if (temp < perfectTemp){

  alert("It's cold!!");
} else {
  alert("It's hot!!");
} // end if

</script>
</head>

<body>
<center><center>
<h1>highOrLow<br></h1>
</center>
<hr>
```

```
<h3>Hit Reload to see another temperature</h3>
</body>
</html>
```

Using the else Clause

The only thing that is new in the High or Low program's code is the `else` clause. Take a look at the segment around the `if` statement:

```
if (temp < perfectTemp){
  alert("Wear a Sweater!!");
} else {
  alert("Wear a Bathing Suit!!");
} // end if
```

The `if` clause works exactly the same as in the previous program, but now there is an `else` clause. The part between `else {` and the closing brace (`}`) will run only if the condition evaluates to false. If the computer evaluates the condition to true, the Sweater message pops up and the next line of code after the `else` clause runs. If the condition turns out to be false, the computer runs only the `else` clause. The `else` clause can contain several lines of code. It is customary to indent the if-else structure as I did in this example. This helps you to see at a glance how the programmer organized the code.

Using Nested if Structures

It's common to have more complex types of conditions. For example, what if you want the program to recommend more than two options for clothing for different conditions? You might want to wear a jacket if it's cold, a sweater if it's cool, short sleeves if it's warm, and a bathing suit if it's hot. You can nest `if` statements inside each other to handle such situations.

Creating the Many Temps Program

Figures 2.9 through 2.12 show the Many Temps program, which displays four different messages to the user depending on the temperature range that the program selects randomly.

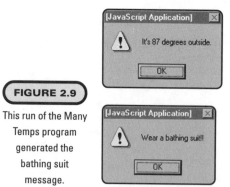

FIGURE 2.9

This run of the Many Temps program generated the bathing suit message.

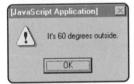

FIGURE 2.10

This time the Many Temps program generated the short sleeves message.

FIGURE 2.11

Here the temperature is cool, so the program recommends a sweater.

FIGURE 2.12

Now the temperature is cold, so the program suggests a jacket.

As you can see, this version of the program is capable of presenting a different message for four different temperature ranges. Look at the code to see how the program accomplishes this:

```
<html>
<head>
<title>manyTemps</title>
<script>
// manyTemps
// Andy Harris
```

```
// Demonstrates the if/else structure

var temp = 0;

temp = Math.floor(Math.random() * 100) + 1;
alert ("It's " + temp + " degrees outside. ");

if (temp < 70){

  if (temp < 30){
    alert("Wear a jacket!!");
  } else {
    alert("Wear a sweater!!");
  } //end 30 if
} else {
  if (temp > 85){
    alert("Wear a bathing suit!!");
  } else {
    alert("Wear short sleeves");
} // end 85 if
} // end 70 if

</script>
</head>

<body>
<center><center>
<h1>manyTemps<br></h1>
</center>
<hr>
<h3>Hit Reload to see another temperature</h3>
</body>
</html>
```

The code begins like most of the earlier programs. An if statement checks for a warm temperature (that for this case is defined as 70 degrees). However, this program includes two other if statements, which enable it to identify four distinct temperatures ranges and provide a different message for each range.

Nesting Layers of if Statements

The first if statement checks whether the temperature is less than 70 degrees:

```
if (temp < 70){
```

Any code between this line and the corresponding right brace (}) will occur only when temp is less than 70. Notice what follows this line:

```
if (temp < 30){
```

This second `if` statement is nested inside the first one. It now checks for temperatures above 30 degrees. Any code placed between this line and its right brace will execute only when the temperature is less than 30 degrees. (Of course, because of the first `if` statement, the program has already determined that the temperature is less than 70 degrees.) The code that executes under these conditions is as follows:

```
alert("Wear a jacket!!");
```

The jacket message appears only when the temperature is below 30 degrees. The next line is an `else` statement:

```
} else {
alert("Wear a sweater!!");
```

The program displays the sweater message only when the temperature is over 30 degrees, because the command to display the message is in the `else` clause of the `if` (`temp < 30`) statement.

To recap, then, the program prints this message only when the temperature is less than 70 degrees (because it's inside the first `if` statement) and greater than 30 degrees (because it's inside the `else` clause of the second `if` statement). For example, if the computer generated a temperature of 47 degrees, the program would evaluate the (`temp < 70`) condition as true. Then the computer would check the condition (`temp < 30`). This would be false, so the program would defer to the `else` clause of the (`temp < 30`) statement and print the message "Wear a sweater!!"

The following line simply ends the inner `if` structure:

```
} //end 30 if
```

You can see how useful indentation and commenting are in such nested statements. Without them, each right brace looks pretty much like another. It's very hard to tell what structure you are ending unless you use indentation and comments.

The next `else` clause relates to the very first `if` statement:

```
} else {
```

The fact that this clause is indented directly under the first `if` statement indicates the clause belongs within the statement. Any code after this `else` line and the corresponding right brace will execute only when the (`temp < 70`) condition is false.

This particular `else` clause contains its own `if` statement, to check where the temperature falls within the 70 to 100 degree range:

```
if (temp > 85){
  alert("Wear a bathing suit!!");
} else {
  alert("Wear short sleeves!!");
} // end 85 if
```

Finally, the program closes the outermost `if` statement with this line:

```
} // end 70 if
```

It is lined up vertically with the `if` (`temp < 70`) statement and the corresponding `} else {` line to help clarify which structure it is ending. I also commented the line to clarify even further what is going on.

TRICK If you're still confused about how these nested statements work, run the program while you're looking at the code. When the computer first outputs the number, see whether you can figure out which line of code will execute next. This technique is very useful, because it helps you find difficult bugs in your programs.

Using the switch Structure

JavaScript supplies one more structure that can be very useful when you have one variable that might have a lot of different values. To illustrate, I wrote a program that adds a very crude graphical interface to the Die Roller program from earlier in this chapter:

Creating the Fuzzy Dice Program

Figure 2.13 shows a fancier die-rolling program. Appropriately enough, I call it the Fuzzy Dice program. You'll get to make even better graphics later, but this program demonstrates how you can at least generate crude images.

As you can see, the program generates a random number, then draws a text-based image of the die on the alert box.

Here's the code that does the work. Although it looks kind of long, it's really very repetitive, so don't let the length of the listing intimidate you.

FIGURE 2.13

Several rolls of the Fuzzy Dice program.

```html
<html>
<head>
<title>fuzzyDice</title>
<script>
// fuzzyDice
// Andy Harris
// Demonstrates switch statement

var roll = 0;
var die = "";

roll = Math.floor(Math.random() * 6) + 1;
switch (roll){
  case 1:
    die = "|--------|\n";
    die +="|        |\n";
    die +="|    *   |\n";
    die +="|        |\n";
    die +="|--------|\n";
    break;
  case 2:
    die = "|--------|\n";
    die +="|      * |\n";
    die +="|        |\n";
    die +="| *      |\n";
    die +="|--------|\n";
    break;
  case 3:
    die = "|--------|\n";
    die +="|      * |\n";
    die +="|    *   |\n";
    die +="| *      |\n";
    die +="|--------|\n";
    break;
  case 4:
    die = "|--------|\n";
    die +="| *    * |\n";
    die +="|        |\n";
    die +="| *    * |\n";
    die +="|--------|\n";
    break;
  case 5:
    die = "|--------|\n";
    die +="| *    * |\n";
    die +="|    *   |\n";
    die +="| *    * |\n";
```

```
    die +="|--------|\n";
    break;
  case 6:
    die = "|--------|\n";
    die +="| *     * |\n";
    die +="| *     * |\n";
    die +="| *     * |\n";
    die +="|--------|\n";
    break;
  default:
    die = "ERROR!"
} // end switch
alert(die);

</script>
</head>


<body>
<center><center>
<h1>fuzzyDice<br></h1>
</center>
<hr>
<h3>reload to see another die</h3>
</body>
</html>
```

The code begins in a now-familiar way:

```
var roll = 0;
var die = "";


roll = Math.floor(Math.random() * 6) + 1;
```

These first few lines set up a variable for the numeric die roll, and roll the die using the technique that you learned earlier in this chapter. (Generating a zero-to-one number, multiplying it by six, and adding one). The die variable contains characters that together create a crude image representing the side of the die that the program rolled.

Using the switch Statement

The new stuff begins with the switch statement:

```
switch (roll){
```

This statement accepts the name of a variable. It tells the computer to start thinking about the value of roll. It ends with a right brace, signifying the beginning of a logical structure. As usual, the code between the braces is indented. The rest of the structure will look at various possible values for the variable:

```
  case 1:
```

This line checks whether roll's value is equal to ()1. The code between this line and the next case statement will execute if roll is equal to 1.

The actual code is simply a bunch of assignment statements that add to the die string variable:

```
die = "|--------|\n";
```

This line assigns a value for the top of the die. The \n part is a special placeholder called *newline*. This placeholder represents pressing the carriage return. I include this newline so that the die image takes up more than one line on the alert dialog box.

The other lines are all pretty similar:

```
die +="|          |\n";
die +="|     *    |\n";
die +="|          |\n";
die +="|--------|\n";
```

The only significant difference between these lines and the first line in the case statement is the += operator. This operator is simply a shortcut for concatenation.

```
die +="|          |\n";
```

is exactly the same as

```
die = die + "|          |\n";
```

Using the break Statement

At the end of each case statement, you will see a line such as the following:

```
break;
```

The break statement tells the computer to move on to the end of the switch structure.

TRAP

Don't forget to put a break **statement at the end of each** case **block. If you don't put a** break **statement there, the computer will also evaluate the next** case **block. This is a very common mistake, especially for people who have programmed using languages based on BASIC, which does not require anything like the** break **command.**

Using the default Clause

You can add a default clause to a switch structure. The computer executes a default clause only when none of the other conditions are true. I added a default clause to this switch structure, although the computer should never execute the clause. If I designed my algorithm correctly, the value will never be anything other than an integer between 1 and 6. Still, I often include a default clause even when I do not expect the program to need it. Then, the program will be ready for the unexpected.

You've learned a lot of new syntax in this chapter. Here's a table of what has been covered so far.

TABLE 2.3 DISPLAYING DYNAMIC CONTENT

Statement	Description	Example
`Math.random()`	Generates a random number between 0 and 1.	`MyVar=Math.random();`
`Math.floor(varName)`	Lops off trailing decimal values, converting a real number to its next lowest integer.	`newVar = Math.floor(oldVar);` `if (condition){    expression`
`}`	Branches program logic based on the value of a condition.	`if (score > 50) {` `alert("Winner!");`
`} else {`	Denotes code within an `if` structure to execute when the condition is false.	`} else {    alert ("Loser");` `} //end if`
`switch(varName){`	Sets up one variable to check against multiple values.	`switch (year){`
`case value:`	Denotes a value for a variable within a switch structure.	`case 1964:` `alert("Correct");`
`break;`	Moves execution directly to the end of the current structure. The `break` statement is used most frequently with `switch` statements.	`break;`
`default:`	Catches any `case` clauses not caught by `case` statements within a `switch` structure.	`default:` `alert("Incorrect");`

Returning to the Fortune Teller Program

Finally you are ready to examine the Fortune Teller program from the beginning of this chapter. It turns out to be incredibly simple after everything you've learned. In fact, it's just like the Die Roller program, except I've used messages instead of images. Here's the code:

```
<html>
<head>
```

```
<title>fortune</title>
<script>
// fortune
// Andy Harris
// The Fortune-teller

var roll = 0;
var fortune = "";

roll = Math.floor(Math.random() * 5) + 1;
switch(roll){
  case 1:
    fortune = "It looks really bad.";
    break;
  case 2:
    fortune = "It's kinda gloomy.";
    break;
  case 3:
    fortune = "Whatever.";
    break;
  case 4:
    fortune = "Things are pretty good.";
    break;
  case 5:
    fortune = "You're in for a perfect day!";
    break;
  default:
    fortune = "ERROR";
} // end switch
alert(fortune);

</script>
</head>

<body>
<center><center>
<h1>fortune<br></h1>
</center>
<hr>
<h3>reload for another fortune</h3>

</body>
</html>
```

Summary

In this chapter, you learned how to generate random numbers and refine them so that they fit within a specific range. You also learned how to make the computer's logic branch. The chapter showed you examples of conditions and explained how programmers use them in `if` statements. You looked at more advanced variants of the `if` statement, including the `else` clause, nested `if` statements, and the `switch` structure. In the next chapter, you'll learn how to use conditions to make the computer repeat certain actions.

EXERCISES

1. Modify the Fortune Teller program so that it contains your own set of fortunes.

2. Write a program that greets the user and asks his or her name. If the user enters your name, compliment him or her on being such a fine programmer.

3. Write a simple quiz program that asks the user five questions. Keep track of how often the user answers correctly, and give the user a score at the end of the quiz.

4. Write a program that randomly pops up a saying as your Web page begins.

5. Write a die program with a "loaded" die. Have the die roll a one half the time and a random number the rest of the time.

6. Certain types of games use multisided dice. Write a program that asks the user how many sides he or she wants, then rolls a die with that many sides and returns the result.

CHAPTER 3

The Number Guesser: for and while Loops

Y ou are starting to learn all the important tasks involved in programming. So far, you have learned how to store information in variables, send messages to the user, retrieve information from the user, and make your program branch. Now you'll add another critical element, which is the ability to make your program repeat itself.

Specifically, you will learn how to do the following:

- Use `for` loops to repeat a given number of times

- Modify `for` loops to skip values

- Make `for` loops go backward

- Use code tracing to verify your understanding of the code's behavior

- Create `while` loops

- Prevent endless loops

- Plan complex programs with pseudocode

Project: The Number Guesser

As usual, you'll start by looking at an example. By the end of this chapter, you will be able to write this program. It's a classic guessing game. The computer will think of a number between 1 and 100 (see Figure 3.1). The user will try to guess the computer's number (see Figure 3.2). After each guess, the computer tells the user whether the user's guess is high, low, or correct (see Figures 3.3 and 3.4). The computer keeps track of the number of turns it takes the user to guess the number.

As you can see, this program repeatedly asks the user for a number until the user guesses correctly. Clearly this program relies on the branching behavior that you learned about in the last chapter. After all, the user gets a different message if he or she guessed high or low. In addition to branching, the program also repeats. It repeats the same set of instructions over and over until the user gets the answer right. This repeating behavior is called *looping*.

Counting Forward

Most programming languages offer a couple of types of loops. The first kind you'll examine is useful for those times when you want something to happen a certain number of times. It's called a `for` loop, and the following program, the Racer, shows it in action.

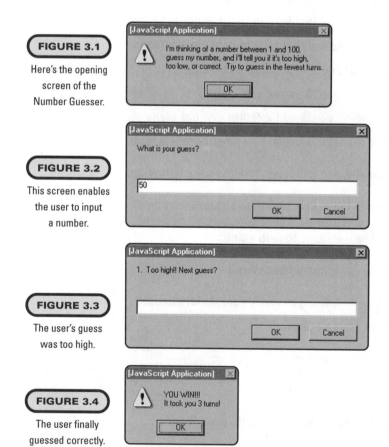

FIGURE 3.1

Here's the opening screen of the Number Guesser.

FIGURE 3.2

This screen enables the user to input a number.

FIGURE 3.3

The user's guess was too high.

FIGURE 3.4

The user finally guessed correctly.

Creating the Racer Program

The Racer program is a silly simulation of a 10-lap race. All it does is present an alert box that tells the user which lap the driver is on. Figure 3.5 shows the program.

Although you could write this program as a series of `alert` statements, the program actually has only one `alert` statement. I got the program to repeat by putting that `alert` statement inside a `for` loop. Here's how the code looks:

```html
<html>
<head>
<title>Racer</title>
<script>
// Racer
// Andy Harris
// Demonstrates the basic for loop

var lap = 0;
for (lap = 1; lap <= 10; lap++){
  alert("Now on lap: " + lap);
} // end for loop

</script>
</head>

<body>
<center><center>
<h1>Racer<br></h1>
</center>
<hr>
</body>
</html>
```

The program has one variable, called `lap`, and one `alert` statement. I nested the statement inside a set of braces. The `for` statement causes the `alert` statement to execute 10 times. The advantage of using a loop rather than a number of `alert` statements is flexibility. If I want the race to be five or 100 laps, all I have to do is change one statement in the code.

FIGURE 3.5

A few of the dialog boxes that pop up as the Racer program runs.

Using the for Statement

The `for` statement sets up a loop. It is especially useful when you know exactly how many times you want something to repeat. Take another look at this line from the Racer program:

```
for (lap = 1; lap <= 10; lap++){
```

`for` loops have three parts inside the parentheses. The first segment initializes a variable. The second part is a condition used to determine when the loop ends. The third part tells the computer how to change the variable each time through the loop.

The initialization segment, `lap = 1;`, specifies the name of a variable that will be used in the loop and the variable's starting value. To make a `for` loop, you must have a numeric variable. In this case, I used the variable `lap`, which will specify which lap the program is currently on. The semicolon separates this part of the `for` loop from the next part.

You specify the condition of the `for` loop code as follows:

```
lap <= 10;
```

The code inside the loop will keep on running as long as this condition is true. In this example, the `lap` variable begins with a value of one, and the code continues executing as long as the value of `lap` is less than or equal to 10.

The last part of the `for` line looks like this:

```
lap++
```

The `++` operator is shorthand for "add 1." So, you could also write `lap++` as `lap = lap + 1`. The function of this part of the `for` loop is to change the value of the variable so the condition will eventually become false. Basically, this is what the line means: "Use the variable `lap`. Start it out at 1, and keep going as long as it is less than or equal to 10. Each time the loop is completed, add 1 more to the value of `lap`."

Tracing Code

To help explain what's going on in this loop, I'll employ a programmer's trick called *code tracing*. This is a good technique to use when you're trying to figure out how a piece of code works or why it isn't doing what you want it to do. To trace code, make a table. (You can draw the table on paper, as it doesn't need to be anything formal.) Write the names of all your variables and conditions along the top of the table, like this:

lap	lap <= 10
____	_____
____	_____
____	_____

Now study the code line by line. Each time the value of a variable changes, write the new value in the table. If the program uses that variable in a condition, write down whether that condition is true or false. The first line of code is as follows:

```
var lap = 0;
```

After the computer evaluates this line, your table will look like this:

lap	lap <= 10
0	true
___	_____
___	_____

The value of lap is now 0, and 0 is less than 10, so lap <= 10 is true. Now go on to the next line, and continue with the process:

```
for (lap = 1; lap <= 10; lap++){
```

After this line executes the first time, here's what your chart will look like:

lap	lap <= 10
0	true
1	true
___	_____

The first time through the loop, the program initializes the value of lap to one. The condition evaluates to true, so the program executes the code inside the braces. The alert statement tells the user the lap value. When the computer encounters the right brace signifying the end of the loop, control automatically reverts to the for loop line.

This time through, the computer increases the value of lap by 1, so by the end of the second time through the for line, here's how your chart will look:

lap	lap <= 10
0	true
1	true
2	true

The value of lap is now 2, and the condition is still true, so the loop will continue to execute. Things get interesting when lap is equal to 10. Look at how the code trace looks up to this point:

lap	lap <= 10
0	true
1	true
2	true
3	true
4	true
5	true
6	true
7	true
8	true
9	true
10	true

The next time through the `for` statement, the value of `lap` becomes 11. This is interesting, because the value of the condition will finally change:

lap	lap <= 10
0	true
1	true
2	true
3	true
4	true
5	true
6	true
7	true
8	true
9	true
10	true
11	false

Now the condition `lap <= 10` evaluates to false, so the loop no longer executes, and program control reverts to the next line of code after the right brace (`}`). As promised, the code executes exactly 10 times, outputting values between 1 and 10.

Skipping Values

The form of the `for` loop in the Racer program demonstrates the most common way to use the `for` loop structure. You can use the `for` loop in other ways, however. The Count by Five program shows one of these ways.

Creating the Count By Five Program

Figure 3.6 shows the Count by Five program, which is a simple application that includes a loop that counts by five with each pass.

This program uses a variation of exactly the same type of loop as in the Racer program. Take a look at its code to see what is different:

```
<html>
<head>
<title>Count By Five</title>
<script>
// CountByFive
```

FIGURE 3.6

The Count by Five program counts by five with each pass through the loop.

```
// Andy Harris
// demonstrates how to vary the for loop

var i = 0;
for (i=5; i <= 100; i += 5){

  alert (i);
} // end for loop

</script>
</head>

<body>
<center><center>
<h1>Count By Five<br></h1>
</center>
<hr>
</body>
</html>
```

This program is very much like the Racer program. The only significant difference is in the `for` loop line. That line looks like this:

```
for (i=5; i <= 100; i += 5){
```

As you can see, the variable is now named i. I chose this name because in this case I'm not necessarily thinking of laps. When programmers need a counter for a `for` structure and that counter does not have any particular meaning except as a counter, it's traditional to name it i.

HINT

It might seem strange that an endeavor as young as computer programming would have tradition and folklore, but this particular tidbit (using i as a `for` loop counter) is an example of the richness of computing lore. The reason that programmers use i in this way dates all the way back to FORTRAN, one of the earliest programming languages. In early versions of FORTRAN, integer variables had to start with i, j, k, and a few other letters. Oddly enough, even though FORTRAN has not been a mainstream programming language for several decades, the practice of using i as a generic name for a counter is still very common.

You might want to determine for yourself what you think the line `for (i=5; i <= 100; i += 5){` means. i starts at 5 and goes to 100. Each time through the loop, the program increases i by five.

Using the += Operator

You have already seen the `+=` operator in action in the context of string concatenation. You can also use this operator with numeric variables. In this context, it means to add five to i. You could also write the code fragment `i += 5` as `i = i + 5`. Most programmers prefer the += operator, because it's faster to type. As you have no doubt deduced, this program works exactly like the Racer program except that the Count by Five program counts from 5 to 100 by five.

Counting Backward

You can also design `for` loops so that they run from larger values to smaller ones. Essentially, all you need to do is to modify the `for` loop line.

Creating the Back Racer Program

Figure 3.7 shows another version of the Racer program, but this one goes backward. It starts at lap 10 and counts down to lap 1.

Making a for Loop Count Backward

The code is very similar to earlier programs in this chapter. Here's the entire program:

```html
<html>
<head>
<title>Back Racer</title>
<script>
// Back Racer
// Andy Harris
// demonstrates counting backward through a for loop

var i = 0;

for (i = 10; i > 0; i--){
  alert(i);
} // end for loop
</script>
</head>

<body>
<center><center>
<h1>Back Racer<br></h1>
</center>
<hr>
</body>
</html>
```

FIGURE 3.7

This time the loop goes from 10 to 1.

As you might expect, the only differences occur in the `for` line. This time I initialized the variable to a large value, which the program decreases each time through the loop.

The initialization part of the loop starts the value of `i` at 10. The condition now checks whether `i` is greater than 0, and the program decreases the variable by 1 each time through the loop.

TRAP

Some programmers misuse the `for` loop. The way that you build `for` loops in JavaScript (and the other languages derived from C) allows you to use the structure in all kinds of other ways. However, doing so is a dangerous practice. Use the `for` loop when you know how many times you want a loop to execute, when you want to have a variable take on every fifth value, or in similar circumstances. If you need any other kind of looping behavior, use the `while` loop, which the next section describes.

Using the while Loop

The `for` loop is an easy structure to build, and it is terrific at certain kinds of repetition. However, sometimes the `for` loop does not provide enough flexibility. Take a look at the following program, the Joke Teller, and see whether you can figure out why a `for` loop would not be a useful structure for controlling the program.

Creating the Joke Teller Program

Figures 3.8 and 3.9 show the Joke Teller program, which asks the user a very old riddle, then asks the user for an answer.

This program needs to keep repeating, but the number of repetitions depends entirely on the user's actions. The part of the program that poses the riddle is inside the loop. That code might execute only once, or it may execute many times. In fact, if the user never enters the correct answer, the loop will continue forever.

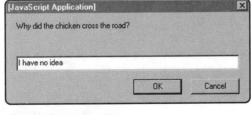

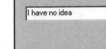

FIGURE 3.8

The Joke Teller program asks the user a riddle, then prints a response if the user guesses incorrectly.

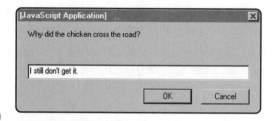

FIGURE 3.9

The program keeps
asking the user for
the correct answer
until he or she
gets it right.

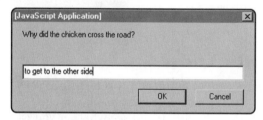

FIGURE 3.10

When the user
enters the
correct answer,
the loop ends.

Looping an Indeterminate Number of Times

Look at the code behind the Joke Teller program. It uses a loop, but not a `for` loop.

```
<html>
<head>
<title>Joke Teller</title>
<script>
// Joke Teller
// Andy Harris
// Demonstrates the while loop

var correct = "to get to the other side";
var guess = "";
while (guess != correct){
  guess = prompt ("Why did the chicken cross the road?", "");
  if (guess == correct){
    alert ("Pretty funny, huh?");
  } else {
    alert ("that's not it...");
```

```
  } // end if
} // end while

</script>
</head>

<body>
<center><center>
<h1>Joke Teller<br></h1>
</center>
<hr>
</body>
</html>
```

The program starts with two variables. One is intended to hold the correct answer. That variable is called `correct`. The other variable is called `guess`.

 TRICK

These choices for variable names are very deliberate. By looking at the variable names, it is clear which one contains the intended correct answer, and which one contains the user's guess. Novice programmers might be tempted to call one of the variables `answer`. The problem with that name is that it does not make it clear whether the variable contains the correct answer or the user's answer. It's surprising how easily you can get confused about what your variables are supposed to contain. Try hard to come up with names that are unambiguous whenever possible.

Using the while Statement

A `while` structure contains the main body of this program. That structure begins with this line:

```
while (guess != correct){
```

The structure ends with a corresponding right brace:

```
} // end while
```

IN THE REAL WORLD

Even if the user knows the correct answer to this riddle, it is very possible that he or she would type it incorrectly and not get credit for knowing the answer. If this were a serious program (one that was meant to do more than demonstrate the `while` loop), I would have added code to check the capitalization, perhaps look at alternate punctuation, and check for multiple spaces. Better yet, I might have designed the program so that the user didn't have to type in the answer at all but could choose it from some sort of menu. Still, the program is really designed to show how `while` loops work. In later chapters, you'll learn some techniques for getting input from the user that do not require as much error checking.

The code between these lines is the part meant to be repeated. The syntax of the `while` statement is much simpler than that of the `for` loop. It simply consists of a condition. In this particular case, the loop should continue to execute as long as `guess` is not equal to `correct`. `while` loops always have a condition, and the code in the loop continues to execute as long as the condition evaluates to true. As soon as the condition evaluates to false, the next line of code after the end of the loop executes.

Recognizing Loops That Never Execute

`while` loops are very simple to build, but they can be dangerous. The design of the `for` loop makes it reasonably safe, because the user is required to put certain elements in it. The structure of the `while` loop is less rigid, which means some bad things could happen. See whether you can guess what would happen if a program contained this code:

```
var i = 10;
while (i < 10){
   alert(i);
   i++;
} // end while
```

The variable `i` is initialized to 10. The condition then checks whether `i` is less than 10. The condition is false, so the computer never executes the code inside the loop. This program will end as soon as it is run, and you'll never see any results. When designing a loop, you have to be careful that your condition can execute at least one time.

Recognizing Endless Loops

Here's another problem that's harder to spot:

```
var i = 0;
while (i < 10){
   alert (i);
} // end while
```

This time the code initializes the variable properly, and the condition in the `while` loop is fine, but there's a worse problem. There's no code to increment the variable, so its value will always be 0. Here's a partial code trace of the program:

i	i < 10
0	true
0	true
0	true

The value of `i` will never become larger than 0, so the condition will remain true forever. The code will never stop spinning through the loop. This is an example of an endless (or infinite) loop. It's reasonably easy to make such a loop accidentally when you're learning to program (or even when you're a professional!). The only way to stop an endless loop is to shut down the program. Press Ctrl, Alt, Delete to go to the task manager in Windows 95/98/00/NT and shut down your browser. Go back and edit your program before you try it again.

Making Well-Behaved Loops

Experienced programmers have learned a few tricks that prevent many of the looping problems noted in this chapter:

- Design your condition carefully. Think carefully about the variables that you will use in your condition, and make sure that they are spelled correctly, with correct capitalization. Make sure that your condition tests what you think it tests.

- Be sure to initialize variables. Any variables used in your condition should be initialized outside the loop, so you can predict what will happen the first time through the loop. If you have a loop that seems as though it never executes at all, check whether the variables have the values that you think they should before the loop starts. (In fact, you may want to include temporarily an `alert` statement informing you what the values of the appropriate variables are.)

- Ensure that the condition can be triggered. The loop must contain some code that changes the value of a variable in the condition so that the condition can become false and the code can exit. This problem is usually the cause of an endless loop.

Returning to the Number Guesser

The number-guessing game that made its debut at the beginning of this chapter is a nice program, because it ties together many concepts used in the first few chapters and incorporates a looping structure. Rather than simply showing you the code, this section will show you how I planned the program. The planning phase is often the most difficult part of programming.

Planning the Program

The first thing I did was think through what the program should do. Then I wrote down a sample transcript of the "conversation" between the user and the computer. That transcript looked a little like this:

Computer	User
I'm thinking of a number.	50
Too high.	25
Too low.	30
That's it! It took three tries.	X

Although this is clearly a simplistic form of the program, it illustrates the basic elements that I need to think about as I build the program. The user needs to be able to input some values, and the computer must evaluate the input. Specifically, the computer must compare the input to some randomly generated number. The code should be capable of executing an unspecified number of times (until the user gets the right answer), and the computer must keep track of how many times the user went through the loop.

TRICK It's a great idea to write down this summary of your program. It will be much easier to put together all the parts of your program if you know what they are.

Writing Pseudocode

The process described in the preceding section might not give you enough information to get started programming. Many programmers like to write a form of their plan in a language called *pseudocode*. Pseudocode expresses the main ideas of the program, but is easier to work with because it does not require you to follow all the strict laws of programming language syntax. Here's my pseudocode representation of the Number Guesser program:

```
make variables
   guess = user's guess
   target = random number generated by computer
   turns = how many turns it takes user to guess


get a random number between 1 and 100
explain game to user
ask user for a guess
as long as user has not guessed right answer,
   increment turn counter
   if user's guess is too high,
     say so
     get another guess
   if user's guess is too low,
     say so
     get another guess
   if user's guess is correct,
     tell user he or she won
     tell how many turns it took
```

You write your pseudocode in English, with each line conveying a specific thought. If you can look at each line of pseudocode and figure out how to translate that line into JavaScript, your pseudocode is detailed enough. If the pseudocode appears to solve the problem at hand, it's probably complete enough.

TRAP

The number one problem of beginning programmers is the tendency to write code too early. If you ever find yourself staring at the computer wondering what you should type next, turn the monitor off and get out some paper. When you have solid pseudocode, you'll write better programs.

It is not a major step to go from the pseudocode to a working program. Here's my version:

```
<html>
<head>
<title>NumberGuesser</title>
<script>
// NumberGuesser
```

```
// Andy Harris
// The classic number guessing game
var guess = 50;
var target = 0;
var turns = 0;
var msg = "";


target = Math.floor(Math.random() * 100) + 1;
//alert(target);

msg = "I'm thinking of a number between 1 and 100. \n";
msg += "Guess my number, and I'll tell you if it's too high, \n";
msg += "too low, or correct.  Try to guess in the fewest turns.";
alert (msg);

guess = eval(prompt("What is your guess?", guess));

while (guess != target){
  turns++;
  if (guess > target){
    guess = eval(prompt (turns + ".  Too high!! Next guess?", guess));
  } // end if

  if (guess < target){
    guess = prompt (turns + ".  Too low!! Next guess?", guess);
  } // end if

  if (guess == target){
    msg = "YOU WIN!!! \n";
    msg += "It took you ";
    msg += turns + " turns! ";
    alert (msg);
  } // end if
} // end while

</script>
</head>
```

Generating the Target

Once I knew that I needed to generate a number between 1 and 100, I remembered the algorithm from Chapter 1, "Variables, Input, and Output." Writing the code turned out to be pretty easy once I knew what I wanted to do.

TRICK

Notice this line in the code:

```
//alert (target);
```

It is a very useful debugging tool. When I first wrote the `target` generation code, I wanted to be sure that it was generating the kinds of values I was looking for. The `alert` statement shows the value of `target`, so it helped to reassure me that the `target` code was working. Also, when the entire program was working, it was nice to know the value of `target` right away, so I could test the program more quickly without having to guess the variable's value every time through the loop. Because this line is so useful, I decided not to destroy it completely after testing my program. Instead, I simply put the comment characters (`//`) in front of the line. This way, if I need the line again, it will be easy to bring back. Whenever you are unsure about the status of a variable, use an `alert` statement like this to make sure that it has the value that you think it does. Of course, don't forget to comment out the line before posting the code to your Web site.

Setting Up the Loop

The pseudocode says, "as long as user has not guessed right answer." The trick of turning this into actual working code is to figure out how to translate that line of English into a condition with which the computer can work. My solution was this:

```
while (guess != target){
```

The condition uses two variables, so I was careful to ensure that both were initialized before the loop began. The computer generated a value for `target`, so it is initialized. I ensured that `guess` had a legal initial value by asking for a guess before the loop began.

Getting User Input

The user input is pretty straightforward. Notice that I immediately evaluated the response from the user (with the `eval` statement) so I wouldn't have to worry about nonnumeric values. Notice also that the user input occurs multiple times. I first ask for a value from the user outside the loop (to initialize `guess`), and then I ask for a value inside the loop. The prompt informs the user whether the current guess is high or low and asks for another guess. This is necessary, because the value of `guess` must change before the loop can end. The prompt also includes the current value of `guess` as the default value, so the user can see what his or her last guess was. This also provides a subtle clue to the user that numeric input is expected.

Evaluating the Input

When the user inputs a guess, the program evaluates that guess to turn it into a numeric value. Then I use a series of `if` statements to compare `guess` to `correct`. If the value is too high or too low, the next prompt informs the user of this situation and asks for another input. If the value is correct, an appropriate message goes to the user, including the number of turns it took to get the correct answer. Note that I use a special variable (`msg`) whenever my output strings involve complicated concatenations. I find that using a variable in such situations decreases the likelihood of syntax errors. As an example of this phenomenon, look carefully at the following line of code:

```
var msg = num1 + " + " + num2 + " = " eval(num1 + num2)
```

It might not be obvious what the line does, and it will be very easy to make a mistake with the quote signs and plus signs. Compare that line to the following series of statements:

```
var msg;
msg = num1;
msg += " + ";
msg += num2;
msg += " = ";
msg += eval(num1 + num2);
```

The second code fragment is longer, but it much more clearly describes what is going on (the program is concatenating a variable which shows the addition of two other variables). If you get a syntax error in the first version, you won't have much more information to go on. If you have a syntax error in the second version of the code, you'll know exactly which part of that complex structure is giving you trouble.

Table 3.1 provides a summary of the new syntax covered in this chapter.

TABLE 3.1 SYNTAX SUMMARY

Statement	Description	Example
`for (init; condition; increment){ repeated code } // end for`	Sets up a loop that executes a set number of times.	`for(i=1; i<10; i++){ }` `// end for`
`Init`	Sets the starting value of a counting variable.	`i++`
`Condition`	Specifies a condition that evaluates to true or false. The loop continues executing as long as condition is true.	`i < 10`
`Increment`	Changes the value of the counter.	`i++`
`while (condition) { code body } // end while`	Creates a loop that continues as long as condition is true.	`While (finished == false){ }`

Summary

In this chapter, you extended the notion of conditions to add looping behavior to your programs. You learned how to use the `for` loop to handle situations involving a specified number of repetitions. You also learned variations of the basic `for` loop, including loops that increment by an arbitrary value and loops that count backward.

This chapter also introduced the powerful `while` loop. You learned how to write programs using the structure, and you learned how to avoid some of the common pitfalls of its use. Finally, you looked at how to use pseudocode to help you write complex programs.

In the next chapter, you will learn how to access the objects inherent in the JavaScript model and learn new ways to get information to and from the user.

EXERCISES

1. Write a program that asks the user for the answer to 2 + 3 (or some other math problem). Your program should keep asking the question until the user enters the correct answer.

2. Change the preceding program so that it generates the numbers to add randomly.

3. Modify this program so it gives a total of five random math problems, but repeats each one until the user gets the right answer. Only move on to the next question when the user gets a question correct. (You'll need a `for` loop *and* a `while` loop for this one.)

4. Improve the Number Guesser so that it asks the user whether he or she wants to play again. Repeat the entire game until the user indicates that he or she is done.

5. Write a version of the Number Guesser with the roles reversed. This time, the user comes up with the random value, and the computer guesses what the number is. Have the user respond with "h" (for high), "l" (for low), or "c" (for correct). You'll need to write pseudocode for this program. The logic is totally different than for this chapter's Number Guesser program.

CHAPTER 4

The Basic Mad Lib Program and Object-Based Programming

The programming principles discussed in the last few chapters have not changed much since the advent of the early programming languages. JavaScript also supports some modern ideas that have revolutionized computer applications and computer programming. Next, you will begin to explore the world of *object-based programming*. Here are some of the things you will learn in this chapter:

- **The basic characteristics of objects**

- **How properties, methods, and events work**

- **How to use some properties of the** document **object**

- **How to use some methods of the** document **object**

- **How to use events**

- **How to write functions to encapsulate your code**

- **How to handle input and output the modern way**

The Project: Mad Lib

The main project for this chapter will be a lot of fun. When the Mad Lib program starts, the Web page contains a form with a number of screen elements (see Figure 4.1).

The Web page consists of an HTML form with a series of text boxes, a command button, and a large text area. This program does not use dialog boxes at all. Instead, the program integrates all of the input and output directly into the Web page itself (see Figures 4.2 and 4.3).

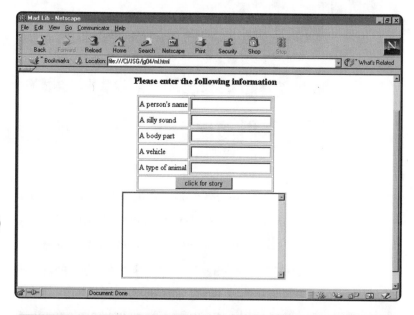

FIGURE 4.1

In the Mad Lib program, the HTML page itself plays a critical role.

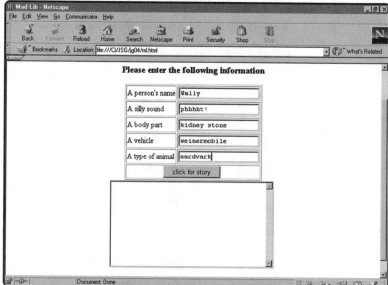

FIGURE 4.2

The user has typed some values into a form.

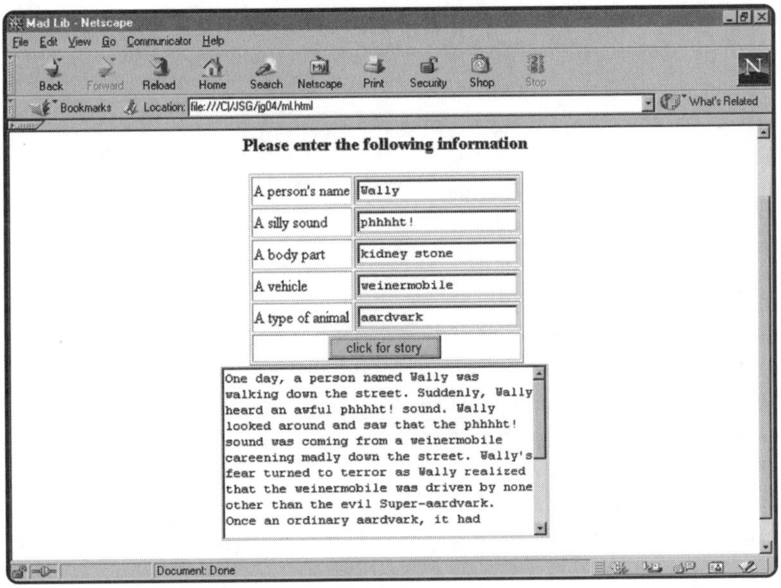

FIGURE 4.3

After the user presses the Click for Story button, the text box displays a silly story.

The results of this program can be very funny. Of course, the program is even more fun when you make up your own story and have the user enter more words.

From a programming standpoint, this game brings a lot of new elements to the table. Before now, your programs have had very little relationship to any other HTML you may have had on your pages. This game tightly integrates HTML and JavaScript.

Objects and HTML

To get your JavaScript programs to interact with the pages in which you place them, you need to understand how JavaScript sees Web pages. This concept might seem a little strange at first, but it is a very important idea, and you'll have a lot of power when you understand it.

The Color Flasher Program

Figures 4.4 and 4.5 show the Color Flasher program, which demonstrates how a JavaScript program can interact with the Web page in which it resides.

The program steps through a number of colors, dynamically changing the Web page's background color. This effect would not be possible with ordinary HTML. Here is the code for this program:

```
<html>
<head>
<title>Color Flasher</title>
<script>
// Color Flasher
// Andy Harris
```

```
// Demonstrates use of the bgColor method

document.bgColor = "red";
alert("ready for another color?");

document.bgColor = "orange";
alert("ready for another color?");

document.bgColor = "yellow";
alert("ready for another color?");

document.bgColor = "green";
alert("ready for another color?");

document.bgColor = "blue";
alert("ready for another color?");

document.bgColor = "indigo";
alert("ready for another color?");

document.bgColor = "violet";
alert("ready for another color?");

document.bgColor = "black";
alert("ready for another color?");

document.bgColor = "white";

</script>
</head>

<body>
<center><center>
<h1>Color Flasher<br></h1>
</center>
<hr>
</body>
</html>
```

The Color Flasher code is very repetitive. The only new concept is demonstrated in a bunch of lines that look like this:

```
document.bgColor = "violet";
```

As you can tell, the program copies the value `violet` to something called `document.bgColor`, which is a special variable-like entity that is used to refer to the background color of the document.

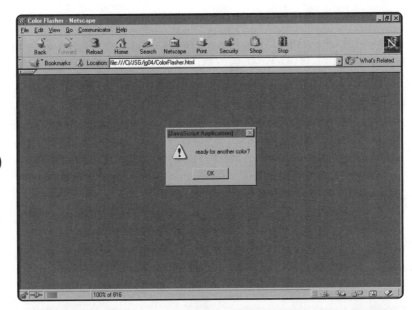

FIGURE 4.4

Although this black and white screenshot doesn't indicate the color, the program is displaying the Web page with a red background.

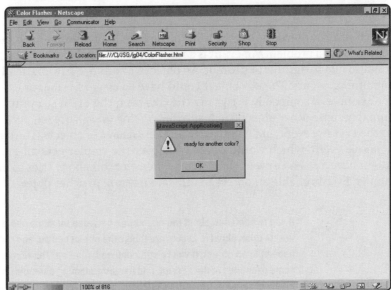

FIGURE 4.5

After the user clicks the OK button, the background changes to another color.

The Characteristics of Objects

JavaScript uses *object-based programming,* a scheme whereby certain elements (such as the parts of a Web page, for example) are defined as *objects.* In the real world, you use objects all the time. Any kind of object—whether it is a Web page, a stapler, or an elephant—has certain defining elements. Programmers call these features of an object *properties, methods,* and *events.* To explain these concepts, I'll start by talking about the kinds of objects you know in the real world (cows and staplers, to be specific). Then I'll explain how JavaScript uses objects to manage the Web page.

Properties

A property of an object is some particular characteristic of an object. A `cow` object might have properties such as `name`, `breed`, `age`, `weight`, and `owner`. A `stapler` object could have properties such as `color`, `manufacturer`, `numberOfStaples`, and `stapleCapacity`. Properties are like adjectives in human languages. They contain data, like variables do. Some properties contain text, and some contain numbers or boolean (true/false) values. Properties give the object the capacity to *hold information.*

Methods

If a property is an adjective, a method is like a verb. A method is something that the object can do. You've already seen some examples of methods in this book. You might recall the `toUpperCase()` method of the `String` object, or `Math.random()`, which is a reference to the `random()` method of the `Math` object. The `cow` object's methods might include `eat`, `moo`, and `giveMilk`. A `stapler` object might have methods like `fasten` (to staple pages together) and `openFlat` (to staple things to the wall). Methods give objects the ability to *do things.*

Events

The closest counterparts to events in the English language are messages such as "Houston, we have a problem. An event is a message that the object can send to other objects. It is also like a stimulus or prompt. An object's events are automatically triggered when something occurs. The `cow` object could have `hungry`, `tipping`, or `givingBirth` events, for example. If somebody is tipping the cow over, the `tipping` event would occur. Presumably some other object (such as a `sheriff` or `farmer` object, perhaps) will respond to the `tipping` event and chase away all the `sophomore` objects. The stapler might have a `jammed` event, which would occur whenever the stapler gets all gummed up. It also might have a `pressed` event that occurs whenever somebody tries to press down on the stapler. Events enable an object to indicate its state to other objects.

TRICK

If you're confused about the distinction between methods and events, here's another way to think about it: Events are things the object can do, and methods are things that happen to an object. If you're still confused, read on. The rest of the chapter looks at some examples in JavaScript, and the programming examples should help you make plenty of sense of properties, methods, and events as they are used in JavaScript.

Reading the Properties of an Object

You actually used some properties already in the Color Flasher program. You repeatedly changed the .bgcolor property of the document object. Document Info is another program that draws a little more deeply from the mysterious `document` object and a few of its key properties.

The Document Info Program

The Document Info program pops up a number of dialog boxes that give information about the page containing the JavaScript code (see Figure 4.6).

JavaScript has an object called `document`. This object refers to the HTML page in which the JavaScript code resides. The `document` object, like most objects, has properties,

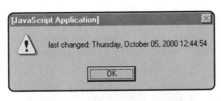

FIGURE 4.6

The Document Info program's dialog boxes describe characteristics of a document that are stored in the `document` object's properties.

events, and methods. Here's the code that demonstrates some properties of the document object:

```
<html>
<head>
<title>Document Info</title>
<script>

  // Document Info
  // Andy Harris
  // Demonstrate some properties of the document object
  alert("background: " + document.bgColor);
  alert("domain: " + document.domain);
  alert("last changed: " + document.lastModified);
  alert("URL: " + document.location);
  alert("Last page: " + document.referrer);
  alert("Title: " + document.title);

</script>
</head>

<body>
<center>
<h1>Document Info<hr></h1>
</center>
<hr>
</body>
</html>
```

The code consists of a series of `alert` statements. These statements all include references to the `document` object.

Document Properties

The `document` object is very important in JavaScript programming. It represents the Web page containing the JavaScript code. The properties of the object reveal important information about the Web page. Table 4.1 details a partial list of the properties of the `document` object.

In addition to these properties, if a Web page contains forms and form elements, they are also available as properties. You will see this soon.

A `document` property is very much like a variable, except that you do not have to define it yourself. The property is built into the browser. Some properties, such as the `bgColor` property, can be written to and read from. You can print out the value of `document.bgColor`, or you can assign a value to it to change the document's background color.

	TABLE 4.1 DOCUMENT OBJECT PROPERTIES
Property	**Description**
bgColor	The background color assigned to the page's body.
taglastModified	The date that the document was last changed.
title	The title of the document.
url	The address of the document.
domain	The domain name of the document's host.
referrer	If the user got to this page via a hyperlink, this property shows the address of the page that referred to the current one.

Platform Issues

Whereas JavaScript itself is a reasonably standard environment, browser manufacturers have been horribly inconsistent in how they define document objects. Netscape Navigator and Microsoft Internet Explorer both have document objects, but these objects are not identical. Each browser manufacturer has implemented different properties, events, and methods for its specific document object. Even when both of the major browsers provide their document objects with properties that share the same name, those properties do not always behave exactly the same. This is a very frustrating problem for JavaScript programmers. Fortunately, there is a subset of document properties that act pretty much the same on both browsers. This book sticks with the properties that work the same on either browser. That way, your Web page won't exclude any users simply because they do not have the browser that you used to create your page.

 TRICK Always check your programs in both the major browsers. Something that works great in one browser won't necessarily work in the other without some tweaking.

Methods

The document object also has some interesting methods. These are things that the document can do. The Document Methods program demonstrates some of the most important of the document object's methods.

The Document Methods Program

The Document Methods program has an old-fashioned prompt for getting input to the user, but the program then incorporates that value directly into the Web page (see Figures 4.7 and 4.8).

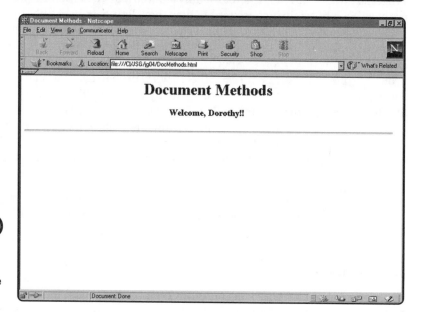

FIGURE 4.7

The Document
Methods program
prompts for the
user's name with a
prompt statement.

FIGURE 4.8

The program
incorporates the
user's name into the
actual Web page.

After getting input from the user, the program uses that input to modify the actual
Web page as it is being written to the browser. The program does so by invoking the
write() method of the document object. Take a look at the code for this program:

```
<html>
<head>
<title>Document Methods</title>
<script>
// Document Methods
```

```
// Andy Harris
// Demonstrates writing to the document

var userName = prompt("Hi!  What's your name?");
</script>
</head>

<body>
<center><center>
<h1>Document Methods<br></h1>
</center>
<h3>
<script>
document.write("Welcome, ");
document.write(userName);
document.write("!!");
document.close();
</script>
</h3>
<hr>
</body>
</html>
```

This document actually has two `script` areas. The first one creates the variable `userName` and gets its value from the user via the `prompt` statement. Inside the document body is another `script` pair. This second `script` invokes the `write()` method of the `document` object several times, then the `close()` method of document. After the script finishes, there is a little more HTML.

TRAP

The preceding code is actually the code used to build this page. If you look at the source code of the page after the program has run, it will not be exactly the same. I'll explain this anomaly in just a moment.

Using document.write()

The `document.write` method allows you to write text to the current document. This is a nice capability, because it means you can modify the actual HTML that the user sees. In addition to writing plain text, you can write HTML tags that the browser will interpret as though they came directly from the original text file.

Using document.close()

HTML documents don't come across the Internet in one big piece. Instead, a Web page comes across as a long stream of text, which the browser then interprets for information about how to lay out the page. When a Web page comes across the Internet, you can't really count on the browser laying it out until the entire page has come across. In fact,

IN THE REAL WORLD

Although the `document.write()` method looks like a great way to interact with the user, it has some serious limitations. The method can't really be interactive, because the document can be closed only one time. Programmers usually use the method only for very simple tasks such as reporting the current time or customizing the page. Chapter 6, "*Petals around the Rose: Dynamic Output*," will show you how you can work with other frames and windows. In these cases, the `document.write()` method will be more useful. Still, it is a good example of a method.

the page sends a signal telling the browser, in effect, that it is finished sending the information necessary to display the page. When you generate portions of a Web page via JavaScript, you are essentially changing the page as it loads. The browser will not necessarily write new information just because a `document.write` method has executed. You can signal to the browser that you are done writing by invoking the `close()` method of the `document` object.

Events

Recall that objects have properties, methods, and events. To demonstrate how events work, I'll move away from the `document` object a little bit and examine the most common kind of event in the graphical programming world, clicking a button.

The Don't Click Program

The Don't Click program poses an irresistible challenge to the user. It incorporates an HTML form with a button, as shown in Figures 4.9 and 4.10.

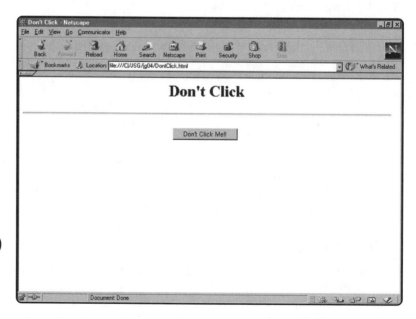

FIGURE 4.9

There's that button, just daring the user to click it.

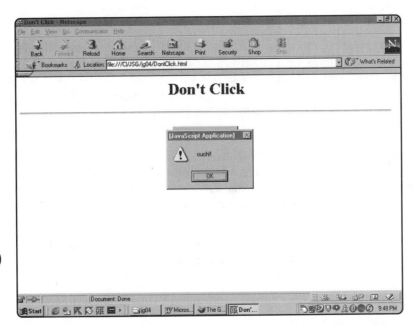

FIGURE 4.10

The user couldn't
resist the
temptation.

When the user clicks the button, the program complains. It then waits for the user to click again. Here's the code for the Don't Click program:

```
<html>
<head>
<title>Don't Click</title>
</head>

<body>
<center><center>
<h1>Don't Click<br></h1>
</center>
<hr>
<form name = myForm>
<input type = "button"
      value = "Don't Click Me!!"
      onClick = 'alert("ouch!!")'>
</form>

</body>
</html>
```

This program is unusual because it does not contain a `script` tag pair. Still, it does have some JavaScript code. The other interesting thing about this program is its use of HTML forms.

The form Object

Many JavaScript programs are related to HTML forms, because forms are containers for interesting components such as text boxes and command buttons. To make a form, just surround a part of your HTML code with a `<form></form>` pair. Inside that form, you can add the `<input>` elements such as text boxes, command buttons, and radio buttons. It's a good idea to name forms and the elements that they contain, so you can refer to these objects in code. Note that I named the `form` object when I defined it:

```
<form name = myForm>
```

The `name` attribute is used to add a name to various HTML elements. I almost always name my forms something like `myForm`. It usually doesn't matter too much what you name a form, but you should name it something.

TRAP

Do not forget to close your form. If you do not include a `</form>` tag, some browsers will display very strange results.

Inside the form, I have placed a command button. Here is the code that does that work:

```
<input type = "button"
      value = "Don't Click Me!!"
      onClick = 'alert("ouch!!")'>
```

The `input` object is a versatile HTML object. It is used to generate several elements; in this example, it creates a button. The `type` attribute determines which type of element to generate. The `value` element describes what to write on the button. The `onClick` attribute is the part that performs the magic.

The onClick Event

HTML buttons have an `onClick` attribute. The value of this attribute is very special. It can contain one line of JavaScript code. Whenever a user clicks the button, the `onClick` event is triggered and the browser runs that one line of JavaScript. In this case, the `onClick` attribute contains the JavaScript code to generate the `alert` statement.

TRICK

Note the use of single and double quotation marks. JavaScript and HTML both allow you to alternate single and double quotes, to avoid confusion.

Although the `onClick` event is very useful, it can be somewhat limiting to be restricted to that one line of JavaScript code. Fortunately, JavaScript, like most languages, enables you to generate new virtual commands, so that just one statement in the `onClick` attribute can call an unlimited number of commands. As usual, an example, the Don't Click Function program, helps to explain this concept better than plain old text.

The Don't Click Function Program

Figures 4.11 and 4.12 show the Don't Click Function program. This variation of the Don't Click program looks very similar to the original program, but it is not identical.

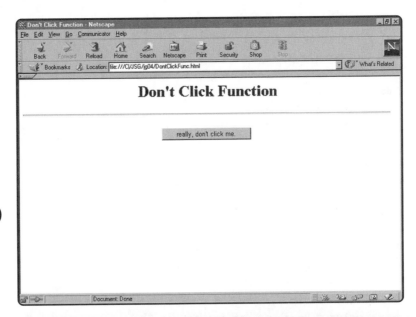

FIGURE 4.11

The Don't Click Function program starts out the same way as the Don't Click program.

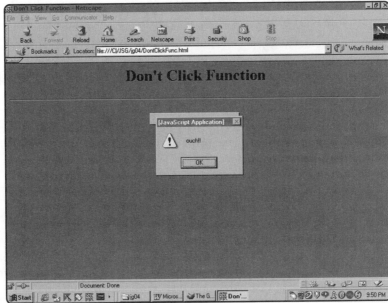

FIGURE 4.12

The alert statement pops up and the background color changes.

When the user clicks the button this time, the program does two things: It displays an alert dialog box and changes the background color. Clearly the one-line limitation will not allow this without some minor trickery. If you look under the hood, you'll see that this program has some new structural elements:

```
<html>
<head>
<title>Don't Click Function</title>
<script>
```

```
function sayOuch(){
  // Don't Click Function
  // Andy Harris
  // demonstrates use of functions
  document.bgColor = "red";
  alert ("ouch!!");
  document.bgColor = "white";
} // end function
</script>
</head>

<body>
<center>
<h1>Don't Click Function<br></h1>
<hr>
<form name = myForm>
<input type = button
       value = "really, don't click me."
       onClick = sayOuch()>
</form>

</center>
</body>
</html>
```

The header area includes a script that the button's `onClick` event seems to invoke. The button still has one line of JavaScript in the `onClick` attribute, but that line of code is not standard JavaScript.

The Purpose of Functions

If someone were to ask you what you did this morning before work, you would probably say something like "I got up, took a shower, got dressed, ate breakfast, and drove to work." You probably wouldn't describe all the details of your breakfast ("I walked into the kitchen, got a spoon and a bowl, found the cereal, got milk from the refrigerator...") because the phrase "ate breakfast" covers all of those details.

Functions work in exactly the same way. You can put together a series of commands and give them a name. Then, whenever you want the computer to follow that series of steps again, you just use the name as if it were a command built into the language. This is exactly how the Don't Click Function program is built.

Creating a Function

Look again at the script inside the header area of the HTML:

```
function sayOuch(){
```

```
// Don't Click Function
// Andy Harris
// demonstrates use of functions
document.bgColor = "red";
alert ("ouch!!");
document.bgColor = "white";
} // end function
```

The header section begins with a function definition. The term sayOuch() is the name of the function. The parentheses are used to indicate that no special values will be sent to this function. (You'll get to send parameters in another chapter.) Most of the code is enclosed inside a pair of braces and indented to indicate it is part of some kind of structure. Most JavaScript programs are actually defined in the header as a function or as multiple functions. These functions are called from events of form elements inside the body of the HTML document. Defining a function in the header area guarantees that the function will be in memory by the time it is needed as the browser is interpreting the rest of the document.

Calling a Function from an Event

Once a function is defined, it is a simple matter to use it. In the rest of the document, the function simply becomes another JavaScript command. Here's where I used sayOuch():

```
<input type = button
       value = "really, don't click me."
       onClick = "sayOuch()">
```

When the user clicks the button, the program automatically calls the sayOuch() function. Program control jumps to that function, which changes the document color, alerts the user, and changes the color back.

Event-Driven Input and Output

The use of HTML forms and event-handling capabilities can be combined to allow more graceful input and output than the dialog boxes that you have been using so far. Dialog boxes are functional, but they tend to annoy the user, because they interrupt the natural flow of the program. It would be much better to have the input and output be more naturally integrated into the Web page.

Creating the Name Grabber Program

Figures 4.13 and 4.14 show the Name Grabber program, which uses text boxes to handle input and output. This program doesn't use any dialog boxes at all.

The Name Grabber program does input and output by manipulating elements of the form. This program introduces only one new feature: HTML text boxes. The text boxes replace both the prompt and the alert dialog boxes.

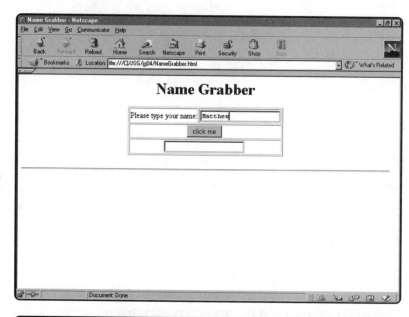

The page that the
Name Grabber
program displays
contains text boxes.
Users type their
name into the first
text box.

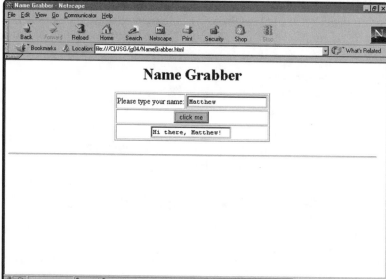

After the user clicks
the button, a
greeting pops up in
the second text box.

Here's the code in its entirety:

```
<html>
<head>
<title>Name Grabber</title>
<script>
function copyName(){
  // Name Grabber
  // Andy Harris
```

```
    // demonstrates form-based I/O
    var userName = document.myForm.txtName.value;
    var greeting = "Hi there, ";
    greeting += userName;
    greeting += "!";
    document.myForm.txtGreeting.value = greeting;
} // end copyName
</script>
</head>

<body>
<center>
<h1>Name Grabber<br></h1>
<form name = myForm>

<table border = 1>
<tr>
  <td>Please type your name:</td>
  <td><input type = "text"
            name = "txtName"></td>
</tr>

<tr>
  <td colspan = 2><center>
  <input type = "button"
        value = "click me"
        onClick = "copyName()">
  </center></td>
</tr>

<tr>
  <td colspan = 2><center>
  <input type = "text"
        name = "txtGreeting">
  </center></td>
</tr>


</table>
</form>
</center>
```

The code consists of a JavaScript function written in the header, with a series of HTML form elements playing parts in the process. The easiest way to understand what's happening is to look at the code as two main segments: the HTML code and the copyName() function.

Writing the HTML Code

First, take a look at the HTML code. When you're looking at somebody else's JavaScript code, it's generally a good idea to look at the HTML code before you worry about the JavaScript code, because the HTML sets the stage. This program's HTML code consists of a form with three elements. The form is named myForm, and it has a text box, a button, and another text box.

TRICK

Tables and forms are a really great combination. Often I hide the table border (<table border = 0>), but I have learned that forms lend themselves to the kind of organization that I want on the screen. As you gain more experience, try other ways of arranging HTML (such as cascading style sheet positionable elements, discussed in Chapter 8, "Dynamic HTML: The Stealth Submarine,") and develop a style that works best for your pages.

Take a look at the code that generated the first text box:

```
<input type = "text"
       name = "txtName">
```

This is another form of the input tag, but this time the type is set to text, giving the text box a totally different appearance and behavior. The browser places a text box on the form. The code specifies no value attribute, so the text box starts out blank but enables the user to type into it. The text box's name attribute is set to txtName. You'll see in a moment that it is critical to name this text box.

TRICK

Many programmers use prefixes such as txt to denote text boxes and cmd to denote command buttons. This convention makes it easier to manage your code when you have a large number of objects defined. When you look at the term txtName, it's easy to guess that it describes a text box that has something to do with a name.

The code that generates the other text box is not terribly different, but the second text box is named txtGreeting. It also has no value specified, so it also starts out blank.

The code for the button is as follows:

```
<input type = "button"
       value = "click me"
       onClick = "copyName()">
```

This code generates a button with the label "click me." When the user clicks the button, the copyName() function should execute. The next section explains what the copyName() function does.

Writing the copyName() Function

The copyName() function is built in the header of the HTML document. It looks a bit different than some of the other scripts that you have seen so far:

```
function copyName(){
```

```
// Name Grabber
// Andy Harris
// demonstrates form-based I/O
var greeting = "Hi there, ";
var userName = document.myForm.txtName.value;
greeting += userName;
greeting += "!";
document.myForm.txtGreeting.value = greeting;
} // end copyName
```

The script starts by creating some variables, `greeting` and `userName`. Take a careful look at the line that gets a value for `userName`. It looks really intimidating, but it actually isn't that complex. `document.myForm.txtName.value` is another name for the contents of the `txtName` text box. The `document` object has as a property the form `myForm`. This object has a `txtName` property, which is the text box. The text box in turn has a `value` property, which represents whatever text is in the text box (see Figure 4.15). It works very much like a complex path in an operating system. If you see a filename like c:\documents\memos\incriminating\extortion.doc, you can tell that the filename is referring to a specific file in a tree structure.

When you build an HTML form, you are also building a complex structure just as you do as you build new folders in a file management system. In HTML, however, the pattern is a little more rigid. The form is a node, and all the objects inside the form are nodes. Each of these objects might have its own properties, such as `value`. It's actually quite an elegant solution. Note the following line:

```
var userName = document.myForm.txtName.value;
```

The net result of this line is to copy the value of `txtName` to the `userName` variable. `document.myForm.txtName.value` essentially becomes a variable that you can assign values to and from, just like any other variable. Once you understand this, the following line makes perfect sense as well:

```
document.myForm.txtGreeting.value = greeting;
```

This line simply copies the value of the `greeting` variable to `txtGreeting`, which makes the value visible to the user.

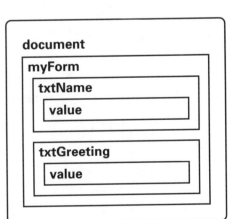

FIGURE 4.15

This diagram illustrates how the various elements of the Name Grabber Web page are connected.

Back to the Mad Lib Program

The Mad Lib program turns out to be very straightforward once you know how to do form-based input and output. Since the code is getting a little long, I will show it to you broken into sections. You should look on the CD included with this book for the entire program. Besides, it's more fun to play the game yourself.

Planning the Game

The first step is to build the story. There are a lot of ways to do this. If you are naturally creative, just write a story and keep track of the words that you want to use as "fill-in" words—the words that you want to replace with the user's choices. Be sure to write out the entire story and the list of "fill-in" words before you start programming. Have the story written out so you know exactly what you will need to be doing in the code. Sketch out the form on paper. Write down the names of any of the objects that you will be using (most likely text boxes, a text area, and a button). This planning will make your coding much easier.

Building the HTML Code

Build the HTML first. Match closely the visual layout of the program that you sketched earlier, with all the text boxes and text areas generally in the right places. Don't forget to name the form, text boxes, and text area. You don't need to name the button, because you will never access any of its properties, but you can if you wish. Here is my HTML code: (Note that it does not yet include any JavaScript code. I will show you that in the next section.)

```
<body>
<center>
<h1>Mad Lib<hr></h1>
<form name = myForm>
<h3>Please enter the following information</h3>
<table border = 1>

<tr>
  <td>A person's name</td>
  <td><input type = text name = txtPerson></td>
</tr>

<tr>
  <td>A silly sound</td>
  <td><input type = text name = txtSound></td>
</tr>

<tr>
  <td>A body part</td>
```

```
      <td><input type = text name = txtPart></td>
   </tr>

   <tr>
      <td>A vehicle</td>
      <td><input type = text name = txtVehicle></td>
   </tr>

   <tr>
      <td>A type of animal</td>
      <td><input type = text name = txtAnimal></td>
   </tr>

   <tr>
      <td colspan = 2><center>
         <input type = button
                value = "click for story"
                onClick = makeML()>
      </td>
   </tr>

</table>

<textarea name = txtStory
          rows = 10
          cols = 40
          wrap>
</textarea>

</form>
</center>

<hr>
</body>
</html>
```

Note especially the use of the text area. The output will be a long story, and I need a place to put it. A text area is perfect for this. Turning on the word-wrap feature (with the `wrap` attribute) ensures that the entire story will be visible without requiring you to put in carriage returns. Also notice that I rigged up the button to trigger the `makeML()` function (which doesn't yet exist). It's a great idea to test your HTML code before you start working on the JavaScript code.

Getting the Inputs

Once the HTML is solid, you can turn your attention to the function itself. Here is the beginning of the function definition:

```
function makeML(){
  // Mad Lib
  // Andy Harris
  // make a silly story from a bunch of input terms

  //get variables from form
  var person = window.document.myForm.txtPerson.value;
  var sound = document.myForm.txtSound.value;
  var part = document.myForm.txtPart.value;
  var vehicle = document.myForm.txtVehicle.value;
  var animal = document.myForm.txtAnimal.value;
  var story = "";
```

This part of the program simply creates variables and extracts them from the various elements of the form. It is not coincidental that `person` and `txtPerson` are so similar. In a repetitive program such as this one, it is wise to generate some kind of naming convention so that you can keep track of all the various form elements and the variables to which they are related. The `story` variable will contain the entire story before it is displayed in the text area.

Building a Long String

Building the story turns out to be one of the easier things to do. Take a look at how I did that:

```
story = "One day, a person named " ;
  story += person;
  story += " was walking down the street. Suddenly, ";
  story += person;
  story += " heard an awful ";
  story += sound;
  story += " sound. ";
  story += person;
  story += " looked around and saw that the ";
  story += sound;
  story += " sound was coming from a ";
  story +=  vehicle;
  story += " careening madly down the street. ";
  story +=  person;
  story += "'s fear turned to terror as ";
  story += person;
```

```
story += " realized that the ";
story += vehicle;
story += " was driven by none other than the evil Super-";
story += animal;
story += ".  Once an ordinary ";
story += animal;
story += ", it had befallen a strange transformation after ";
story += "being dropped in a vat of nuclear waste. ";
story += "Super-"
story += animal;
story += " continued to taunt ";
story += person
story += " with the horrible ";
story += sound;
story += " noise, but ";
story += person;
story += " was unconcerned. \"You can't bother me, Super-";
story += animal;
story += "!  I know how to turn the other ";
story += part;
story += "!\"  \nThe End."

    document.myForm.txtStory.value = story;
```

`} // end makeML`

I alternated text and variables. It would be very tempting to write long concatenations, as in the following example:

```
story += "Super-" + animal + " continued to taunt ";
```

The problem is that lines like this can be very difficult to debug.

TRAP

The reason lines like these can be difficult to debug is that it gets hard to figure out what is inside the quotes and is meant to be interpreted as a literal value, and what is outside the quotes, which will be interpreted as a variable or function name. For example, will the preceding line actually print the word "animal" or will it print the value of the `animal` variable? It all depends on the placement of the quotes and the plus signs.

One more interesting thing to note is the use of \" in the last line of the story (as well as a few other places). The backslash character indicates that the quotation mark should not be interpreted as the end of the string, but literally as a quotation mark.

Once the story is built, it is a simple matter to copy it to the `txtStory` text area for output.

Table 4.2 provides an easy reference of the new syntax covered in this chapter.

TABLE 4.2 SYNTAX SUMMARY

Statement	Description	Example

`function funcName() { }`	Creates a new function.	`function doIt(){`
		`   alert("I did it");`
		`} // end function`

Summary

This chapter covered some major territory. You learned about the notion of objects and their principal characteristics. You began to explore properties, methods, and events. You took a first look at the `document` object, and at how event-driven programming ties JavaScript more closely to the Web page. You also learned how to copy values to and from text fields and text areas. In the next chapter, you will learn how to work with other kinds of screen components, such as radio buttons, check boxes, and drop-down lists. The next chapter continues to develop the Mad Lib program by adding a number of other user interface elements to the screen.

EXERCISES

1. Write a program that uses a prompt to ask the user's favorite color, then changes the form's background to that color.

2. Modify the preceding program so that the user types the color into a text box and then clicks a button to get the color.

3. Write a program that gets the user's first, middle, and last names, and returns the user's full name in another text box.

4. Write a program that writes the current date and time at the top of a Web page. (Hint: `var theTime = new Date()` will create a variable with the date in it.)

5. Modify the Number Guesser game from Chapter 3 so that it uses form-based input and output. (Tip: It will *not* need a loop!)

CHAPTER

5

Advanced Mad Lib: Using the Other Form Elements

In the last chapter, the programs accepted all user input in text boxes and text areas. Although the basic text elements are extremely flexible, HTML and JavaScript allow you to use a number of other screen components. In this chapter, you will learn how to work with other elements of an HTML form, and how JavaScript interacts with them. Specifically, you will learn how to do the following:

- Use other text-based elements, such as password and hidden input boxes

- Create and interact with forms that use check boxes

- Use radio buttons and understand how they differ from check boxes

- Organize screen elements into arrays

- Build and use selection lists for user input

Project: The Advanced Mad Lib

In this chapter, you will build a variation of the Mad Lib game from Chapter 4, "The Basic Mad Lib Program and Object-Based Programming." The basic idea will be the same, but the form on this version will have a number of elements that users expect from a graphical user interface (see Figure 5.1).

These elements make the user interface a little more convenient for users, because they usually do not have to type as much. The elements are also convenient for the programmer, because they limit the user's choices to only legitimate values.

Working with Text-Like Objects

You learned how to manipulate the text box and text area in the last chapter. JavaScript has a number of elements that are very similar from the programmer's perspective. These elements (like most form components) are created with variations of the HTML `<input>` tag.

The Password Program

The Password program demonstrates some of the text-like input elements (see Figure 5.2). Although only four elements are visible on the page, the page actually includes five elements.

The user chooses an option from a drop-down list.

Here the user selects one or more elements from a group of checkboxes.

The user can choose only one of these options.

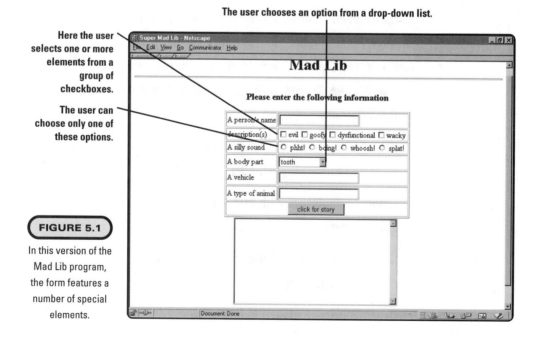

FIGURE 5.1

In this version of the Mad Lib program, the form features a number of special elements.

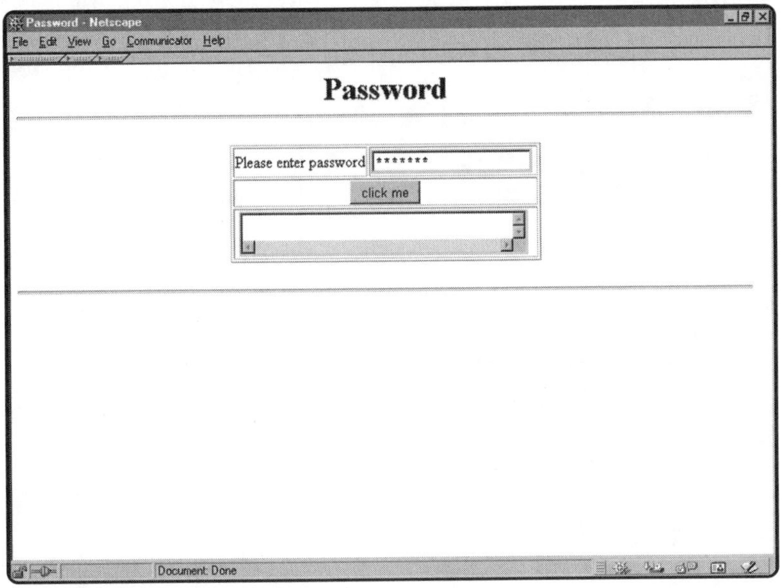

FIGURE 5.2

The Password program's interface features several text-like input elements.

The layout of the screen is reasonably straightforward. Here is the HTML code that generates the screen layout:

```html
<body>
<center>
<h1>Password<hr></h1>
<form name = "myForm">
<table border = 1>
<tr>
  <td>Please enter password</td>
  <td><input type = "password"
             name = "pwdGuess"></td>
</tr>

<tr>
  <td colspan = 2><center>
    <input type = "button"
           value = "click me"
           onClick = "checkPass()"></center>
  </td>
</tr>

<tr>
  <td colspan = 2>
```

```
      <center>
      <textArea name = "txtOutput"
                rows = 1
                cols = 35>
      </textarea>
      </center>
   </td>
</tr>
</table>
<input type = "hidden"
       name = "hdnSecret"
       value = "JavaScript">
</form>
<hr>


</center>
</body>
```

The form is laid out inside a table, and the table contains four elements. The first is a password box, then a button, and finally a text area. Outside the table is a fifth input element, a hidden field. This fifth field contains the correct password. When the user clicks the button, a function called checkPass() is executed. Here is the code for the checkPass() function:

```
<head>
<title>Password</title>
<script>
function checkPass(){
  // Password
  // Andy Harris
  // demonstrates several textlike elements

  var guess = document.myForm.pwdGuess.value;
  var secret = document.myForm.hdnSecret.value;
  if (guess == secret){
    document.myForm.txtOutput.value = "You may proceed.";
  } else {
    document.myForm.txtOutput.value = "That is incorrect.";
  } // end if
} // end checkPass
</script>
</head>
```

This function extracts the relevant details from the various form elements, compares the values, and returns an appropriate message.

Password Boxes

Password boxes are almost identical to text boxes as far as HTML and JavaScript are concerned. The only real differences are that an `<input type = password>` HTML statement generates the password and that asterisks (*) replace any values that the user types into the text field. The actual characters that the user types are still recorded, but the field displays only the asterisks. This prevents the KGB, Mafia, aliens, or whoever else from stealing your password by looking over your shoulder as you enter your password into the page. Password fields have a `value` property, and you can use JavaScript to copy values to and from the password in exactly the same way as you do with an ordinary text field.

TRAP

The password field is notoriously insecure, especially when used in JavaScript. The user can figure out the correct password by looking at the source code. JavaScript is not secure enough for any transaction that involves real security, but the password field can still be fun in game programming. You might use it as a "mood enhancer" if you're writing a game where the player is supposed to be a hacker, for example. You might also use the field in other instances where you want light security but secrecy isn't vital, such as to allow players to skip levels in an arcade game.

Hidden Fields

The other interesting element in this example is the hidden field. If you look closely at the HTML code, you will see this element listed:

```
<input type = "hidden"
       name = "hdnSecret"
       value = "JavaScript">
```

The code is much like that of text boxes and password boxes, but the hidden field has different behavior. It stores a value in a form, but the value is not visible at all to the user. In this example, I used the hidden field to store the correct password. You can use hidden fields in game programming to store values in the form. However, as a JavaScript programmer, you can do the same thing with variables, so hidden fields usually aren't necessary in JavaScript programs.

HINT

Why does the hidden field exist? If the hidden field isn't necessary, you might be surprised that it is supported at all in HTML. HTML supports the hidden field because programmers can attach HTML forms to programs written in many other kinds of languages. Sometimes an HTML form is connected to a program on the Web server. In these kinds of programs, hidden fields can be very useful, because the program can store information in the form that the program will need later.

Using Check Boxes

In some situations, the user should be able to choose from a group of elements. In other situations, the user should be able to choose any number of available options. The Music Chooser program presents users with check boxes that enable them to do both.

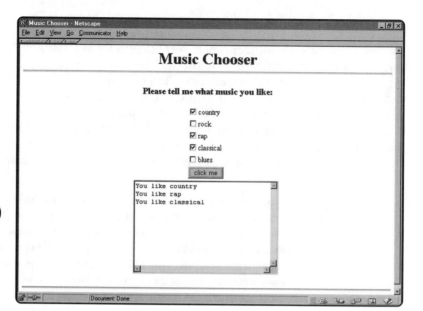

The form accepts any number of check-box inputs and returns an appropriate output.

The Music Chooser Program

As shown in Figure 5.3, the Music Chooser program asks users to select their favorite music genre through a group of check boxes.

The user can choose any of a series of check boxes. It's important to note that these boxes are not mutually exclusive. The status of any one check box has no particular effect on all the other check boxes. Most users have seen this type of input element before and know the kind of behavior to expect from it.

The Code for Creating Check Boxes in HTML

To understand how to write code for a group of check boxes, it is helpful to look at the HTML code. Check boxes are another variant of the `input` element. The HTML code that generates the Music Chooser screen looks like this:

Note that this code is only the HTML. The JavaScript code will be added in the next section.

```
<body>
<center>
<h1>Music Chooser<hr></h1>
<form name = myForm>
<h3>Please tell me what music you like:</h3>
<table border = 0>
<tr>
  <td><input type = "checkbox"
         name = "chkCountry"
```

```
              value = "country">country
    </td>
  </tr>


  <tr>
    <td><input type = "checkbox"
          name = "chkRock"
          value = "rock">rock
    </td>
  </tr>


  <tr>
    <td><input type = "checkbox"
          name = "chkRap"
          value = "rap">rap
    </td>
  </tr>


  <tr>
    <td><input type = "checkbox"
          name = "chkClassical"
          value = "classical">classical
    </td>
  </tr>


  <tr>
    <td><input type = "checkbox"
          name = "chkBlues"
          value = "blues">blues
    </td>
  </tr>


  <tr>
    <td><input type = "button"
          value = "click me"
          onClick = "processMusic()">
    </td>
  </tr>
</table>
<textarea name = "txtOutput"
          rows = 10
          cols = 35>
</textarea>


</form>
```

```
</center>
<hr>
</body>
```

The preceding is reasonably straightforward HTML code. It includes the expected form, with a series of check boxes. Each check box has a name and a value. Note that the value of a check box is not visible to the user. If you want to connect a label to a check box, you need to write that label as ordinary HTML code. It is very common to put checkbox elements in a list or table as I did here, to keep them neat. The code also contains a button to trigger the processMusic() function and a text area to contain the output of that function.

The Behavior of Check Boxes

The code to manipulate check-box components is also reasonably straightforward. The checkbox object has a value property, which corresponds to the value stored when the object was created in HTML. Check boxes also have another important property, checked. This property contains a true or false value. If the user selects the check box (and it was previously unchecked), the checked property is true. Usually you will want your program to do something only if the user has selected the check box. In this program, you want to execute the processMusic() function if the user selects a check box.

Here's the code for the processMusic() function:

```
function processMusic(){
  // Music Chooser
  // Andy Harris
  // demonstrates check boxes

  document.myForm.txtOutput.value = "";

  if (document.myForm.chkCountry.checked == true){
    document.myForm.txtOutput.value += "You like ";
    document.myForm.txtOutput.value += document.myForm.chkCountry.value;
    document.myForm.txtOutput.value += "\n";
  } // end if

  if (document.myForm.chkRock.checked == true){
    document.myForm.txtOutput.value += "You like ";
    document.myForm.txtOutput.value += document.myForm.chkRock.value;
    document.myForm.txtOutput.value += "\n";
  } // end if

  if (document.myForm.chkRap.checked == true){
    document.myForm.txtOutput.value += "You like ";
    document.myForm.txtOutput.value += document.myForm.chkRap.value;
    document.myForm.txtOutput.value += "\n";
```

```
} // end if

if (document.myForm.chkClassical.checked == true){
  document.myForm.txtOutput.value += "You like ";
  document.myForm.txtOutput.value += document.myForm.chkClassical.value;
  document.myForm.txtOutput.value += "\n";
} // end if

if (document.myForm.chkBlues.checked == true){
  document.myForm.txtOutput.value += "You like ";
  document.myForm.txtOutput.value += document.myForm.chkBlues.value;
  document.myForm.txtOutput.value += "\n";
} // end if

} // end processMusic
```

Although this looks like a lot of code, the function isn't nearly as complex as it seems at first glance. If you examine the code more closely, you can see that it really is very repetitive. The code is basically nothing more than a series of if statements. Each one checks a specific check box to see whether the user has selected it. If so, the function writes the value of that check box to the text area.

 Check boxes are usually used to let the user turn certain options on or off. You might use a check box in a preferences screen, for example, to indicate a number of options that the user can turn on or off.

It is important to remember that each check box is basically an independent entity. The values of the various check boxes are not related in any particular way, and each check box must be evaluated independently in the code.

Using Radio Buttons

Check boxes have a cousin called radio buttons. Radio buttons are similar to check boxes, but they behave differently when you place them in groups. They are used when you want the user to choose only one element from a group. Radio buttons get their name from the old car radios that had little buttons sticking out for the preselected stations. When you pressed a button, all the others would automatically stick out, because radios can be tuned to only one station at a time.

Creating the Size Chooser Program

The Size Chooser program provides an example of an HTML-JavaScript radio button group in action. Figures 5.4 and 5.5 show the program.

When the user clicks the OK button, the program agrees to get the appropriate size of whatever it is the user is ordering.

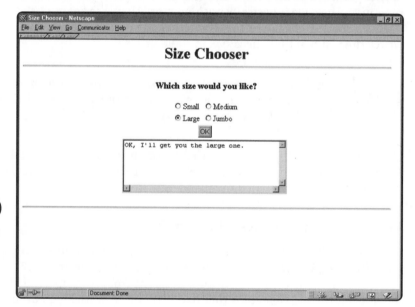

FIGURE 5.4

The user has selected a small size.

FIGURE 5.5

When the user then selects Large, the Small option is automatically unchecked.

Generating Radio Buttons in HTML Code

The HTML code to make radio buttons starts out very much like that of the other screen components that you have seen. But see whether you can spot the one significant difference in the code:

Please note that this is simply the HTML code for this program. I'll show you the JavaScript in the next section.

```
<body>
<center>
```

```
<h1>Size Chooser<hr></h1>
<form name = myForm>
<h3>Which size would you like?</h3>
<table border = 0>
<tr>
  <td>
    <input type = "radio"
           name = radSize
           value = "small">Small
  </td>

  <td>
    <input type = "radio"
           name = radSize
           value = "medium">Medium
  </td>
</tr>

<tr>
  <td>
    <input type = "radio"
           name = radSize
           value = "large">Large
  </td>

  <td>
    <input type = "radio"
           name = radSize
           value = "jumbo">Jumbo
  </td>
</tr>

<tr>
  <td colspan = 2>
    <center>
    <input type = "button"
           value = "OK"
           onClick = "processSize()">
    </center>
  </td>
</tr>
</table>
<textarea name = "txtOutput"
          rows = 5
          cols = 40>
```

```
</textarea>

</form>
</center>
<hr>
</body>
```

If you didn't see the strange new feature, take another look at the names of the radio buttons. All the radio buttons have the same name! I'll explain in the next section why I did that. For now, just note that the rest of the HTML code is pretty straightforward. There is a button attached to a function and a text area for output, just as in all the other programs in this chapter.

Placing Buttons in Arrays

What makes radio buttons special is the way that they act when placed in groups. Check boxes, as you recall, are pretty independent creatures. They don't really care whether the user has selected any other neighboring check boxes. Radio buttons, on the other hand, are team players. Each radio button expects to be part of a group. Whenever one button in the group is turned on, all the others will be turned off. Somehow you need to make all the buttons in a group aware of which group they are in. In HTML code, you make all the radio buttons part of a group by giving them all the same name.

Although it seems kind of strange to have a bunch of things with the same name, it isn't really all that unusual. If you're playing golf, you might have a scorecard that looks something like Figure 5.6.

A small golf course might have nine holes. The holes are usually numbered. Each golfer keeps track of how many strokes it takes to get the ball in the cup. In effect, the golfer has a score for each hole. The golfer might refer to the first score as the score for hole 1. The next score would be the score for hole 2, and so on.

Hyper Links

Hole	Score
1	4
2	3
3	5
4	
5	
6	
7	
8	
9	

FIGURE 5.6

A scorecard for a golfer.

Programming languages usually refer to this kind of structure as an array. An array is a group of similar things, all with the same name, but with different numeric indices. JavaScript refers to an array with square bracket (`[]`) notation. By generating a series of radio buttons all with the same name, you have created an array. Programming languages usually count beginning at 0, so the Small radio button is also known as `radSize[0]`, the Medium radio button is `radSize[1]`, and so on.

Using Variables to Simplify the Code

The code for a series of radio buttons looks a little bit intimidating, but when you look at it a little bit at a time, it isn't too bad. Before you see the code itself, here's the strategy. I'll use a `for` loop to generate numbers from 0 to 3. Each time through the loop, I'll look at the appropriately numbered radio button. If the user selected that button, I'll remember the value associated with that button in a variable. After the loop completes, the variable will contain the value of whichever button the user clicked. Take a look at the code, and you'll see how I did it:

```
<script>
function processSize(){
  // Size Chooser
  // Andy Harris
  // Demonstrates radio buttons
  var size;
  var i;
  var theOption;
  for (i = 0; i <= 3; i++){
    theOption = document.myForm.radSize[i];
    if (theOption.checked == true){
      size = theOption.value;
    } // end if
  } // end for loop
  document.myForm.txtOutput.value = "OK, I'll get you the ";
  document.myForm.txtOutput.value += size + " one.";
} // end function
</script>
```

The function starts out simply enough. The `size` variable will eventually contain the size of object that the user is ordering. The variable `i` is used in the `for` loop. (This is one of those instances where the actual value of the `for` loop counter does not matter, so `i` is an appropriate variable name.) The last variable, `theOption`, is a little more puzzling. JavaScript allows you to store many kinds of things in variables. You can even store an object in a variable. Doing so can make your life quite a bit simpler, as you will see in a moment.

The following line begins a `for` loop that will repeat three times:

```
for (i = 0; i <= 3; i++){
```

The value of `i` will (at various times) be 0, 1, 2, and 3. Remember that JavaScript begins counting at 0. Because there are four radio buttons, they will be numbered 0 to 3.

The following line gets the i *th* button:

```
theOption = document.myForm.radSize[i];
```

When i is 0, `document.myForm.radSize[0]` (the radio button associated with the value small) will be copied to the variable theOption. Every time through the loop, i will have a different value, and another radio button will be copied to the theOption variable.

The next line checks whether the user has selected the current radio button:

```
if (theOption.checked == true){
```

If the value is true, the following line copies the value property of the object to the size variable:

```
size = theOption.value;
```

If the current radio button is not selected, nothing happens. The loop continues until all four radio buttons have been checked.

The last two lines generate output for the txtOutput text area:

```
document.myForm.txtOutput.value = "OK, I'll get you the ";
document.myForm.txtOutput.value += size + " one.";
```

You can replicate the following general strategy any time you want to get the value of the currently selected radio button:

1. Create variables for the loop, for the result, and to hold a reference to a radio button.
2. Make a for loop that steps from 0 to the number of buttons in the group minus 1.
3. Assign the current button to the button variable.
4. If the button is selected, copy the value to the result variable.
5. Repeat the loop until it has checked all buttons.

Of course, for every group of radio buttons that you use on the page, you will need to repeat this procedure. Fortunately, you can copy and paste it and just modify the new version to fit each particular group of radio buttons.

Using the select Object

The last of the new elements that you will look at in this chapter is the select object. This is also known as a list box in many programming languages. The Color Chooser program is an example that uses a select object.

Creating the Color Chooser Program

The Color Chooser program displays a list of colors (see Figure 5.7). When the user clicks the list box, the list of colors drops down. After the user selects a color from the list, the selected color is then displayed in the list box. When the user clicks the OK button, the document's background color is reset to the selected color (see Figure 5.8).

This type of selection object is efficient because it takes up less space on the screen than the equivalent set of option buttons.

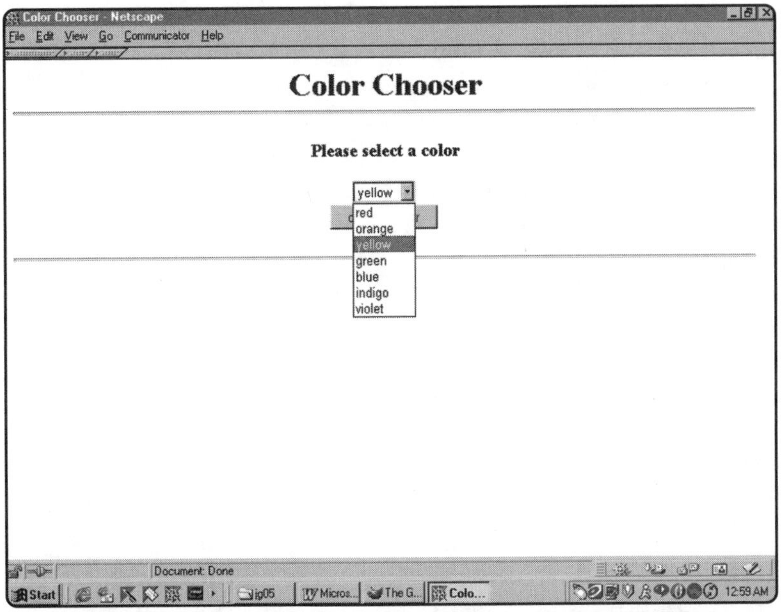

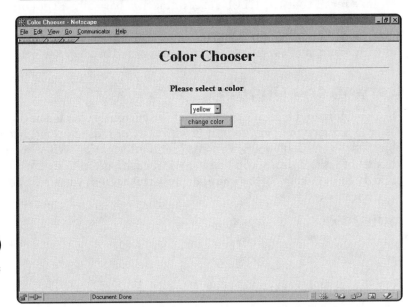

FIGURE 5.7

The user is about to select yellow from the drop-down list.

FIGURE 5.8

The background has changed to the selected color.

Creating the select Object in HTML

Here's the HTML that was used to generate the select object:

```
<body>
<center>
<h1>Color Chooser<hr></h1>
<h3>Please select a color</h3>
<form name = "myForm">
```

```
<select name = selColor>
  <option value = red>red</option>
  <option value = orange>orange</option>
  <option value = yellow>yellow</option>
  <option value = green>green</option>
  <option value = blue>blue</option>
  <option value = indigo>indigo</option>
  <option value = violet>violet</option>
</select>
<br>
<input type = "button"
       value = "change color"
       onClick = "changeColor()">
</form>
</center>
<hr>
</body>
```

You may recall that the HTML `select` object is basically a container for a series of `option` objects. The `select` object should have a name, and each `option` object will have a value. It is not necessary to name each `option` object. Because the `select` object contains a bunch of `option` objects, they are stored as an array.

Getting the Choice

The procedure for obtaining the value of the currently selected option is actually a bit easier in a selection object than it is with a set of radio buttons, because the `select` object itself can supply you with some useful information. When you wanted to evaluate a set of radio buttons, you had to look at each button to figure out which one was clicked. The `select` object has a built-in property that tells you which button was clicked. Here's my code:

```
<script>
function changeColor(){
  // Color Chooser
  // Andy Harris
  // demonstrates select object used as a drop-down list box
  var theSelect = document.myForm.selColor;
  var theOption = theSelect[theSelect.selectedIndex];
  var theColor = theOption.value;
  document.bgColor = theColor;
} // end changeColor
</script>
```

This code's brevity might surprise you. Essentially, the code simply picks apart the selection object until it gets the value that I need. Then the code stores the value in the `theColor` variable. The following line of code begins this process:

```
var theSelect = document.myForm.selColor;
```

This line creates a variable called `theSelect`. That variable is a reference to the selection object itself. This line isn't absolutely necessary, but it makes the following lines much easier to read, because you don't have to write all that `document.myForm.selColor.blah.blah` business every time.

The next line is similar:

```
var theOption = theSelect[theSelect.selectedIndex];
```

This line generates a variable to hold an option button. The variable contains the currently selected element. The `select` object has a `selectedIndex` property, which returns the index of the selected element. The `theSelect` variable has an array of options, and by indicating the `theSelect.selectedIndex` value, this line copies to the `theOption` variable a reference to the option that the user selected.

It then becomes a simple matter to retrieve the value of this option, with the following line:

```
var theColor = theOption.value;
```

Once the color is stored in a variable, you can copy it to the `bgColor` property of the document and thus change the page's background color:

```
document.bgColor = theColor;
```

Using Multiline Select Boxes

The select box turns out to be a very adaptable feature. In addition to the behavior that you have just seen, a select box can be set up to show multiple lines on the screen, and to allow the user to select more than one option at a time. The Color II program described in this section is a variation of the Color Chooser program that takes advantage of these capabilities.

Creating the Color II Program

The Color II program is modified from the Color Chooser program. Figure 5.9 shows this modified program.

For this program, you change the select box so that it can accept multiple values. Also, the program adds a text area for output. The user can select a series of elements in the select box, using Shift+click or Ctrl+click combinations. When the user clicks the button, the selected element nearest to the top of the box will be used as the form's new background, and all the selected values will be copied to the text area.

Modifying the HTML to Handle Multiple Selections

It just takes a couple of modifications in the `select` object's HTML code to get the desired effect:

```
<select name = selColor
        multiple
        size = 7>
```

The `multiple` attribute tells the browser to allow multiple selections. However, multiple selection doesn't make sense in a typical drop-down list box. To have a number of

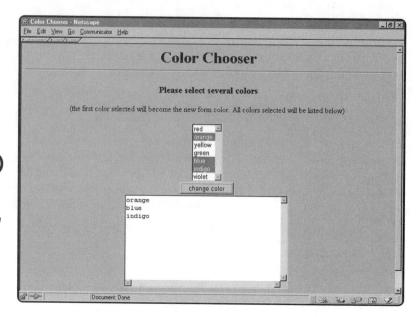

FIGURE 5.9

The user has chosen several colors. The first one was applied to the form's background. All selected colors are listed in the text area.

options visible at the same time, you must set the `size` attribute to some value. This page has seven elements, so I set the `size` attribute to seven, although any number larger than 1 would do the trick. To get multiple selections, you must set the `size` larger than 1 and also specify the `multiple` attribute.

The only other change to the HTML code is the creation of the text area for output. You've already seen this code several times in this chapter.

Writing Code to Handle Multiple Selections

The JavaScript code for the multiple selection Color II program starts just like the original Color Chooser program. It uses exactly the same code to extract a color for the background. When you set a select box for multiple selections, the `selectedIndex` property returns the index of the first selected item found. Here's the code:

```
function changeColor(){
  // Color Chooser
  // Andy Harris
  // demonstrates select object used as a multiline list box

  //change color to the first selected color
  var theSelect = document.myForm.selColor;
  var theOption = theSelect[theSelect.selectedIndex];
  var theColor = theOption.value;
  document.bgColor = theColor;

  //list all the selected colors
  var colorList = "";
```

```
  var i = 0;

  for (i = 0; i < theSelect.length; i++){
    theOption = theSelect.options[i];
    if (theOption.selected == true){
      colorList += theOption.value + "\n";
    } // end if
  } // end for loop
  document.myForm.txtOutput.value = colorList;
} // end changeColor
```

The new code appears after the comment to list all selected colors. If you look carefully at this code, however, you will see that it is not as new as it might at first appear. The code looks very similar to the code used to check a series of radio buttons. First, I set up some variables to make a `for` loop counter and a string to contain the text that the program is to print to the text area. Then, I started a `for` loop:

```
for (i = 0; i < theSelect.length; i++){
```

This loop continues as many times as there are elements in the `select` object. The `length` property indicates the number of elements in the `select` object. The i variable gets values from 0 up to the number of options in the `select` object minus one.

The next line grabs the current option, then puts the option in the `theOption` variable:

```
theOption = theSelect.options[i];
```

Next I use an `if` statement to check whether the user has selected the current option:

```
if (theOption.selected == true){
```

If the user selected the option, the next line copies the value related to that option to the colorList variable, which the program prints in the text area:

```
colorList += theOption.value + "\n";
```

Returning to the Advanced Mad Lib Program

The advanced Mad Lib program becomes simple to understand once you learn how to read the various elements. It introduces absolutely nothing new, but just combines the elements that you have already seen.

The HTML Code for the Advanced Mad Lib Program

The HTML code sets the stage. It is not that complex, but you must plan it well or it will cause you great difficulty when you are writing the JavaScript code. Here is the HTML code: (I'll show you the JavaScript in the next section)

```
<body>
<center>
<h1>Mad Lib<hr></h1>
<form name = myForm>
<h3>Please enter the following information</h3>
```

```
<table border = 1>

<tr>
  <td>A person's name</td>
  <td><input type = text name = txtPerson></td>
</tr>

<tr>
  <td>description(s)</td>
  <td>
    <input type = "checkbox"
           name = "chkEvil"
           value = "evil">evil
    <input type = "checkbox"
           name = "chkGoofy"
           value = "goofy">goofy
    <input type = "checkbox"
           name = "chkDysfunc"
           value = "dysfunctional">dysfunctional
    <input type = "checkbox"
           name = "chkWacky"
           value = "wacky">wacky
  </td>
</tr>

<tr>
  <td>A silly sound</td>
  <td>
  <input type = "radio"
         name = "optSound"
         value = "phht!"> phht!
  <input type = "radio"
         name = "optSound"
         value = "boing!"> boing!
  <input type = "radio"
         name = "optSound"
         value = "whoosh!"> whoosh!
  <input type = "radio"
         name = "optSound"
         value = "splat!"> splat!
  </td>
</tr>

<tr>
```

```html
    <td>A body part</td>
    <td>
      <select name = selBody>
        <option value = "tooth">tooth</option>
        <option value = "kidney stone">kidney stone</option>
        <option value = "cheek">cheek</option>
        <option value = "elbow">elbow</option>
        <option value = "brain">brain</option>
      </select>
    </td>
  </tr>

  <tr>
    <td>A vehicle</td>
    <td><input type = text name = txtVehicle></td>
  </tr>

  <tr>
    <td>A type of animal</td>
    <td><input type = text name = txtAnimal></td>
  </tr>

  <tr>
    <td colspan = 2><center>
      <input type = button
             value = "click for story"
             onClick = makeML()>
    </td>
  </tr>

</table>

<textarea name = txtStory
          rows = 10
          cols = 40
          wrap>
</textarea>

</form>
</center>

<hr>
</body>
```

The entire form is wrapped in a table. It is very difficult to create a professional-looking form without using tables. If you aren't already comfortable with tables, now is a good time to learn. It's also a great idea to get used to the `colspan` and `rowspan` attributes (which allow cells to take up more space than they normally would be allotted). These attributes give you reasonable flexibility in your page design.

> ### IN THE REAL WORLD
>
> Your choice of user interface elements can be more than a matter of aesthetics. Using the correct type of input element can greatly simplify the user's life by allowing mouse input instead of typing.
>
> These elements (the check box, radio group, and select element) are also very useful from the programmer's point of view, because they give the user very limited input options. Recall from the last chapter the warnings about how difficult it is to check information typed into text boxes and `prompt` statements. If you use the input elements described in this chapter, you can be assured that all inputs will be legitimate, because the values were designed into the program.

The form contains a number of standard text input elements. These were copied directly from the program in the last chapter and need no modification.

The `description` element is new. I introduced it into the story just so you could see how you might use check boxes. The user can choose any combination of `checkbox` elements. It makes sense to group them together on the page, but such grouping is not absolutely necessary. Note that each `checkbox` element has a different name.

The program retrieves the `sound` value via a radio button set. Although the story can easily make use of more than one descriptive word, it requires only one sound. Because you want the user to select only one sound, the `sound` value is a good candidate for a radio button set. Placing all radio buttons of a group together makes sense. Note also that the code assigns all of the radio buttons the same name, so that they can be accessed as an array.

The user selects the `body part` value with the assistance of a drop-down `select` object. This makes sense for this particular story element, because the story requires only one body part.

The other elements, such as the button and the text area for output, remain identical to those of the original Mad Lib program.

The JavaScript Code

All the JavaScript code for this project derives directly from the projects in the chapter. Here is the function:

```
function makeML(){
    // Mad Lib
    // Andy Harris
    // make a silly story from a bunch of input terms

    //create variables
    var sound;
    var part;
    var descrip;
```

```
var vehicle;
var animal;
var story = "";

//get text box variables
person = window.document.myForm.txtPerson.value;
vehicle = document.myForm.txtVehicle.value;
animal = document.myForm.txtAnimal.value;

//get description
descrip = "";

if (document.myForm.chkEvil.checked==true){
  descrip += document.myForm.chkEvil.value;
  descrip += ", ";
} // end if

if (document.myForm.chkGoofy.checked==true){
  descrip += document.myForm.chkGoofy.value;
  descrip += ", ";
} // end if

if (document.myForm.chkDysfunc.checked==true){
  descrip += document.myForm.chkDysfunc.value;
  descrip += ", ";
} // end if

if (document.myForm.chkWacky.checked==true){
  descrip += document.myForm.chkWacky.value;
  descrip += ", ";
} // end if

//story += "descrip: \t" + descrip + "\n";

//get sound
for (i = 0; i <= 3; i++){
  if (document.myForm.optSound[i].checked == true){
    sound = document.myForm.optSound[i].value;
  } // end if
} // end for loop

//story += "sound: \t" + sound + "\n";

//get body part
```

```javascript
var theSelect = document.myForm.selBody;

var theOption = theSelect[theSelect.selectedIndex];

part = theOption.value;

//story += "part: \t" + part + "\n";
story = "One day, a person named " ;
story += person;
story += " was walking down the street. Suddenly, ";
story += person;
story += " heard an awful, ";
story += descrip;
story += "mysterious ";
story += sound;
story += " sound. ";
story += person;
story += " looked around and saw that the ";
story += sound;
story += " sound was coming from a ";
story +=  vehicle;
story += " careening madly down the street. ";
story +=  person;
story += "'s fear turned to terror as ";
story += person;
story += " realized that the ";
story += vehicle;
story += " was driven by none other than the evil Super-";
story += animal;
story += ". Once an ordinary ";
story += animal;
story += ", it had befallen a strange transformation after ";
story += "being dropped in a vat of nuclear waste. ";
story += "Super-"
story += animal;
story += " continued to taunt ";
story += person
story += " with the horrible ";
story += sound;
story += " noise, but ";
story += person;
story += " was unconcerned. \"You can't bother me, Super-";
story += animal;
story += "!  I know how to turn the other ";
story += part;
```

```
story += "!\"  \nThe End."

    document.myForm.txtStory.value = story;

} // end makeML
```

The program has very little that is new.

As a program gets large, it becomes more important to document carefully what is happening inside the program. Note the comments that explain what each part of the code is supposed to be doing. It's also a good idea to use vertical space (that is, blank lines) to separate parts of the code from each other.

I made all the variables necessary for the story. The only new variable is the `descrip` variable, which did not exist in the original story.

TABLE 5.1 OBJECTS AND PROPERTIES USED FOR INPUT		
Object.property	**Description**	**Example**
Checkbox.value	Returns the value associated with a specific check box object (defined in HTML).	theVar = myCheck.value;
Checkbox.checked	Returns true or false depending on whether the box is currently checked.	if (myCheck.checked){ theVar = myCheck.value; } // end if
Radio[i].value	Returns the value associated with a specific radio button object (defined in HTML). Radio buttons are usually defined in an array.	for(i=0; i <5; i++){ theVar = myRadio[i].value; } // end for loop
Radio[i].checked	Returns true or false depending on whether the radio button is currently checked. Radio buttons are usually defined in an array.	for(i=0; i <5; i++){ if (radio[i].checked){ theVar = myRadio[i].value; } // end if } // end for loop
Selection. selectedIndex	Returns the index of whichever option is currently selected.	alert ("you chose option # " + mySelect. selectedIndex);
Selection[i]	Returns the *i*th option in the array.	myOption = mySelect[3];
Option.value	Returns the value of a specified option (usually called as part of an array).	alert (myOption.value);

It is very easy to get values from ordinary text boxes, so I extracted values from the text boxes first and copied them all to the appropriate variables.

To get a value for the `descrip` variable, I needed to evaluate all the check boxes. I checked whether each check box's value was true; if the value was true, I copied the check box's value to the `descrip` variable.

TRICK

Take a careful look at the following line:

```
//story += "descrip: \t" + descrip + "\n";
```

The line is commented out, but it fulfills a very useful purpose. As I was testing the program, I wanted to be sure that the program was generating the value of the `descrip` variable correctly. I didn't want to worry about all the string concatenation until I was sure that the variables were right, so I just wanted a simple version of the story that would just output the correct values. This line is part of that simple version that I used for debugging. I commented it out when I finished the debugging. However, I didn't remove it completely, because I might want it back if I find something else is going wrong. This kind of feedback line makes a great debugging tool.

I got values for the `sound` and the `body part` by using variations of exactly the same code that you saw earlier in this chapter. To reuse the code, all I had to do was change a few variable names. This is a very good strategy.

I built the story just as I did for the original Mad Lib program, with a series of string concatenations. One neat trick is to embed the `descrip` list inside another list so that I don't have to worry about whether a particular element needs a trailing comma.

Summary

In this chapter, you learned much more about integrating HTML form elements into JavaScript. You got a feel for several of the main elements in GUIs, including check boxes, radio buttons, and selection objects. You also learned general strategies for getting values from each of these elements in your JavaScript code. In the next chapter, you will look at some new ways to send output to the user.

EXERCISES

1. Build a version of the Number Guesser program that uses radio buttons for input instead of text fields.

2. Create a prototype order form that involves all the screen elements that you have learned about so far. Have a text area return a summary of the information on the form.

3. Write a Rock Paper Scissors game using form elements for input.

Petals around the Rose: Dynamic Output

In this chapter, you will add the ability to use HTML code itself as a form of output. Up to now, all your output has been through text areas. Although this use of text areas is reasonably straightforward, it is limited. You will learn how you can use HTML itself as an output medium. Specifically, you will explore how to do the following:

- Incorporate JavaScript and HTML frames

- Write code that writes to another frame

- Generate external windows

- Control the behavior and appearance of external windows

- Write to external windows

- Generate graphic images for games

- Incorporate graphics in a simple game

Project: Petals around the Rose

The game that you will write in this chapter is based on an old dice game. It is actually more like a puzzle. When played by humans, one person rolls five dice and asks "How many petals around the rose?" There is a specific pattern to the correct answers. The game turns out to be remarkably simple, but it can take you some time to figure out the solution. Figures 6.1 through 6.4 show the game's interface.

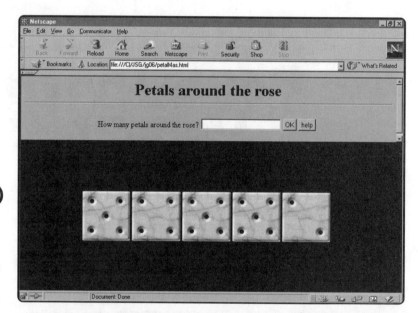

FIGURE 6.1

The Petals around the Rose program opens in two frames, with a form on the top and five dice on the bottom.

FIGURE 6.2

When the user asks for help, a new window pops up.

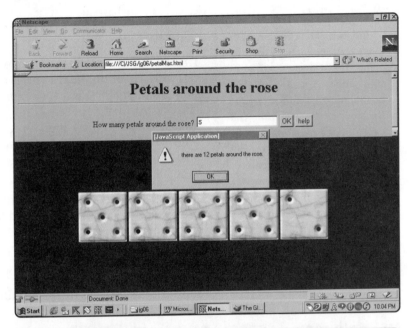

FIGURE 6.3

After the user clicks the OK button, the computer determines whether the guess was correct.

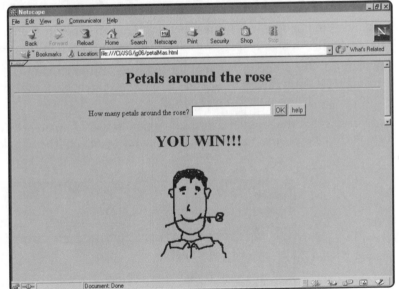

FIGURE 6.4

Finally the user has figured out the pattern.

The game introduces a lot of new elements. It is the first game in this book that relies heavily on graphics. It also is the first game that integrates at least some of the output directly into the Web page itself, without using a text area or `alert` statement. The game also introduces a pop-up help screen, which is implemented as a second Web page. To build this game, you will need to spend some time on each of these new elements. Fortunately, the game itself is reasonably easy to build once all the pieces are in place.

Generating Output in Frames

The first skill to master is to generate a page that can write HTML on the fly. This is a very important skill, because HTML is a very expressive language. If you want to incorporate graphics into your programs, or have your program repeatedly build pages on-the-fly, you will need HTML, because it just isn't possible to do these things well with the techniques that you've learned so far.

As you might remember from Chapter 4, you can use the `document.write()` method to write HTML to a document. However, this method has a significant drawback: It does not allow you to write to a document after it finishes loading to the browser. This is a big problem, because you cannot run functions until the browser has finished loading the page.

Creating the HTML Frame Tester Program

It would seem impossible to write functions that can generate Web pages, but there is a loophole. Take a look at the Frame Tester program shown in Figures 6.5 and 6.6.

The Frame Tester program is a tool for teaching and practicing HTML. When you're learning HTML, you can type any code into the text area, click the button, and see the results. You don't even need a text editor.

The secret is that the input and output happen in two completely different pages. The form with the text area, the button, and the function is in the left side of a frameset,

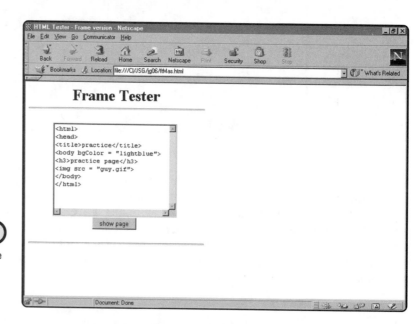

FIGURE 6.5

The left side of the page has a text area filled with HTML code.

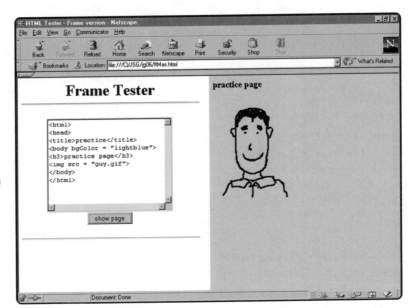

FIGURE 6.6

When the user clicks the Show Page button, the code in the text area is used to build a new page on the right side.

and the right side is rebuilt by the function. Creating this program is not as complicated as it might sound.

Building the Frames

Perhaps it will be helpful to review quickly frames in HTML. As you recall, a frameset involves a number of documents. Here's the source of the main page in the Frame Tester program. The file name is ftMas.

```
<html>
<head>
<title>HTML Tester - Frame version</title>
<frameset border = 0
          cols = "50%, 50%">
  <frame src = "FrameTester.html">
  <frame src = "blank.html"
         name = "frameOutput">
</frameset>
</html>
```

The page has no body area, only a head. The page contains a frameset element with two frames. The first frame contains the FrameTester.html page, and the second is set to blank.html. Note that I set the page to hide the frame border (border = 0). Such hiding is common when you are working in JavaScript if you want the results to look like one page. I have named the second frame frameOutput. It is especially important that you name frames that will handle output if you'll be working with the frame through JavaScript. The blank.html page is simply an empty page that I use to initialize framesets.

Writing to a Second Frame

The HTML code in FrameTester.html is very standard. As usual, the JavaScript will come later.

```html
<body>
<center>
<h1>Frame Tester<hr></h1>
<form name = "myForm">
<textArea name = txtInput
          rows = 10
          cols = 30>
<html>
<head>
<title>practice</title>
<body bgColor = "lightblue">
<h3>practice page</h3>
<img src = "guy.gif">
</body>
</html>
</textarea>
<br>
<input type = "button"
       value = "show page"
       onClick = "buildPage()">
</form>
</center>
<hr>
</body>
```

The HTML code simply sets up a text area and button. Note that the browser does *not* directly interpret the code between the `<textarea>` and `</textarea>` tags as HTML code, but simply as the text inside the text area. The button triggers the `buildPage()` function. Here is how that function looks:

```javascript
function buildPage(){
  // Frame Tester
  // Andy Harris
  // Demonstrates how to write HTML to another frame

  var theCode = document.myForm.txtInput.value;
  var theDoc = window.parent.frameOutput.document;

  theDoc.open();
  theDoc.write(theCode);
  theDoc.close();

} // end buildPage
```

The first line gets the text from the text area and copies it to the `theCode` variable. The second line is a little trickier:

```
var theDoc = window.parent.frameOutput.document;
```

This line also creates a variable, but this variable is a reference to the document in the `frameOutput` frame. When a page has multiple frames, it becomes necessary to refer to the frameset itself. In this instance, I did so by adding a reference to `window.parent`. `frameOutput` is the name of the specific frame, and it has a `document` object. So, `window.parent.frameOutput.document` is a reference to the `document` object of the `frameOutput` frame of the browser's frameset.

HINT

This whole naming scheme seems pretty unwieldy, but it isn't really all that new. Think of the children's song *The Green Grass Grows All Around*. That song describes "a wing on a bird in a nest on a branch on a tree in a hole in the ground." If it helps, you can think of the document syntax in the same way.

The `window.parent.frameOutput.document` syntax is very ugly and difficult to work with. I copied the whole mess over to a variable called `theDoc` so I wouldn't have to worry about typing that long reference correctly anymore.

Once I have a reference to the output document, I can invoke its methods to manipulate it. The call to `theDoc.open()` clears out any existing contents in the document and prepares the document for new text. `theDoc.write(theCode)` simply writes the contents of `theCode` to the page. Finally, the call to `theDoc.close()` signals the browser that the page is complete and that the browser can begin rendering the document.

TRAP

You cannot count on any `document.write()` output being visible to the user until you have closed the document. Don't forget to close the document with the `close()` method. This method is the equivalent of the signal sent to the browser that tells it that the document is done loading. If you don't close the document, there is no guarantee that all the elements will be shown in the right places, or at all.

All it takes to write output to another frame is some careful planning. Just set up the frameset, making sure to name any frames that will contain output. Then, build a function that assembles a Web page in a string variable. Make a reference to the frame, then open the frame, write to it, and close it.

TRICK

If you simply want to load a page into a frame, set a value to the document's `location.href` property. For example, the following line of code would launch my main page in the `frameOutput` frame from a function:

```
theDoc.location.href = "http://www.cs.iupui.edu/~aharris"
```

This technique can be useful when the page that you need is already complete and available on the Web. You might use the technique to create a Help screen or to load different parts of a complex program onto the main frame of your page.

JavaScript Programming for the Absolute Beginner

Displaying Output in Separate Windows

Although it is nice to be able to write HTML code into another frame, you might instead wish to have another window pop up altogether. This can be done easily in JavaScript.

Showing an Existing Page

You can easily create a new window to display an existing page. This is exactly how I implemented the Help screen in the Petals around the Rose game. The help screen is simply an HTML page. Figures 6.7 and 6.8 show the Show Help program, which pops up that page into a new window.

The ability to pop up a page like this can be very useful, because it displays output without disturbing the current page layout.

HINT

The HTML code for the Show Help program is quite predictable (it consists of a button that calls the showHelp() function). You may want to look at this program on the CD-ROM.

Here is the code for the showHelp() function:

```
<script>
function showHelp(){
  // Show Help
  // Andy Harris
  // demonstrates opening an HTML page in a new window
  var winHelp = window.open("petalHelp.html",
      "pHelp", "width=450,height=450,resizable");

  winHelp.focus();

} // end showHelp
</script>
```

The code is very short, but very powerful. The first line generates a variable called winHelp. It invokes the window.open() method, which simply opens a new window. The method takes three parameters. The first is the name of the file to load. The second parameter is the HTML name for this document. You would use the HTML name if you had HTML hyperlinks to the document in the new window. (Generally you will not have such hyperlinks, but you will need to specify a value for this parameter anyway.) The last parameter is a list of features for the new window. Table 6.1 lists the most important features that you might want to use.

HINT

This table includes only attributes that are common to both of the major browsers, Netscape Navigator and Microsoft Internet Explorer. A few more attributes are available that work in only one browser or the other, but those listed in Table 6.1 should serve most of your purposes.

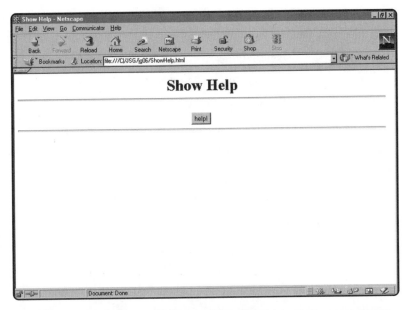

FIGURE 6.7

The Show Help program is just a page with a button.

FIGURE 6.8

The user asks for help by clicking the button, and a page appears.

To determine the features of your new window, create a string that contains a list of the features that you want, separated by commas. For example, if you want a 300×300 window with no menus or toolbars, you would use this string:

```
height=300,width=300
```

To add the standard toolbar, you would instead use this string:

```
height=300,width=300,toolbar
```

TABLE 6.1 COMMON ATTRIBUTES OF THE FEATURE PARAMETER

Attribute	Description	Example
height	How high the window will be.	height=200
width	How wide the new window will be.	width=200
location	Whether the location toolbar will be shown.	location
menubar	Whether the menubar will be shown.	menubar
resizable	Whether the user will be able to resize the window.	resizable
scrollbars	Whether scrollbars will be present (if needed).	scrollbars
status	Whether the status bar will be present.	status
toolbar	Whether the standard toolbar will be present.	toolbar
directories	Whether a directory toolbar will be present.	directories

IN THE REAL WORLD

You might think that a page with no toolbars is kind of useless, but it is actually a very common device. When you don't include menus or toolbars, the user doesn't know that the page is actually another browser window. Instead, the user gets the impression that your program popped up a window. Often, this is exactly the impression that you want to give the user. Of course, the page that you pop up can contain any HTML and JavaScript elements that you want.

Note that there are no spaces between values. Also note that only those elements that you include in the list will be added. If you do not specify a feature string, the new window will have exactly the same features as the window that contains the JavaScript code.

There's one more line of code in the function:

```
winHelp.focus();
```

This line tells the new window to seek the focus as if the user has clicked it. The first time that a window is created, it automatically has the focus; however, the user might call the Help screen and then pull the main program to the foreground, thus obscuring the Help screen. Without the `focus()` command, the next time that the user clicks the Show Help button, the page will be updated, but it will remain in the background. The `focus()` command ensures that the Help window is brought to the forefront.

Building the Window Tester Program

You can combine the page-writing features of the HTML tester with the ability to open a new window. Figures 6.9 and 6.10 show another version of the HTML tester. This version creates a new window to which the browser writes the Web page.

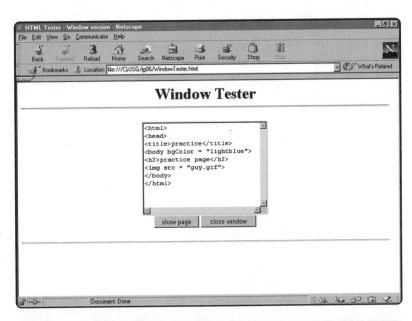

FIGURE 6.9

This program looks just like the Frame Tester, but it does not have any frames.

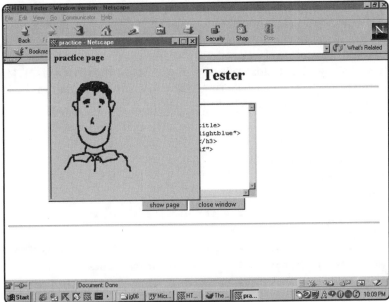

FIGURE 6.10

When the user clicks the Show Page button, the HTML is printed to a new window.

The program's code is mainly just a combination of the Frame Tester and the Show Help programs. It involves only one file. Here's the HTML code of that document:

```
<body>
<center>
<h1>Window Tester<hr></h1>
<form name = "myForm">
<textArea name = txtInput
          rows = 10
          cols = 30>
```

```
<html>
<head>
<title>practice</title>
<body bgColor = "lightblue">
<h3>practice page</h3>
<img src = "guy.gif">
</body>
</html>
</textarea>
<br>
<input type = "button"
       value = "show page"
       onClick = "buildPage()">
<input type = "button"
       value = "close window"
       onClick = "closePage()">
</form>
</center>
<hr>
</body>
```

As you can see, this HTML code is just like that of the code page of the Frame Tester program. I added a Close Window button, but otherwise this HTML is much like the Frame Tester page. The JavaScript code is also similar to that in the Frame Tester, but it includes some new instructions for making a window.

```
var theWindow;

function buildPage(){
  // Window Tester
  // Andy Harris
  // Demonstrates how to write HTML to a new window

  theWindow = window.open("", "practice", "height=300,width=300");
  var theCode = document.myForm.txtInput.value;
  var theDoc = theWindow.document;

  theDoc.open();
  theDoc.write(theCode);
  theDoc.close();

  theWindow.focus();
} // end buildPage

function closePage(){
  theWindow.close();
} // end function
```

This code has a few features that you haven't seen yet in this book. For the first time, more than one function is defined in the page. You can in fact define as many functions as you want. In this case, I made a different function for each button. Doing so is a reasonably common practice. Notice also that I defined one of the variables outside of either function. This is because both of the functions need access to the variable that refers to the new window. I'll talk a little more about how variables and multiple functions are related shortly. For now, make sure that you understand the rest of the code.

Opening a New Window

The `buildPage()` function is much like the `buildPage()` function in the Frame Tester program. Notice that there are two different calls to the `open()` method. The first opens up a new window by invoking the `open()` method of the `window` object.

```
theWindow = window.open("", "practice", "height=300,width=300");
```

The second call opens the document for writing.

```
theDoc.open();
```

The `window` object and the `document` object both have `open()` methods, but the meaning of the term *open* is different.

After opening the document, I wrote the HTML code to it, closed it, then set the focus to the new window. Note that I closed the *document,* which tells the browser that the document has finished loading and can be rendered.

Closing a Window

The user triggers the `closePage()` function by clicking the Close button. The function is simple once you understand polymorphism. It invokes the `close()` method of the window created by `buildPage()`. The `close()` method of a `window` object makes the window disappear.

Designing the Petals around the Rose Game

The Petals around the Rose game that you saw at the beginning of the chapter uses the techniques of this chapter to make a much more impressive front end for the dice games that you started making in Chapter 2. In addition, it is the first program in the book that takes advantage of graphics.

In the Real World

It might seem disconcerting that `window.open()` is different from `document.open()`. It is completely legal for different kinds of objects to have methods with the same name as well as similar but not identical behavior. This demonstrates a concept of object-oriented programming called *polymorphism.*

Polymorphism can be defined in a couple of ways, but, basically, it means that objects can adapt the way that they perform certain functions.

While the term *open* is reasonably universal, the way that different objects invoke the method may be different. Think about how you would open a garage door, a treasure chest, and a birthday present. You open all these objects, but the details of opening are different in each case.

TRAP

If you haven't played the Petals around the Rose game yet, you should do so before reading the rest of this chapter. The next section will reveal the secret of the game, which might spoil your fun. Try the game out first, then come back and read about how it was made.

Understanding the Overall Design Strategy

Here's the spoiler for the Petals around the Rose game: The center dot of the die is the rose, and any dots around it are petals. So, only the values 1, 3, and 5 have a rose. The value 1 has no petals, 3 has two petals, and 5 has four petals. The program determines the number of petals around the rose by counting how many total petals are around the rose in the currently visible set of dice. If this description doesn't clarify the program's scheme, try running the game for a little while and you will understand.

The game is all housed inside a frameset, in a page called petalMas.html. It divides the main page into two sections. The top section has the user interface, with a text box and a couple of buttons. This page contains all the JavaScript code. The bottom of the frameset shows five dice (and the winning screen). Usually, the code in the top frame generates the HTML code in the bottom frame. The bottom frame does not contain any code. The program also features a Help screen, which is implemented as a new browser window. Here is the HTML for the frameset (petalMas.html):

```
<html>
<head>
<frameset rows = "30%, 70%"
          border = 0>
  <frame src = petals.html>
  <frame src = "begin.html"
         name = "output">
</frameset>
</head>
</html>
```

The top frame contains petals.html, which has all the JavaScript code. The bottom frame is called output. It will usually contain very simple HTML, with <img> tags for five dice.

The HTML code in the top frame sets up the user interface. The code is as follows:

```
<body bgcolor = "tan">
<center>
<h1>Petals around the rose<hr></h1>

<form name = "myForm">
How many petals around the rose?
<input type = "text"
       name = "txtGuess">
<input type = "button"
```

```
        value = "OK"
        onClick = "rollEm()">
<input type = "button"
        value = "help"
        onClick = "helpScreen()">
</form>

</center>
</body>
```

As you can see, the form is very basic, with a text box and two buttons. Each button calls a different function.

Creating Graphics for JavaScript Games

The most obvious new feature in the Petals around the Rose game is the addition of graphics. Images add tremendously to the feel of a program. By learning a few tricks, you can add really great graphics to your games even if you aren't a terrific artist.

You can add images in a couple of ways. First, you can use images that somebody else has generated. There are numerous archives of images on the Web that depict nearly anything that you might want in a game. It is very easy to use any image you can see on the Web. Simply right-click on the image (or, if you are using a Macintosh, click and hold down on the image); a menu then pops up. One of the options allows you to save the image locally.

However, just because you *can* use an image easily doesn't mean that you *should* do so. Many images available on the Web are the intellectual property of somebody, and might be copyrighted material. Now that you are producing intellectual property of your own, you should be especially sensitive to the rights of other authors. You should get permission from the original author of any kind of work before you use it in your own projects.

IN THE REAL WORLD

Although image manipulation is especially important in game programming, the ability to include corporate logos, product images, or other graphical information can be an important asset to your Web site.

You can also buy the services of a professional artist. For commercial-quality games, this may be required. You can get very good results from a professional artist, but they will be expensive

Finally, you can generate graphics on your own. Although I have an art disability, I have found this to be the best option for a number of reasons. First, because you are the images' creator, you will have no problem obtaining permission for them. Second, modern image-creation programs do a lot to help you make at least passable graphics. Third, the specific needs of game art are a little different from those of other kinds of programs, and nobody will know the requirements of your game better than you.

Even if I hire a professional artist to create images for me, I still usually design some crude mock-ups of my own, just to illustrate what I want the artist to accomplish.

Making the Dice

Figure 6.11 shows the tools that I book's used to build the dice.

I used The GIMP (included on the CD-ROM) as my main image-editing tool. It is not in a final release, but it is free and exceptionally powerful, so I don't mind the fact that it crashes once in a while. I started by making a rectangle. I then inserted a texture onto the background of the rectangle. Using a special tool called the *bump map* filter, I then generated the three-dimensional effect.

HINT

A bump map is a gray-scale image. When you apply the bump map to another image, all the dark areas are interpreted as concave, and the white areas are left alone. The graphics editor then applies a shading effect. The effect is a very realistic-looking texture. I actually applied two bump maps to the die images, using one to round off the die's edges and the other to create the depressions for the dots.

Of course, you can just paint the dots if you prefer. Notice that I drew all the dots first. I saved this file, and then erased dots as needed to get each particular face of the die.

Finally, I saved the images as die1 through die6. You need to save your image files in a jpeg or gif format. In general, a photorealistic image works better as a jpeg, and an image created from scratch (or one that requires transparency) is better as a gif file. For this particular set of images, it doesn't matter too much which format you choose. It is important to make your image files as compact as possible, because they will all have to be downloaded. If the downloading takes too long, the user will never play your game.

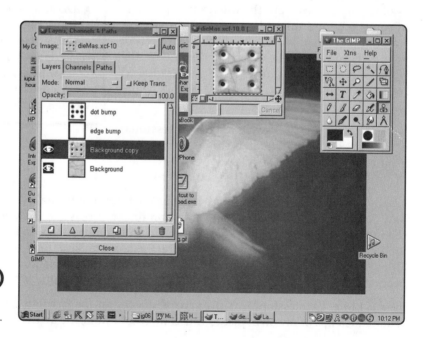

FIGURE 6.11

Using The GIMP, I create a master die.

Making the Cartoon Figures

Although the dice are very nice, what really gives this game its tone is the cartoon figure. The figure shows up originally in the Help screen and when the player wins. Caricatures such as this are terrific for games for a number of reasons. First, they are reasonably easy to learn how to draw. Also, they are very forgiving. The image is a cartoon, so nobody expects it to be perfect. My base image looks like Figure 6.12.

The guy in the drawing is a very straightforward cartoon. I stuck with a set of features I knew I could replicate: tall skinny head, short hair, goofy smile, and bushy eyebrows. (Any resemblance to a certain programming author is purely coincidental.)

I drew the image in black on a transparent background. This made the image easier to draw, because no shading was involved. Also, the transparent background makes it easy to reuse the image in other programs. Finally, an image with a transparent background integrates easily into your page.

If you know how to use layering tools in your graphics editor, you can put each feature (eyes, mouth, nose, and so on) in another layer so that it is reasonably easy to modify one feature without changing the rest. This gives you an easy way to generate, for example, a frowning version of the figure when the player loses.

I concentrated on the head but deliberately gave myself room on one side of the image for a hand. I then saved this image in the gif format, because the gif format supports a transparent background.

For the Petals around the Rose program, I decided not to use the original image at all, but instead made two variants. The first is the guy holding a rose, as shown in Figure 6.13. I use this image in the Help screen.

FIGURE 6.12

This is the basic form of the cartoon image.

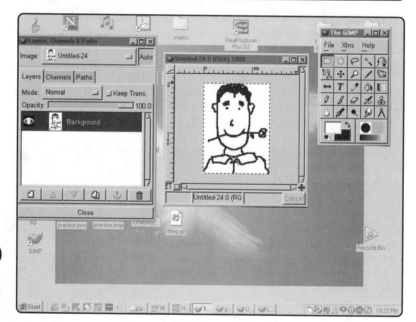

FIGURE 6.13

The Help screen shows the man holding a rose.

FIGURE 6.14

The winning screen shows the man with a rose in his mouth.

For the winning screen, I decided to go for sort of a tango flavor and put the rose in the guy's mouth, as shown in Figure 6.14.

As you can see, a little imagination and some clever use of the tools in a graphics editor can amplify even poor drawing skills enough to achieve very usable images.

Generating the Dice-Rolling Routine

The functions in petals.html do all the real work. One function is called `rollEm()`. It is activated every time that the user clicks the OK button. The pseudocode for the `rollEm()` function is as follows:

```
get the user's guess from the text area
If the user was correct,
  Send the "winner" screen to the output variable
If the user was incorrect,
  Tell the correct answer in a dialog box
  Clear the output frame
  Do this five times:
    Get a random value between 1 and 6
    Add the appropriate graphic to the output variable
  End of the loop
End If
Write out the output variable to the bottom frame
```

TRICK

This kind of plan is called *pseudocode*. The number one mistake that beginning (and advanced) programmers make is to write code without a plan. Now that your programs are starting to get longer, they are going to be harder to keep track of. You should write out in English the basic steps in your program before you even open your editor. Once you have a list of steps, it's reasonably easy to convert the pseudocode into actual JavaScript code. It is a really great habit to write out your steps as I have done here. It can prevent those moments when you are staring at a blank screen, trying to figure out what to do next.

Checking User Input

The first task of the `rollEm()` function is to get the user's guess. I do this with a text box. Here's the code for the first part of the function:

```
var numPetals = 12; //stores the correct answer

function rollEm(){
  // Petals around the rose
  // Andy Harris
  // An adaptation of an old dice game
  // requires that a document named "output" is available

  var theSource = "";
  var roll = 0;
  var guess = 999; //stores the user's guess
  //check user's guess

  guess = eval(document.myForm.txtGuess.value);
```

This program declares one variable outside any function. The variable `numPetals` contains the current correct number of petals. The starting value of `numPetals` is set to 12, because the default page in the bottom frame has the answer 12. Whenever a new set of dice is generated, the program changes the value of `numPetals` appropriately. The `numPetals` variable is declared outside the function because the program needs to preserve its value even when the function is not running. Remember that any variables declared inside a function do not preserve their values when the function has finished. The `numPetals` variable will be defined during one run of the function, and the value is needed the next time that the user clicks the OK button, so this variable needs to be declared outside the function.

The function begins with the normal comments and generates a number of more traditional variables. `theSource` is a string variable that will contain the source code of the output frame. I find it easier to compile an HTML page into a long string, then write that string to the page in one command. `theSource` is the string variable that contains that page.

The variable `roll` is an integer that contains the current randomly generated die roll. One more variable, `guess`, is used to hold the user's guess. Notice that I initialized `guess` to 999, which is guaranteed to be incorrect. I did that to ensure that the program does not start with the winner screen so that the user gets at least one chance to guess the answer.

The following line pulls the user's guess from the text box, evaluates it into a numeric variable, and assigns it to the variable `guess`:

```
guess = eval(document.myForm.txtGuess.value);
```

Dealing with the Winning Position

The program then contains the following `if` structure:

```
if (guess == numPetals){
    theSource += "<html>";
    theSource += "<body bgColor = tan>";
    theSource += "<center>";
    theSource += "<H1>YOU WIN!!!</H1>";
    theSource += "<img src = 'guyTeeth.gif'>";
    document.myForm.txtGuess.value = "";
} else {
    //player is incorrect
} // end if
```

The `if` statement checks whether the player has guessed correctly. If the user's guess is the same as the previously stored value of `numPetals`, the function creates the HTML for the winning page and stores that HTML code in the `theSource` variable. The following line resets the text box to blank, to remove whatever value the user last had in the text box:

```
document.myForm.txtGuess.value = "";
```

Generating the Dice Page

A bit more work is involved if the user's guess was incorrect, because the program will have to generate a new puzzle. Fortunately, most of this process should be familiar to you, since it uses a number of techniques from Chapter 2. Here is the code:

```
if (guess == numPetals){
  // user got it correct
  } else {
    alert("there are " + numPetals + " petals around the rose.");
    numPetals = 0;
    document.myForm.txtGuess.value = "";
    theSource += "<html>";
    theSource += "<body bgColor = black>";
    theSource += "<center>";
    theSource += "<br><br><br><br>";
    for (i = 1; i <= 5; i++){
      roll = Math.floor(Math.random() * 6) + 1;
      switch (roll){
        case 1:
          theSource += "<img src = die1.jpg> ";
          break;
        case 2:
          theSource += "<img src = die2.jpg> ";
          break;
        case 3:
          theSource += "<img src = die3.jpg> ";
          numPetals += 2;
          break;
        case 4:
          theSource += "<img src = die4.jpg> ";
          break;
        case 5:
          theSource += "<img src = die5.jpg> ";
          numPetals += 4;
          break;
        case 6:
          theSource += "<img src = die6.jpg> ";
          break;
        default :
          theSource += "ERROR!!";
      } // end switch
    } // end loop
  } // end if
```

If the user did not guess correctly, the first order of business is to inform the user what the correct answer was. I decided to use an `alert` statement, because that would hold the rest of the code's processing until the user clicked the button. This means that the user can still see the last puzzle while looking at the correct answer. As soon as the user clicks the OK button in the alert box, the program puts the new set of images in the output frame.

I then reset the value of `numPetals` to 0, because the program will determine the appropriate value of the variable as it generates the screen.

Next I generate a `for` loop, because I want five die on the screen. The procedure for generating each is identical. I use the algorithm from Chapter 2 for generating a number from 1 to 6, and then use a `switch` structure to add the appropriate image to the page. Take a careful look at the code for case 3 and case 5. These are the only dice that have "petals around the rose," so whenever a 3 is generated, I add 2 to `numPetals`. Whenever a 5 is generated, I add 4 to `numPetals`. I put a default case in the `switch` structure, even though it should never occur.

TRAP

I designed my algorithm so the only possible values should be 1 to 6, but it is possible that there is a mistake in my algorithm that will occur in very rare cases (What if the `Math.random` turns out to be exactly 0?).

Finally, I added code to close up the HTML page when the loop is finished, then wrote the value of `theSource` to the output frame.

Making the Online Help

The Online Help is simply a Web page that I already made. To make it appear, I use the same code as in the Show Help program from earlier in this chapter. Here's the version in the Petals around the Rose program:

```
function helpScreen(){
  //pop up a new window with a help screen in it
  //requires petalHelp.html

  var helpWindow = window.open("petalHelp.html", "pHelp",
    "height=450,width=450");
  helpWindow.focus();
} // end helpScreen
```

The function generates a new pop-up window, then sets the focus to that window. Nothing else is necessary.

Table 6.2 provides you with an easy reference for the new syntax used in this chapter.

	TABLE 6.2 SYNTAX SUMMARY	
Object.property	**Description**	**Example**
`window.parent.` `framename.document`	Refers to the `document` object of the `frameName` frame.	`window.parent.frameOutput.` `document.write` `("I'm a frame");`
`document.open()`	Opens up a document for writing.	`window.parent.frameOutput.` `document.open();`
`document.close()`	Signals that nothing else will be written to the document, and that the browser can render the document.	`window.parent.frameOutput.` `document.close();`
`window.open` `(url, targetName,` `properties)`	Opens a new window. The starting address `url.targetName` refers to the name of the window if you are using the window as an HTML target. You describe window characteristics in `properties`.	`myWindow = window.open("",` `"goofyWin", "height=400,` `width=400,resize");`
`windowName.close()`	Destroys the window called `windowName`.	`myWindow.close();`
`windowName.focus()`	Pulls the window called `windowName` in front of all other windows.	`myWindow.focus();`

Summary

In this chapter, you looked at how to generate output external to the function's own page. Specifically, you learned how to write to another frame, and how to write to a new browser window that you created through the code. The benefit of external output is that you can build an entire Web page as the output of your program, which enables you to incorporate any HTML features into your program's output. You examined the object-oriented programming concept of polymorphism, and you took a first look at the special characteristics of graphics for JavaScript games. Finally, you got a look at a reasonably complete game and saw many of the features from earlier chapters put together to build one program.

EXERCISES

1. Design graphics for the Number Guesser game so that rather than printing words, the program provides the user an up arrow for "too low," a down arrow for "too high," and a medal or certificate when the user guesses correctly.

2. Write online help for one of your earlier programs and use a pop-up window to display the text to the user.

3. Make a graphical version of a Rock, Paper, Scissors game. For each round, the computer will guess and display a rock, paper, or scissors symbol, and the user will have to input some value to indicate rock, paper, or scissors. The program should then display the values as graphics and determine a winner for the round. Scissors cut paper; paper covers rock; and rock breaks scissors. Have the game continue indefinitely, with the program keeping track of the number of rounds.

4. Write a program that deals a poker hand. Have it choose five values between 1 and 52, and display a card corresponding to that value. You can use one of the many card deck graphics available on the Web, or you can make your own.

Image Swapping and Lookup Tables: The Basketball Game

In this chapter, you will use two of the most powerful features of modern programming. *Image swapping* is the ability to change images dynamically. You will see how these effects are used in traditional Web design and how you can apply them to game development. You will also learn one way that a computer program can store and retrieve complex information: *lookup tables*. The specific skills you will learn in this chapter include:

- Using the DOM image object

- Changing an image with the .src property

- Using the `onload`, `onMouseOver`, **and** `onMouseOut` event handlers

- Building arrays of variables and Making two-dimensional arrays

The Project: The Basketball Game

Figures 7.1 through 7.3 show the Basketball program. The game enables the user to play a crudely simulated game of basketball. The user controls five players that compete against an (unseen) computer-operated opponent.

The interface has very few controls. The user controls the action by clicking the players and the basket. The ball appears to move from one player to the next. A text box at the bottom of the screen displays current information. The game goes to 21 points. As simple as the game seems, it is surprisingly engaging.

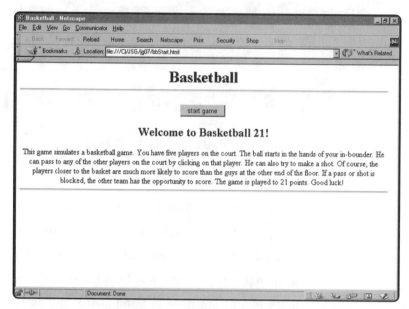

FIGURE 7.1

When the program starts, it shows a Help screen with a Start Game button.

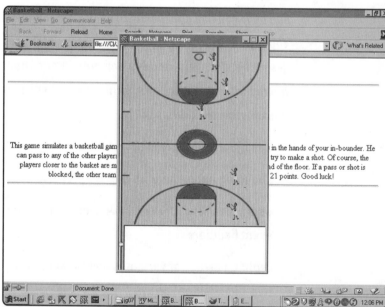

FIGURE 7.2

A new screen pops up with a basketball court.

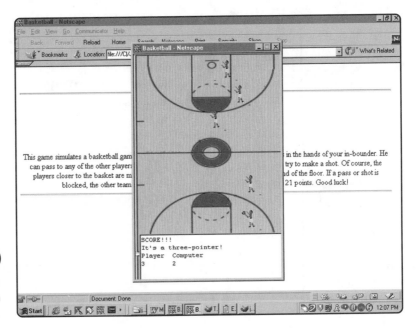

FIGURE 7.3

The user clicks on a player to pass, or on the basket to shoot.

Swapping Images

You have already learned that it is difficult to change much in a Web page (besides form elements such as text boxes) once it has finished loading. There is one very important exception to this rule. You can use JavaScript to change images on the fly. Figures 7.4 and 7.5 show a program, Simple Image Swap, that demonstrates how you can accomplish this.

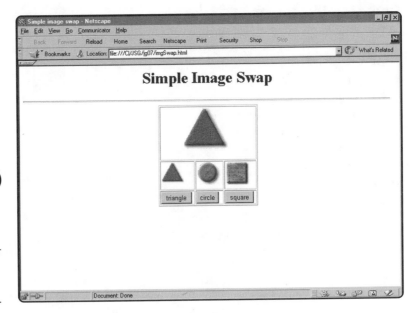

FIGURE 7.4

The Simple Image Swap program's interface displays a triangle in the larger image, then three other images with buttons below them.

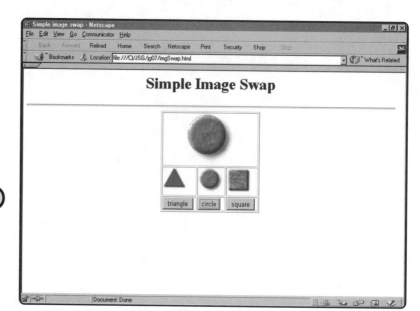

FIGURE 7.5

When the user clicks a button, the corresponding image shows up in the larger image area.

The HTML Code

The code behind the Simple Image Swap program is especially interesting, because it illustrates three different ways that you can manipulate images through JavaScript. As usual, you start with the HTML code:

```
<body>
<h1>Simple image swap</h1>
<form name = theForm>

<hr>
<table border = 1>
<tr>
  <td colspan = 3>
  <center>
  <img name = imgDisplay
       src = "triangle.gif"
       height = 100
       width = 100>
  </center>
</tr>

<tr>
  <td><img src = "triangle.gif"
           height = 50
```

```
                width = 50
                name = "imgTriangle">
    </td>


    <td><img src = "circle.gif"
                height = 50
                width = 50
                name = "imgCircle">
    </td>


    <td><img src = "square.gif"
                height = 50
                width = 50
                name = "imgSquare">
    </td>
</tr>

<tr>
    <td><input type = "button"
                value = "triangle"
                onClick = "showTriangle()">
    </td>


    <td><input type = "button"
                value = "circle"
                onClick = "showCircle()">
    </td>


    <td><input type = "button"
                value = "square"
                onClick = "showSquare()">
    </td>
</tr>

</table>
</form>
</body>
```

The page is a basic form with one button on it. The interface displays one large image and several smaller ones. Note that each image has a name associated with it. Each of the smaller images has a button underneath it. The onClick event of each button calls a different function. As you will see, each of these functions uses a different technique to display the image. I'll show you the functions one at a time, so you can see how they work.

The Triangle Technique

The code for the `showTriangle()` function is as follows:

```
function showTriangle(){
    window.document.imgDisplay.src = "triangle.gif";
}   //end showTriangle
```

The code here is simplicity itself. Images are objects in the `document` object model. They live right below the document. An image can be referred to as *document.imageName* and have an `src` property, which can be read from and written to. If you assign a new URL to the `src` property, the effect is to change the image on the page.

TRAP

The size of the image on the screen can be something of a problem. If you expect to change a particular image through JavaScript code, be sure that the HTML image tag has height and width properties set. In fact, adding these properties to any HTML image is a very good idea anyway, as it prevents a number of unpleasant surprises.

The Circle Technique

The code for the circle function is slightly different. Here's how it is written:

```
function showCircle(){
    window.document.theForm.imgDisplay.src =
    window.document.theForm.imgCircle.src;
} // end showCircle
```

The code here is similar to the code in the previous function. There is one significant difference: Instead of assigning a URL to the `src` property of `imgDisplay`, the function copies the source property of `imgDisplay` from the source property of the circle image. This particular approach is used to copy an image from one image on the screen to another. This technique can be useful if you already have an image on the screen that can be copied.

The Image Object and the Square

The `showSquare()` function relies on a different technique. Essentially, I created a new object to hold an image, and I preset the image variable's source to be the rectangle image. Here is the code.

```
var imgObjectSquare = new Image(100,100);
imgObjectSquare.src = "square.gif";


function showSquare(){
    window.document.theForm.imgDisplay.src = imgObjectSquare.src;
} // end showSquare
```

First, I created the image object outside any functions, so that it is available to other functions. When you create an image object, you use the `new` keyword and specify a height and width for the image. After creating an image object, you can refer to its `src` property as you would for any other image. This technique has one very important advantage: As you create the image object, it is not displayed on the page. Using this approach, you can preload an image into a variable object and copy the `src` property whenever you wish.

Using the MouseOver Events

Figures 7.6 and 7.7 show another version of the Simple Image Swap program. The MouseOver Image Swap program has a couple of differences from the Simple Image

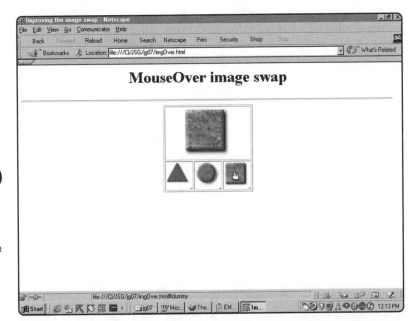

FIGURE 7.6

The MouseOver Image Swap program has no buttons. Instead, the main image changes when the mouse moves over the smaller images.

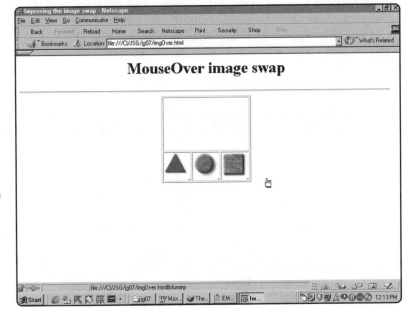

FIGURE 7.7

When the mouse is not over a particular element, the program simply leaves the main display area blank.

Swap program. First, the page has no buttons! The main image changes when the user moves the mouse over the smaller figures. When the mouse is not over a particular element, the display reverts to blank.

Creating Images with Event Handlers

The lack of buttons is the most obvious new feature, but the code also introduces a number of other improvements. First, take a look at the HTML code. The only part that is different is that which surrounds the smaller images. All the images call exactly the same function, so the key differences are embedded in the HTML code itself. The triangle code follows; the code for the other images is all pretty much the same. Of course, you really should look at the actual program on the CD-ROM that accompanies this book.

```
<a name = "dummy">
...
<tr>
  <td><a href = "#dummy"
          onMouseOver = show("imgObjTriangle")
          onMouseOut = "document.imgDisplay.src = 'blank.gif'">
      <img src = "triangle.gif"
        height = 50
        width = 50
        name = "imgTriangle"
        border = 0>
    </a>
  </td>
```

A couple of interesting features are apparent in this code. The essential problem is this: You want the main image to change when the mouse moves over the triangle image. It would be great if the image object had some sort of "the mouse is over me" event. Unfortunately, images do not have any events at all. Web authors have devised a clever way to work around this problem. Anchors (created with the <A> tag) have some event handlers built into them. Here are the key event handlers of the anchor object:

TABLE 7.1 KEY EVENT HANDLERS OF THE ANCHOR OBJECT

Event	Description
onClick	The user clicks the anchor.
onDblClick	The user double-clicks the anchor.
onMouseOver	The mouse moves over the anchor.
onMouseOut	The mouse moves off of the anchor.

Note that other event handlers are possible, but those listed in the table are the most commonly used, and they are proven to work well in both the major browsers. Use online references to check for the existence of other event handlers.

The other interesting feature of the anchor tag is that it can surround images or text, so if you want to apply an event handler to an image, you can simply surround the image with an anchor tag and apply the events to the anchor.

 HINT

In this particular situation, the URL used in the anchor's href attribute is irrelevant—you don't really intend for the user ever to click the anchor, but just to move over it. There are a number of ways to deal with this situation. You can simply point the href attribute back to the file that contains the code. A more elegant solution (the one I used in this code) is to build a named anchor in the current page and link to that anchor. As long as the page all fits on the screen, the user will not notice the jump to the anchor at all.

To pull off the illusion well, you need to make sure that the anchor isn't obvious. Setting the image's border to 0 eliminates the blue border that would normally appear when an image serves as a hyperlink. Notice that I added the onMouseOver event handler. This calls a function that will change the image. I also added an onMouseOut event handler. This second event handler changes the display image's source to blank as soon as the mouse exits the triangle image.

IN THE REAL WORLD

Several variations of this technique have become staples in the Web world recently. The most prevalent of these is the MouseOver technique. No doubt you have seen many pages that use the effect: When your mouse goes over a certain part of the screen, the particular word or image changes color, swells, glows, or does something similar. To achieve this effect, you attach both an onMouseOver and an onMouseOut event to the image. The code might look something like this:

```
<a href = "http://www.whatever.com"
    onMouseOver = "document.theImage.src = 'glow.gif'"
    onMouseOut = "document.theImage.src = 'normal.gif'">
    <img src = "normal.gif"
        name = "theImage">
</a>
```

This code displays the glowing image whenever the mouse is over the anchor object. As soon as the mouse exits the image and anchor, the onmouseOut event triggers the image to revert to its default value. Note the nested single and double quotation marks.

Writing JavaScript to Change the Images

Now that you know how to set up an image with an event handler, you need to look at the code that will call it. Here's the JavaScript code for the imgOver page:

```
<script>
//create the image objects
var imgObjSquare = new Image(100,100);
var imgObjTriangle = new Image(100,100);
var imgObjCircle = new Image(100,100);

//initialize the image objects
imgObjSquare.src = "square.gif"
imgObjCircle.src = "circle.gif"
imgObjTriangle.src = "triangle.gif"

function show(imgToShow){
  //receives image as a parameter

  //copy the value to the display image
  document.imgDisplay.src = imgToShow.src;
} // end show
</script>
```

Before starting the function, I created a series of image objects and initialized them. The function code will refer to these image objects.

Using Parameters with Functions

It would have been reasonably easy to make a separate function for each image. The code would be almost identical in every function, except that it would replace the display image with a different value. Although it would be easy to build these functions with the copy and paste features of your editor, experienced programmers often try to find ways to avoid such code repetition. Imagine if you had written the code five (or 500) times and then discovered that there was a problem. You would then have to make five (or 500) changes. There is a better way.

The show() function is a little unique, because it contains a *parameter*. In most of the programs in this book, you created functions with empty parentheses. The parameter allows you to create a function that can work with a special value. By changing the value sent to a function, you can make it operate on a number of different things. You've already seen this many times in your programming career. Think about the alert() function. It always pops up a message box with a message in it, but the value in the parentheses determines the specific message. To specify a function that will work with a parameter, just write a variable name in the parentheses when you define the function. Then, when you call the function, specify a value. When the function is running, the parameter variable will be automatically created, and it will contain the value specified by the function call.

Here's how parameters are used in the show() function: The function will always be used to copy the src property of an image object to the imgDisplay picture. The problem is that the specific image to be copied will differ based on which of the smaller images the mouse passed over. The onMouseOver events each specify the name of the object to be displayed. When the user passes the mouse over the triangle image, for example, its onMouseOver event triggers the show() function with the value imgObjTriangle sent as a parameter. Likewise, the square image code sends the imgObjSquare, and so on. When the show() function runs, whatever value was sent in the parentheses is stored in the variable imgToShow. The src property of whatever image object that the imgToShow variable contains is copied over to display the image. Function parameters are often used to make a function more flexible, as I have done in this example.

Creating Simple Arrays

The programs that you are writing are becoming more complex, and they are beginning to have a large number of variables. To make the variables more manageable, programmers tend to use structures such as arrays. You might recall arrays from Chapter 5, "*Advanced Mad Lib: Using the Other Form Elements*". In that chapter, you simply built a series of HTML components with the same name, and they automatically became an array. You can also make arrays out of any type of JavaScript variable. Figures 7.8 and 7.9 show a simple program, Simple Array Demo, that features an array of strings.

The program switches from blank to triangle, circle, square, and back to blank when the user clicks the button. In a moment, you'll add matching images, but for now, just concentrate on the structure that will give you the captions in sequence.

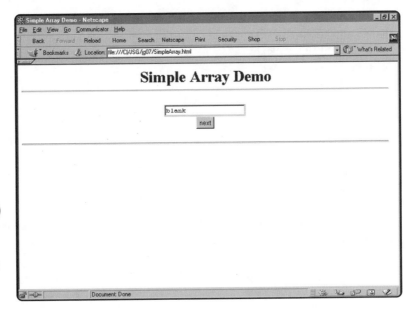

FIGURE 7.8

The Simple Array Demo program starts with the word "blank" visible in a text box.

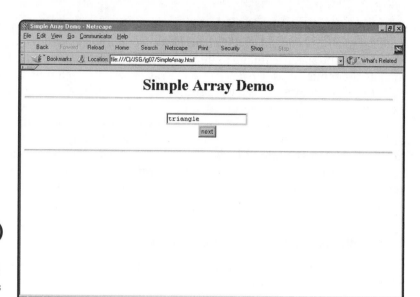

Simple Array Demo

FIGURE 7.9

As the user clicks the button, the text box changes values in a set pattern.

The HTML consists of one text area, named `txtDescription`, and one button, which calls the `upDate()` function when clicked. Here's the JavaScript for the program:

```javascript
var description = new Array(3)
var counter = 0;

function initialize(){
  // sets up the array with some starting values
  // Andy Harris
  description[0] = "blank";
  description[1] = "triangle";
  description[2] = "circle";
  description[3] = "square";
} // end initialize

function upDate(){
  //increments the counter and shows the next description
  counter++;
  if (counter > 3){
    counter = 0;
  } // end if
  document.myForm.txtDescription.value = description[counter];
} // end upDate
```

Creating a Variable Array

The first line of code creates a variable called description:

```
var description = new Array(3)
```

This is a very special type of variable, because it houses an array. To make an array, you use the `new Array()` syntax. The value inside the parentheses indicates the number of elements in the array. JavaScript does not actually require the number, so the following line would work just as well:

```
var description = new Array()
```

Still, most languages require the programmer to state the number of elements in an array when it is created, so it is traditional to do so even in a more lenient language such as JavaScript.

TRAP

Don't forget to capitalize the term `Array`! This is a very easy mistake to make, and it can be very difficult to debug.

Populating the Array

Once an array is created, it is essentially a list of variables. Somehow, you will need to fill up the array with values. In this program, I chose to use a special function called `initialize()`. The function contains a series of assignment statements that fill up all the array elements with the appropriate values. JavaScript arrays are extremely flexible. You can mix and match variable types in the same array, and you can even add more elements than you specified when creating the array.

TRAP

Be aware that JavaScript's cavalier attitude toward arrays is not typical. Most other languages are much pickier about how arrays are defined. It's fine to take advantage of the lax rules in JavaScript, but don't be surprised when you find that the habits you learned in JavaScript array creation are seen as a bit sloppy in some other language.

The `initialize()` method needs to occur early. I chose to attach it to a special event handler to force the initialize() function to occur as soon as the page is loaded. The HTML `body` tag has an `onLoad` event. Any function in the `onLoad` event will execute as soon as the browser loads the body. Therefore, this function is a perfect place for initialization code. Although I did not show you the HTML code for this program, here is the relevant line:

```
<body onLoad = "initialize()">
```

IN THE REAL WORLD

In any kind of program that requires some code to execute before the user gets control of the environment, you might want to consider this kind of `initialize()` function. Such a function is useful any time you want to set up variables, initialize form values, or get some kind of initial information from the system (such as the current time or the user's domain name).

Showing the Next Element

The button calls the `upDate()` function. The job of this function is to show the next array element. To do this, the function keeps track of a variable called `counter`. Note that `counter` is created outside any functions, because the program must retain the variable's value through multiple function calls. Each time that the user clicks the Next button, the program increments `counter`. Then the program checks whether the value of `counter` has gotten too large. If it has, the program resets `counter` to 0. Finally, the program updates the text box with the member of the array related to the `counter` variable.

Any time that you increment or decrement a variable, you should consider using some kind of boundary checking to make sure that the variable does not get too large or too small. You should follow most increment or decrement operations with some kind of `if` statement checking for a boundary, and take action if the value exceeds that boundary.

Creating Arrays with Images

JavaScript supports arrays of anything that can be placed in variables, even images. Figures 7.10 and 7.11 show an improved version of the array program called the Image Array Demo. This version supports graphics.

This program sports two arrays. One array contains all the descriptions, and the other contains all the images. I carefully designed the arrays to be in exactly in the same order, so that `image[1]` refers to the same thing as `description[1]`.

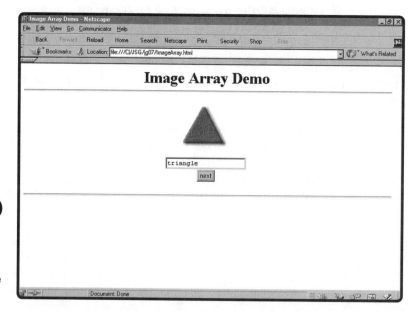

FIGURE 7.10

When the description in the text field is "triangle," a triangle image appears.

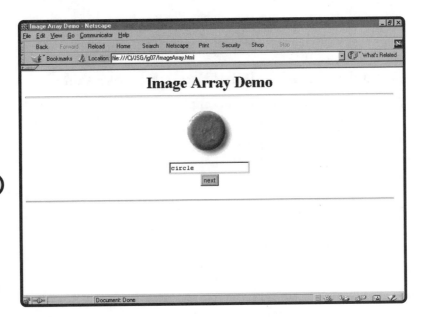

The Image Array
Demo program
synchronizes the
circle image with
the circle
description in the
text box.

Writing the HTML Code for the Image Array Demo Program

The HTML for this version of the array program is reasonably straightforward:

```html
<body onLoad = "initialize()">
<center>
<h1>Image Array Demo<hr></h1>
<form name = "myForm">
<img src = "blank.gif"
     name = "imgDisplay"
     height = 100

     width = 100>
<br>

<input type = "text"
       name = "txtDescription"
       value = "blank">
<br>
<input type = "button"
       value = "next"
       onClick = "upDate()">
</form>
</center>
<hr>
</body>
```

The most significant features are the initialization function in the body `onLoad()` method and the image object called `imgDisplay`.

Creating and Initializing the Arrays

The Image Array Demo program contains an array of strings and an array of images. The code initializes the two array types differently. Take a look at this code:

```
var description = new Array("blank", "triangle", "circle", "square");
var pictures = new Array(3);
var counter = 0;


function initialize(){
  // sets up the array with some starting values
  // Andy Harris
  pictures[0] = new Image(50, 50);
  pictures[0].src = "blank.gif";
  pictures[1] = new Image(50, 50);
  pictures[1].src = "triangle.gif";
  pictures[2] = new Image(50, 50);
  pictures[2].src = "circle.gif";
  pictures[3] = new Image(50, 50);
  pictures[3].src = "square.gif";


} // end initialize
```

The `counter` variable is created as you would expect, and the `pictures` array creation looks much like you would guess, but the `description` array is a little bit different. JavaScript allows you to define arrays on the fly in certain circumstances. Since I already know the values that I want in the `description` array, I simply list them in the array creation statement, and the array is automatically built for me.

Sadly, image objects require a bit more work, because I need to create the image object and then assign a value to its source property. For the picture array, I decided to use the standard initialization function.

Updating the Page

The `upDate()` function is very similar to that in the Simple Array Demo program, but I added one line to update the image. Here's the entire function:

```
function upDate(){
  //increments the counter and shows the next description
  counter++;
  if (counter > 3){
    counter = 0;
  } // end if
  document.imgDisplay.src = pictures[counter].src;
  document.myForm.txtDescription.value = description[counter];
} // end upDate
```

The only new line is the one that refers to imgDisplay. Here's what that line means: Take the member of the pictures array referred to by counter. Grab the source property of that image and copy it to the source property of imgDisplay. This has the net effect of changing imgDisplay so that it shows the current image.

Using Lookup Tables

Arrays can be exceptionally useful when you have large amounts of data to manage. As an example, think back to the Basketball program featured at the beginning of this chapter. To illustrate how arrays can be useful, I started with a simpler program, Lookup Table Demonstration, that determines the likelihood that a given player will succeed with a shot or a pass to another player.

Creating the Basketball Lookup Table Demonstration Program

Figures 7.12 and 7.13 show the Lookup Table Demonstration program. The drop-down lists enable the user to choose a shooter (the player who is passing the ball) and a target (either the basket or the player to whom the user is passing the ball). Then, when the user clicks the Throw It button, the text screen analyzes the likelihood (expressed as a percentage) that the play will succeed.

HINT

When you are writing complex programs, it is often a great idea to isolate new ideas into smaller test programs, so that you can ensure that each of the main concepts works in isolation before you piece all the tested concepts together in potentially more complex ways.

You'll see the code for the lookup program in a moment, but it is important to understand the underlying concepts first.

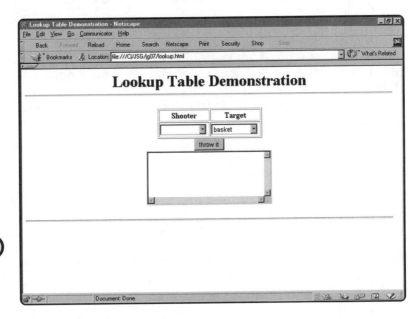

FIGURE 7.12

The user can choose a shooter and receiver.

Lookup Table Demonstration

Shooter	Target
guard	center

throw it

```
Shooter: 4 guard
Target: 1 center
Percentage: .4
Result: 0.09480183556226512
Made it!
```

FIGURE 7.13

The Lookup Table Demonstration program calculates how likely it is that the pass will succeed.

Encoding One Player's Percentages

Imagine that the in-bounder has the ball. This player can choose to pass to each of the other four players on the team, and can even attempt to score by directing a shot at the basket (at least in the very simplified form of basketball that I modeled in my game). It is very likely that the in-bounder will succeed in a pass to the nearest player. It is much less likely that the player could make a basket from the other end of the court. You could summarize the likelihood (expressed in a percentage) of each of this player's options in a chart such as the following:

Player	Basket	Center	Forward	3-Pt	Guard
In-bounder	.01	.05	.10	.30	.90

This table describes the likelihood of the in-bounder passing a ball to each of the other players. In other words, I am suggesting that there is a 1% (.01) chance that the in bounder would successfully complete a basket. The same player would have a 5% chance of completing a pass to the center, a 10% chance of passing successfully to the forward, a 30% chance of a successful pass to the 3-point shooter (maybe a shooting guard standing outside the three-point arc), and a 90% chance of a successful pass to the guard.

It is good that these values are expressed as percentages, because percentages can be thought of as values between 0 (0%) and 1 (100 %).

You already know how to get a random number between 0 and 1, so if you want to simulate that a certain pass is successful 30% of the time, all you need to get is a 0-to-1 random number and compare it to .3. The random number will be less than .3 30% of the time and larger than .3 70% of the time.

You can store this information in an array that looks like this:

```
var INVals = new Array(.01, .05, .10, .30, .90);
```

Then, if you want to see whether the in-bounder succeeded in passing to the center, you could use code like this:

```
//inbounder passes to center
if (Math.random() < INVals[1]){
  alert("pass from inbounder to center succeeded!");
} // end if
```

Adding the Other Players

Of course, you have five players on the court, so you need five of these charts to manage all the possible pass permutations. I made another chart combining my estimates of each player's chances for each type of pass or shot. My complete chart looks like this:

Player	Basket	Center	Forward	3-Pt	Guard	In-bounder
Center	.50	−1	.70	.30	.80	.80
Forward	.30	.60	−1	.70	.80	.80
3-Pt	.25	.50	.70	−1	.80	.80
Guard	.05	.40	.50	.70	−1	.80
In-bdr	.01	.05	.10	.30	.90	−1

Each row represents a shooter, and each column represents a target. A cell in the table designates the likelihood, expressed as a percentage, that a particular shooter will succeed with a particular pass or shot attempt. For example, to find out how likely it is that the three-point shooter will successfully pass to the center, find the 3-Pt row, then read across to the Center column. The value that you will find is .50, so this means that there is a 50% chance this particular pass will succeed.

The center has a 50% chance at a basket, whereas the in-bounder has a 1 in 100 chance. I decided that a player should never pass to himself, so I set those values at −1.

HINT

There is absolutely no scientific method behind the assignment of these values. I sat down and wrote this chart just off the top of my head. It seemed to me that these were reasonable assumptions, and after testing the completed game, they made an interesting game. Of course, in a more realistic simulation, you would find ways to get more accurate percentages, perhaps by researching actual basketball statistics.

Coding a Lookup Table

This kind of two-dimensional chart is called a *lookup table*. To make one in JavaScript, you simply create a series of arrays (one per row) and then join these arrays together in a bigger array. A look at the source code should help you understand how this works. The first thing I did was to make a set of variables to represent the players on the court:

```
//define constants for positions
var BK = 0; //basket
var CT = 1; //center
var FD = 2; //forward
```

```
var TP = 3;   //three point shooter
var GD = 4;   //guard
var IN = 5;   //in-bounder
```

I'll be making a lot of arrays, and in each array the 0 element represents the basket and the fifth element represents the in-bounder. To make the coding easier to read, I named some of the variables using mnemonics for the positions.

Sometimes, though, I might really want the position names, so my first array will be a list of the actual player names:

```
var plName = new Array( "basket", "center", "forward", "three point
shooter", "guard", "in-bounder");
```

Note that the player names are in order, so plName(BK) is "basket." You can also modify this array so that it contains the actual names of players on your favorite team.

Next, I'll make a series of arrays that encode the percentages for each player:

```
//define arrays to hold rows
var CTVals = new Array(.50, -1, .70, .30, .80, .80);
var FDVals = new Array(.30, .60, -1, .70, .80, .80);
var TPVals = new Array(.25, .50, .70, -1, .80, .80);
var GDVals = new Array(.05, .40, .50, .70, -1, .80);
var INVals = new Array(.01, .05, .10, .30, .90, -1);
```

Each array specifies one row in my original chart. The order of values in the arrays is very important. If you want to know the likelihood of the guard successfully passing to the center, you could write a code statement such as alert(GDVals[CT]);.

Finally, I combined all the individual player arrays into one larger array.

```
var allVals = new Array (0, CTVals, FDVals, TPVals, GDVals, INVals);
```

<table>
<tr><td>

IN THE REAL WORLD

Lookup tables are useful any time you want to deal with some sort of a chart of information. You could use such a structure to look up shipping cost information, tax rates, customer information, or nearly anything that could be written in a two-dimensional table. In fact, lookup tables are not limited to two dimensions. By placing the large arrays into even larger arrays, you can create lookup tables with three, four, or even more dimensions. (In Chapter 12, "The Game Creation Process: The Brick Game," you will see an example of a three-dimensional lookup table.)

</td><td>

Note that the elements in the arrays are other arrays. Also note that the 0 value is just a placeholder, because the basket won't ever shoot. Now all the data about all the players is stored into one big variable called allVals. You can determine any value in the table by referring to the allVals array of arrays. For example, alert(allVals[IN][CT]) would return the likelihood of a pass from the in-bounder to the center. The [IN] value would specify use of the fifth element of allVals (remember, IN is just a shortcut for 5). Since the fifth element of allVals is another array, you can ask for the [CT] (or first) value of that array. This type of structure (an array of arrays) is a two-dimensional array. Other languages use other techniques to generate two-dimensional arrays, but most languages support them.

</td></tr>
</table>

Getting Values from the Lookup Table

It is very easy to use a lookup table once you have defined it. Here's the `throwIt()` function in the Lookup Table Demonstration example:

```
function throwIt(){
  // Lookup Table Demonstration
  // Andy Harris

  //  alert("got to throwIt");
  var scoreboard = document.m+yForm.txtOutput;
  var shooter;
  var target;
  var rndVal = Math.random();
  var result;

  //theSelect = document.myForm.selShooter;
  shooter = document.myForm.selShooter.selectedIndex;
  target = document.myForm.selTarget.selectedIndex;

if (rndVal < allVals[shooter][target]){

    result = "Made it!";
  } else {
    result = "Failed";
  } // end if

  scoreboard.value = "Shooter: " + shooter + " " + plName[shooter] + "\n";
  scoreboard.value += "Target: " + target + " " + plName[target] + "\n";
  scoreboard.value += "Percentage: " + allVals[shooter][target] + "\n";
  scoreboard.value += "Result: " + rndVal + "\n" + result;
} // end
```

The function generates variables for the shooter, the target, and a random value. The values for `shooter` and `target` are extracted from the two `select` objects. The following is the key line:

```
if (rndVal < allVals[shooter][target]){
```

It compares the randomly generated value to the appropriate percentage from the lookup table. If the condition is true, the function considers the pass or shot complete.

All the rest of the code simply sends information to the text box to clarify what is happening.

IN THE REAL WORLD

Beginning programmers are often put off by the notion of arrays and lookup tables. You could in fact write this program without any arrays at all. On my first attempt at this program, I did exactly that. I used a `switch` statement to figure out who had the ball, and inside that `switch` statement I placed another `switch` statement to figure out which player was the target of the pass. Each receiver `switch` statement took 22 lines of code, and the passer `switch` statement had five of these receiver structures, plus some of its own overhead. The entire logic structure for determining the percentages required over 130 lines of code, with logic structures sometimes four and five layers deep. Even though I'm a reasonably experienced programmer, I was having a hard time keeping the logic structure straight. Updating the code would have been really difficult, and tweaking the code so that it performed exactly as I wanted would have been nearly impossible. In contrast, the version that uses a lookup table requires a total of 15 lines of code. All the data is in the same place, where it can be easily modified. Sometimes spending a little bit of time up front designing a more elaborate data structure can save you a huge amount of grief down the road.

Putting Together the Basketball Game

The Basketball game is simply a combination of the main ideas in this chapter. Its basic core is the lookup table described in the previous section. I added a graphical interface and scorekeeping capabilities to turn the table into a game.

The Game Window

The graphical appearance of the game is important, if it is to feel like a basketball simulation. I started by drawing a basketball court with my painting program. This court is intended as a background image, because the other images (the players) are superimposed on top of it.

The tricky thing about background images is the way that they automatically tile. This means that if the basketball court image is smaller than the window, the image will appear more than once. If the background image is too large, the entire court will not be visible. I needed a way to guarantee the size of the browser window, so I decided to make the actual game appear in a secondary window. The screen that the user sees first has only one button. The code for that button pops up a secondary window, which is pre-sized to be the right size for the background graphic and the scoreboard. Because the user cannot resize the new window, the tiling effect of the background image will not be a problem. Here's the code that pops up the game window:

```
function startGame(){
  // Basketball
  // Andy Harris
  // loads up basketball court in new window

  var stadium = window.open("bball.html", "bbAnch",
"height=450,width=300");
  stadium.focus();
} // end startGame
```

Displaying a game in a separate window is a pretty standard technique.

You have no control of the browser's configuration when the user first comes to your Web page. You can only achieve precise control of a window that you create. By creating a window, you can determine its exact size, and you can ensure that the user cannot resize the screen.

The Graphic Design

The basketball court is the background of the main game page. The page also contains figures for the five positions on the court. Getting the images placed on the court correctly is a real challenge using standard HTML techniques. To position these images correctly, I relied on a few tricks of the HTML designer. Figure 7.14 shows the basketball page with some modifications to illustrate how I placed the figures.

Each player is in a table. The tables each have one row containing a blank image and a player image. In Figure 7.14, I changed the blank image to an all-white image, so you could see more clearly how the spacing was done. By changing the size of the spacing image, I gave myself a fair degree of control over the placement of the player. For example, the height of the white image over the basket ensures that the forward will be completely below the basket. The width of the image to the left of the forward ensures that the forward will be placed to the right of the basket. Of course, the white bars are distracting, so once I got all the players positioned correctly, I replaced the all-white image with a completely transparent gif image.

In the Real World

HTML is a wonderfully expressive language. The HTML author can be reasonably confident that the content of his or her page will be displayed on a wide variety of platforms. The cross-platform flexibility comes at a cost, however. It is very difficult to control exactly how elements are positioned on a page. In Chapter 8, "Dynamic HTML: The Stealth Submarine," you will learn about how cascading style sheets (CSS) technology can be used to position elements. For this chapter, though, I will rely on techniques that are used even in the older browsers that do not support CSS elements.

HTML authors discovered that tables were a very nice way to position elements onscreen. Many of the forms in this book have been created with tables. It is theoretically possible to exactly determine the height and width of a table cell in pixels. It would seem that this would give the HTML author a terrific way to place things more precisely on the screen, but the browsers are notoriously inconsistent in their support for these table features.

You can also directly determine the size of an image in pixels, and all the major browsers do this very well. HTML authors began using blank images to put blank space in their Web pages. By building a table with blank images in it, you can achieve a surprising amount of control of your screen layout without use of CSS or other advanced techniques.

You will learn several more elegant solutions to positioning HTML elements as you go through the book, but this technique is still useful in some situations.

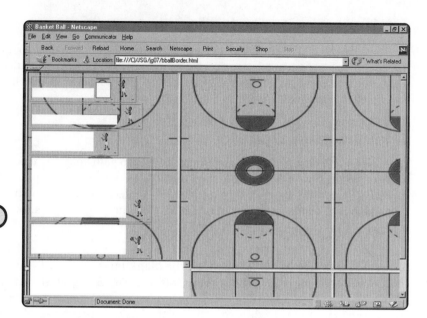

FIGURE 7.14

The images are placed in tables with invisible images as placeholders.

Here's the HTML code that shows the placement of the images:

```
<body background = court.gif
    onLoad = "resetGame()">
<form name = myForm>

<!--   basket and center -->
<table border = 0>
<tr>
  <td>
  <img src = "blank.gif"
      height = 20
      width = 130>
  <a href = javascript:throwTo(BK)>
  <img src = "blank.gif"
      name = "img0"
      height = 30
      width = 20
      border = 0>
  </a>
  <a href = javascript:throwTo(CT)>
  <img src = "player.gif"
      name = "imgPlay1"
      height = 40
      width = 40
      border = 0>
  </a>
```

```
    </td>
  </tr>
</table>


<!-- Forward -->
<table border = 0>
<tr>
  <td>
  <img src = "blank.gif"
       height = 20
       width = 180>
  <a href = javascript:throwTo(FD)>
  <img src = "player.gif"
       name = "imgPlay2"
       height = 40
       width = 40
       border = 0>
  </a>
  </td>
</tr>
</table>
```

This code fragment handles only the first two tables, but shows the technique that I used for all the tables. You can check the CD-ROM for the full source code. Note that I hid the borders of the images and tables so that the graphics would appear to be integrated into the page. Note also the use of JavaScript:throwTo() as the bref of the anchor tags. Any place you can put a url or an href, you can also put "JavaScript:" and a line of JavaScript code. In this case I called the throwto() function. All the images call the same function but send their own ID as a parameter.

HINT

In later chapters, I will describe some more precise positioning techniques that use positional style sheet elements. It is good also to know the more "old-fashioned" technique used in this example, as the technique is still reliable and useful for certain situations.

The player image is very crude but does the job (see Figure 7.15). I drew the image at 100×100 resolution with a blank background. I saved versions with and without the basketball.

The Global Variables

The lookup table is the key to this program. I started by defining the lookup table exactly as it was in the Lookup Table Demonstration program. I also added a few other variables for scorekeeping:

```
//define main variables
var playerScore;
```

```
var opScore;
var currentPlayer;

//define constants for positions
var BK = 0;  //basket
var CT = 1;  //center
var FD = 2;  //forward
var TP = 3;  //three point shooter
var GD = 4;  //guard
var IN = 5;  //in-bounder

//define array for player names
var plName = new Array( "basket", "center", "forward", "three point
shooter", "guard", "in-bounder");

//define arrays to hold rows
var CTVals = new Array(.50, -1, .70, .30, .80, .80);
var FDVals = new Array(.30, .60, -1, .70, .80, .80);
var TPVals = new Array(.25, .50, .70, -1, .80, .80);
var GDVals = new Array(.05, .40, .50, .70, -1, .80);
var INVals = new Array(.01, .05, .10, .30, .90, -1);

//make an array of arrays
var allVals = new Array (0, CTVals, FDVals, TPVals, GDVals, INVals);
```

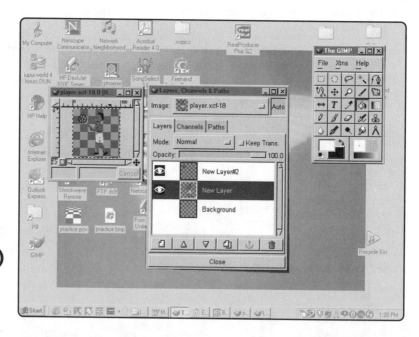

FIGURE 7.15

Using The GIMP to create the original player image.

The resetGame() Function

The program must initialize all the variables to suitable starting values. The program will also need to execute the exact same code whenever the user wins or loses the game. So, I put all the code for resetting the game into a function, resetGame(). Here's the code for that function.

```
function resetGame(){
  //reset all game variables
  playerScore = 0;
  opScore = 0;
  currentPlayer = IN;
  document.myForm.scoreBoard.value = "";
  updateScreen(currentPlayer);
} // end resetGame
```

The code just sets up key variables with the values necessary to start up the game. ScoreBoard is a reference to a text box that displays all information to the user. The function ends with a call to another function, updateScreen. You'll see what that function does in just a moment.

The updateScore() Function

Another function is meant to be called each time the player or the computer scores a basket. Here's how it works:

```
function updateScore(){
  var scoreCard = "";
  scoreCard += "Player \tComputer \n";
  scoreCard += playerScore;
  scoreCard += "\t" + opScore;
  document.myForm.scoreBoard.value += scoreCard;

  //check for win
  if (opScore >= 21) {
    alert ("You LOST!!!");
    resetGame();
  } else if (playerScore >= 21) {
    alert ("You WIN!!!");
    resetGame();
  } // end if
} // end updateScore
```

The function builds a string with scoring information. Because this function is called after every score, it's a great place to check for winning and losing positions.

The updateScreen() Function

The program calls the `updateScreen()` function every time that the ball is supposed to change hands. The player who is to receive the ball is passed as a parameter to the function. Here is the function's code:

```
function updateScreen(currentPlayer){
  //clears all the images, shows only current player with ball

  //clear all images
  for (i = 1; i <= 5; i++){
   var imgPlayer = eval("document.imgPlay" + i);
   imgPlayer.src = "player.gif"
  } // end for loop

  //show current image
  imgPlayer = eval("document.imgPlay" + currentPlayer);
  imgPlayer.src = "ball.gif";
  window.status = plName[currentPlayer];
} // end updateScreen
```

The program puts the player image (with no ball) in every position, then puts the ball image in the position specified by the `currentPlayer` parameter. Notice the use of the `eval` statement. The images for the players are called `imgPlay1`, `imgPlay2`, and so on. I concatenated the string variable `document.imgPlay` with the variables `i` (in the loop, this variable will have values between 1 and 5) and `currentPlayer`. I then used the `eval` statement to force the computer to evaluate the resulting string as a JavaScript statement. The evaluation generates an image object, which I stored to a variable for convenience.

The throwTo() Function

Every time the user clicks one of the player images, the program calls the `throwTo()` function. This function's job is to determine whether the pass or throw should be completed. Here's the code for the function:

```
function throwTo(receiver){
  if (Math.random() < allVals[currentPlayer][receiver]){
    //successful pass or shot
    //check for score
    if (receiver == BK){
      document.myForm.scoreBoard.value = "SCORE!!! \n";
      playerScore += 2;

      //look for three pointers!
      if (currentPlayer >= TP){
        document.myForm.scoreBoard.value += "It's a three-pointer! \n";
        playerScore +=1;
      } // end three point if
```

```
      updateScore();
      currentPlayer = IN;
    } else {
      document.myForm.scoreBoard.value = "made the pass to " +
plName[receiver] + "\n";
      currentPlayer = receiver;
    } // end score if

  } else {
    //pass or shot did not succeed
    currentPlayer++;
    document.myForm.scoreBoard.value = "blocked!!";
    if (currentPlayer > IN){
      currentPlayer = IN;
    } // end opponent scores
    //give opponent a random chance of scoring
    if (Math.random() < .20){
      document.myForm.scoreBoard.value += "Opponent scored!! \n";
      opScore += 2;
      updateScore();
      currentPlayer = IN;
    } // end if

  } // end if
  updateScreen(currentPlayer);

} // end throwTo function
```

The function expects a receiver to be sent as a parameter. All the calls to this function include the code variable for whichever player is supposed to receive the ball.

The main order of business is to determine whether the shot succeeded. That is done in the following line of code.

```
if (Math.random() < allVals[currentPlayer][receiver]){
```

currentPlayer is a global variable, and it will always contain the code for the player that currently has the ball. The code line makes a reference to the lookup table and retrieves the percentage stored for this combination of passer and receiver. The program then compares this value to a random value.

If the pass succeeded, the program must check whether the pass was an attempt to score. This is easy to do, because the pass will be a score only if the receiver is the basket. In all other cases, the pass is simply a pass to another player. If an attempt for a basket succeeds, the program should increment the score by two. One more check determines whether the scoring player was behind the three-point line. If so, the program tacks on another point. Since the score has changed, the program makes a call to upDateScore() so that the user knows the current score.

	TABLE 7.2 SYNTAX SUMMARY	
Statement	**Description**	**Example**
`varName = new Image (height, width)`	Creates a new image object called `varName` with the specified height and width.	`var myImage = new Image(100, 100);`
`imgVar.src = URL`	Assigns the URL as the source of the given image object. The URL must point to a valid image file.	`myImage.src = "face.gif";`
`varName = new Array()`	Creates a new array variable called `varName`.	`var myArray = new Array();`
`varName = new Array (length)`	Creates a new array variable called `varName` with the specified number of elements.	`var myArray = new Array(3);`
`varName = new Array (valA, valB, valC)`	Creates a new array variable called `varName` preloaded with the values in the parentheses.	`var myArray = new Array("small", "medium", "large");`

If the receiver was not the basket, the attempt was a pass. In this case, the program simply sends a message to the scoreboard indicating the pass and changes the `currentPlayer` variable to reflect the player that currently has the ball.

If the pass or shot failed, the program moves the ball back one position. For example, if the three-point shooter missed a shot, the ball goes to the guard. If the passer was the in-bounder, I chose to let that player keep the ball. Any time a shot or pass is blocked, the opponent has the opportunity to make a score. I chose to give the opponent a 20% chance of scoring. This seems to give balanced game play. The player wins often enough to stay interested, but not every time. The opponent's likelihood of scoring is the single easiest way to change the difficulty of the game. If you make this number larger, the opponent will score more often. If you make it smaller, the opponent will not score as frequently.

Summary

In this chapter, you looked at two very useful concepts. The first concept was that of image swapping. You learned about the JavaScript image object, and how to manipulate the source property of that object to make new images appear on the screen. You also learned how to add event handlers to an image by surrounding the image with an anchor tag, and you learned how to make your functions more flexible by adding parameters to them.

The other main concept of the chapter was the use of data arrays as lookup tables. You learned how to build basic one-dimensional arrays of normal variables and of image objects. You wrote code that allows you to step through an array one value at a time, and you learned how to build two-dimensional arrays to encapsulate larger data structures.

You also learned a few graphics tricks to make the Basketball program work. You learned how a custom window can be useful in controlling the size of a game window. You also learned how to position images with blank gif files and tables. Finally, you explored a reasonably involved simulation of a basketball game and saw how a number of utility functions can come together to make a reasonably interesting game program.

In the next chapter, you will see how cascading style sheets and other advanced HTML topics can be used to add motion and sound to JavaScript programs.

EXERCISES

1. Modify the Basketball game so that it reflects the names of players on your favorite basketball team.

2. Modify the percentage table to reflect the characteristics of your team. For example, you might have a three-point shooter who's a great shot, but who does not pass well. You can tweak the data in all kinds of ways to simulate this characteristic.

3. Add multiple levels of difficulty to the game. For the easier levels, make the opponent less likely to score a basket. At the more difficult levels, make an opponent score more likely.

4. Modify the graphics and the data table to simulate another similar sport, such as soccer, hockey, or water polo.

5. Add randomly occurring penalties.

6. Many role-playing games and war games rely on two-dimensional data tables and dice throws. Modify the lookup program so that it simulates one of these tables and returns the results.

Dynamic HTML: The Stealth Submarine

So far, this book has tread on reasonably safe ground. All the projects done so far should work even with the older browsers. For more sophisticated programs, you need to push the limits of JavaScript's capabilities. In this chapter, you begin to do exactly that. Specifically, you will be looking at how to do the following:

- Write cross-browser code

- Write a browser-detection routine

- Create positionable style sheet elements

- Move floating elements

- Change the text in floating elements

- Work with sound files

All these techniques (and a few others) constitute dynamic HTML (*DHTML*). The tricks in this chapter pretty much push the modern browsers to their limits. As you read through the chapter, you will see a lot of detail, but don't get overwhelmed. You should get a flavor for how to accomplish these tasks in typical DHTML, so that you can appreciate the library approach taken in the rest of the book. If you find the chapter a bit too challenging, feel free to skip ahead, then come back again after you have read some of the later chapters in the book.

The Project: The Stealth Submarine Program

The program you will build is a strategy-puzzle game called Stealth Submarine. Here's the premise: The player is a spy who has finished a dangerous mission. The player gets into a stealth minisub and has to maneuver the sub out of the harbor. Unfortunately, the enemy has been tipped off, and patrol boats lurk everywhere. If the player moves into a square occupied by an enemy patrol, the patrol will recognize the sub with a sonar ping.

If the enemy manages to get three pings on the submarine, the game is over. The spy has a device in the sub that tells how many patrol boats are in the vicinity. The player must use this device to find a safe way to the open ocean. When the player reaches the ocean, a nuclear submarine picks up the spy, and the player has won. Figures 8.1 through 8.3 show the game's interface.

The Stealth Sub game introduces some new challenges. The submarine figure actually moves around on the screen under program control. In addition, the scoreboard and control pad are special elements that can also be moved and specially modified. The game also features sound.

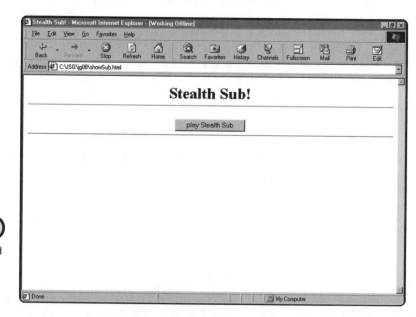

FIGURE 8.1

The instruction and startup screen for the Stealth Sub program.

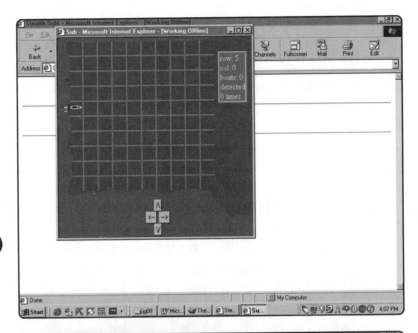

FIGURE 8.2

The player must
sneak through a
10×10 patrol grid
to win.

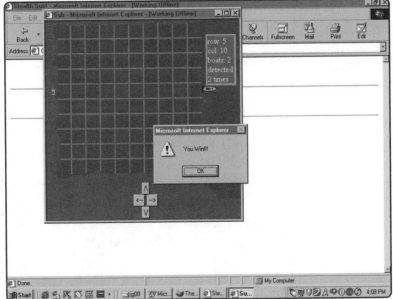

FIGURE 8.3

In addition to seeing
dialog boxes, the
player hears various
sound effects
associated with
winning, being sunk,
and sonar pings.

Dealing with Browser Dependency

The interesting new features of the sub program come at a cost: Both of the major
browsers can do all the necessary tasks, but they do them in completely different ways.
For example, you can store a sound file in a property of the Internet Explorer browser,
but you must embed all sound files as plug-ins for Netscape Navigator. I'll take you
through that mess later in the chapter, but this is a good illustration of the major

plague troubling client-side Web developers. The browser manufacturers have selectively ignored standards bodies in their attempts to build more powerful browsers. Although this means that each of the browsers has many interesting features, it is very difficult to write code that works properly on both browsers at the same time. Often you will find yourself having to write completely different code for the two main browsers. One solution is simply to write code for one browser or another. This solution is fine on an intranet, or when you don't mind losing part of your audience. On the other hand, many would claim that the Internet is all about inclusiveness, and getting beyond hardware and software boundaries. In that spirit, I've tried to write every program in this book so that it works with both browsers. In this chapter, you'll see how you can write such code.

Creating the Browser Detective

The key to writing cross-browser code is to have a browser detection script. Figures 8.4 and 8.5 show the interface for such a program.

The program is simple but very important. It determines by looking at the `document` object model which browser is running the script, then returns an appropriate message.

Here is the code that generates the Browser Detective program.

```
<html>
<head>
<title>Browser Detective</title>
<script>
var bVersion = 0;
var isNav = false;
var isIE = false;


function checkBrowser(){
```

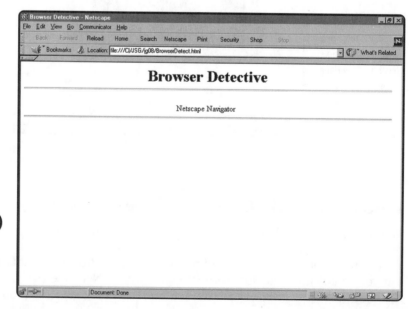

FIGURE 8.4

The page recognizes that it is in Netscape Navigator.

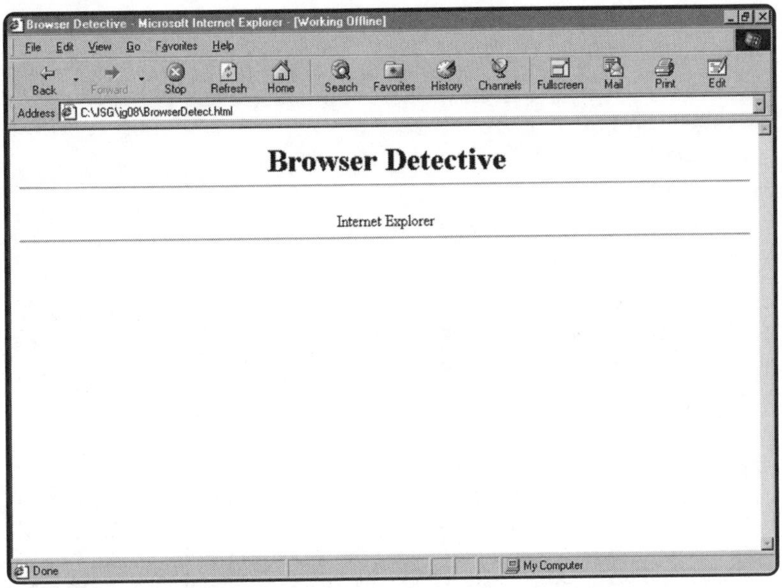

FIGURE 8.5

This time the page was brought up in Internet Explorer.

```
// Browser Detective
// Andy Harris
// Checks which browser is working
if (navigator.appName == "Netscape"){
  isNav = true;
} else {
  if (navigator.appName == "Microsoft Internet Explorer"){
    isIE = true;
  } // end IE if
} // end Netscape if

bVersion = parseInt(navigator.appVersion);

if (bVersion < 4){
  alert("Consider getting a newer browser! This code might not work!");
} // end if

if ((!isNav) && (!isIE)){
  alert("I do not recognize this browser. This code might not work");
} // end if
}  // end checkBrowser

</script>
</head>

<body>
```

```
<center>
<h1>Browser Detective<hr></h1>
<script>
checkBrowser();

if (isNav){
  document.write("Netscape Navigator");
} else {
  if (isIE){
    document.write("Internet Explorer");
  } // end if
} // end if

</script>
</center>


<hr>
</body>
</html>
```

Detecting Which Browser Is Being Used

There are many ways to do browser detection, but I prefer to work with three variables. I created a Boolean variable called isNav. This variable will be true when the program confirms that it is running in the Netscape Navigator browser. Another variable, called isIE, will be true only after the browser is confirmed as Internet Explorer. Another variable checks the version number of the browser. Since most dynamic HTML (including that which you will write throughout the rest of this book to accomplish many other tasks) requires version 4+ of one of these two browsers, it makes sense to check all these things.

Both of the major browsers have a navigator object, which contains information about the browser. The navigator object has a property called appName, which holds the name of the current browser, and another called appVersion, which holds the version number. The checkBrowser() function simply looks at these properties and assigns appropriate values to the three variables. Note that the version number is returned as a string value, so the program forces it into numeric format. To see how the program uses the checkBrowser() routine, take a look at the body of the HTML document. You can see a second script that starts with a call to the checkBrowser() function. The program then sends an appropriate message to the screen, based on the browser type detected.

Using Cascading Style Sheets

Many of the most intriguing capabilities of JavaScript come from an understanding of cascading style sheets (CSS). This technology was intended to add flexibility to HTML. It does that, and it also adds a number of interesting possibilities for the JavaScript program.

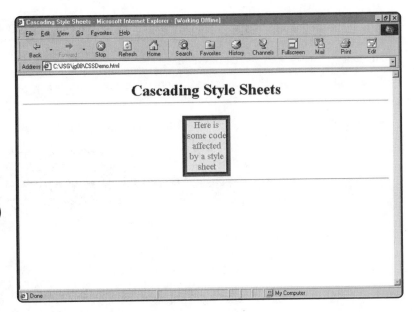

FIGURE 8.6

A CSS style tag manages all the special effects, the border, the colors, and the large font.

The Basics of CSS

One use of CSS is simply to extend the capabilities of HTML. Figure 8.6 shows an example of a page that uses this basic form of cascading style sheets.

CSS elements extend HTML. The basic idea of CSS elements is that you can use them to extend any HTML tag. The CSS elements add an entirely new set of property characteristics to a document. Although there are a number of interesting CSS elements, the list of such elements that both browsers support is quite short. Table 8.1 illustrates a few of the key CSS options.

How to Add CSS Styles to an HTML Page

There are a number of ways to incorporate style sheet elements into an HTML document. The easiest is to place a string containing CSS commands into an HTML tag's style attribute. You should use semicolons (;) to separate the commands. For example, to display a paragraph with green letters on a yellow background, you could use this variant of the <p> tag:

```
<p style = "color:green; background-color:yellow">
This is the green text on the yellow background
</p>
```

If you want to add a CSS style to an otherwise unremarkable piece of text, you can surround the text with the <span></span> or <div></div> tags and then attach a style to these tags. span and div are very useful as placeholders for CSS, because they do not have any other side effects of their own.

TABLE 8.1 CSS OPTIONS

Element	Description	Example
background-color	Sets the color of whatever element is being described.	background-color:blue
background-image	Adds a background image to the element.	background-image: bg.gif
border-color	Sets a border of the specified color around the element.	border-color:blue
border-style	Sets the type of border. Both browsers support double, groove, inset, outset, ridge, and solid borders, or you can specify the none variable if you don't want any border.	border-style: double
border-width	Describes the width of the border in pixels (px), inches (in), or centimeters (cm).	border-width: 3px
color	Defines the foreground color of the element.	color:red
font-family	Sets the font of the element to the first font in the list that is found on the browser's system.	font-family:'Arial', 'Times New Roman'
font-size	Determines the size of the font in points.	font-size: 20pt
height	Defines the minimum height of the element in inches(in), centimeters(cm), or pixels (px).	height: 2in
width	Defines the minimum width of the element in percent (%), inches (in), centimeters (cm), or pixels (px).	width:2%
left	Determines where the element is placed horizontally.	left:2.5cm
top	Determines where the element is placed vertically.	top: 4in
position	Makes the element positionable. Legal values are absolute and relative.	position:absolute

Here's the HTML that generated the CSS demonstration program.

```
<html>
<head>
<title>Cascading Style Sheets</title>

</head>


<body>
<center>
<h1>Cascading Style Sheets<hr></h1>
<span style = "height: 50px;
               width: 100px;
               border-style: groove;
               border-color: blue;
               border-width: 9px;
               background-color: yellow;
               color: red;
               font-size: 14pt">
Here is some code affected by a style sheet
</span>

</center>
<hr>
</body>
</html>
```

The span tag's style attribute controls all the characteristics of the special text.

Working with Positionable CSS Elements

CSS technology gives a level of control over HTML output that is very welcome to HTML authors. There is a special category of CSS commands that are even more important to a game author, because they enable elements to move around dynamically in the Web page. Figure 8.7 shows an example of this phenomenon, the Move Sub program.

Standard HTML (without CSS) does not let you move images (or anything else, for that matter) around on a page. Both of the major browsers allow a form of this behavior using elements that are formatted with special CSS characteristics. Start by looking at the HTML.

```
<body>
<center>
<h1>Move Sub<hr></h1>

<form name = "myForm">
<input type = "button"
```

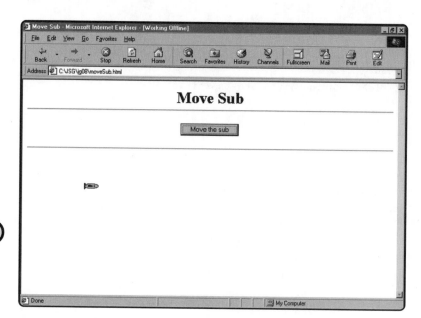

FIGURE 8.7

When the user clicks the button, the sub moves to the right.

```
        value = "Move the sub"
        onClick = "moveSub()">
</form>
</center>
<span name = "sub"
      id = "sub"
      style = "position: absolute;
               left: 50px;
               top: 200px;
               height: 30;
               width: 30;">
<img src = "sub.gif">
</span>
<hr>
</body>
</html>
```

Creating a Positionable Element

The page features a form with a button on it and a span object containing the sub graphic. A span object is a special HTML container that has almost no characteristics of its own. This makes it a great container for a style.

Notice the position: absolute part of the style definition. The position attribute specifies that the element it describes can be positioned on the screen. Rather than having the sub follow the normal rules of HTML positioning, you can use the `left` and `top` CSS attributes to define the sub's position. You can set the position as `relative` or `absolute`. `Relative` positioning means that the left and top positions are calculated from where the HTML element would normally go. `Absolute` positioning refers to distance from the top-left corner of the current document, window, or frame. For game programming, you will usually be concerned with `absolute` positioning.

The `left`, `top`, `height`, and `width` elements are used to describe the position and size of the object. Like most CSS elements, these tags can use a variety of units of measurement, including inches (`in`), centimeters (`cm`), and pixels (`px`).

TRICK

For game elements, I prefer to use pixels, because then the relationships among various objects on the screen remain constant even though the screen resolution is unpredictable. (You don't know the resolution of every player's screen, but a pixel is always a pixel.)

IN THE REAL WORLD

Cascading style sheets were developed as a way to give more control to more advanced HTML authors without compromising the basic simplicity of the language. Positionable elements can give the programmer fine-grained control over page layout of any type of Web page—a level of control that is not possible with standard HTML. Still, you should be very careful to test any pages that you build with CSS elements, because the major browsers do not follow the standards in exactly the same way.

Moving a Positionable CSS Element with Code

Once you have defined an HTML element with a positionable style, you can write code to move this element around the screen. Although both Netscape Navigator and Internet Explorer support this behavior, they differ in the implementation details. The Browser Detective script from earlier in this chapter will be an important part of this page.

```
var bVersion = 0;
var isNav = false;
var isIE = false;

function checkBrowser(){
  // Browser Detective
  // Andy Harris
  // Checks which browser is working
  if (navigator.appName == "Netscape"){
    isNav = true;
  } else {
    if (navigator.appName == "Microsoft Internet Explorer"){
      isIE = true;
    } // end IE if
```

```
      } // end Netscape if

      bVersion = parseInt(navigator.appVersion);

      if (bVersion < 4){

        alert("Consider getting a newer browser! This code might not work!");
      } // end if

      if ((!isNav) && (!isIE)){
        alert("I do not recognize this browser. This code might not work");
      } // end if
    }  // end checkBrowser

checkBrowser();

function moveSub(){
  // Move Sub
  // Andy Harris

  if (isNav){
    document.sub.moveBy(20, 0);
    if (document.sub.left > 300){
      document.sub.moveTo(50, 200);
    } // end if
  } else {
    document.all.sub.style.pixelLeft+= 20;
    if (document.all.sub.style.pixelLeft > 300){
      document.all.sub.style.pixelLeft = 50;
    } // end if
  } // end if
} // end moveSub
```

The first part of the code is the checkBrowser() function copied directly from the earlier example in this chapter. The browser-detection variables are also copied verbatim from the Browser Detective example.

HINT

Copying and pasting code is often not such a great idea. When you find yourself replicating code, it's usually a sign that you could write the code more efficiently. Even though it is very easy to copy and paste code, you will almost always end up spending a great deal of time and effort making small modifications to each of the copies. A little bit of time spent designing the code to be reused can reap large benefits down the road. You'll learn a way to import code from an external library in the next chapter. For now, however, the copying and pasting technique is acceptable for a code fragment as small as this one.

The `checkBrowser()` line runs the `checkBrowser()` function to determine which browser is active.

Moving an Element in Netscape Navigator

Both of the major browsers allow you to work with positionable elements, but they use different syntax. Ultimately, they use a different object model to describe the same kinds of elements. Figure 8.8 shows how Netscape Navigator sees positionable elements.

Netscape Navigator provides a special object called a `layer`. This is essentially a floating frame that can be positioned dynamically. When you assign the `position` attribute to a CSS style in Netscape Navigator, the browser automatically converts that element to a `layer` object. The `name` attribute of any element contained in the `style` tag becomes the name of the `layer` object.

The `layer` object has some very useful properties and methods. If you want to move a `layer` object to a specific spot, you can use the `moveTo()` method to move to a specific x,y coordinate (in pixels). If you want to move a specific amount, you can use the `moveBy()` method instead. Additionally, you can directly access the `left` and `top` properties of the layer to determine where the `layer` object is or to set the object's position.

Here again is the Netscape Navigator-specific code for the Move Sub program:

```
if (isNav){
    document.sub.moveBy(20, 0);
    if (document.sub.left > 300){
      document.sub.moveTo(50, 200);
    } // end if
```

The element in question is called `sub`. Because it has a `position` attribute, Netscape Navigator treats it as a `layer`. The `moveBy` command moves the object 20 pixels to the left. An `if` statement checks to see if the sub has moved past pixel 300. If so, it resets the sub's position.

TRICK

Remember, whenever you have code that increments or decrements a variable, you should think about checking for boundaries.

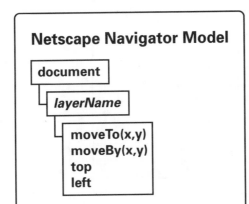

FIGURE 8.8

A positionable element in Netscape Navigator becomes a `layer` object.

Netscape Navigator Model

document

layerName

moveTo(x,y)
moveBy(x,y)
top
left

The Internet Explorer Approach

Internet Explorer has a different but similar way of looking at positionable elements. IE does not recognize `layer` objects, but can directly move an element specified by a positionable style. Figure 8.9 shows how the Internet Explorer document model sees positionable elements.

IE has a special feature called `all`, which is a container for all the objects on the form. The `sub` object is one of the elements on the form, so you can reach it from `all`. Note that IE does not use `layer` objects, but allows you to consider any object potentially moveable. However, the element with the positionable CSS style does not have the `left` and `top` properties directly. These properties belong to the `style` property of the object. Finally, the properties are not called `left` and `top`, but `pixelLeft` and `pixelTop`. The IE-specific code in the Move Sub program looks like this:

```
document.all.sub.style.pixelLeft+= 20;
if (document.all.sub.style.pixelLeft > 300){
  document.all.sub.style.pixelLeft = 50;
} // end if
```

The first line moves the `sub` element 20 pixels to the left. The `if` statement checks whether the sub is past pixel 300. If so, the statement resets the position.

HINT

If you are a Netscape Navigator fan, you might be feeling smug about how much easier this process is in Netscape than in IE. Moving an object is easier in Netscape Navigator, but you'll find a lot of other tasks to be easier in Internet Explorer. If you want to write cross-browser programs, it doesn't really matter which is easier; you have an obligation to write for both browsers.

FIGURE 8.9

The element is part of something called `all` and has a `style` property with some useful features.

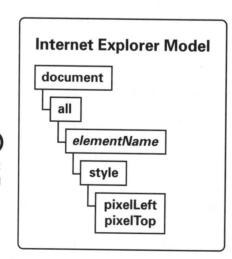

IN THE REAL WORLD

If you think it's crazy that the browser manufacturers cannot agree on how to move an object around, you are not alone. Most of the interesting things you can do in dynamic HTML require you to consider similar problems.

You could choose to write your programs for only one browser, but then you might lose part of your audience. You could also write two complete versions of each program, but users would still end up at the wrong version of the page.

My preferred technique is to check the browser type, then put a branch in each function that has browser-specific techniques. Executing this technique is a pain, but it will have to do until the browser manufacturers decide to agree on a standard.

Starting with the next chapter, you'll see another solution that eliminates some of these problems, but I want you to see how to build browser-independent code yourself so that you can appreciate the code library techniques that you'll see in the later chapters.

Changing the Text in a Positionable Element

Once you have defined an HTML element with a position style, you can also write new HTML to that element. This is (of course) done differently in Netscape Navigator and Internet Explorer, but the result is the same. Figures 8.10 and 8.11 show the interface for the program that illustrates how you can write new HLML to a defined element.

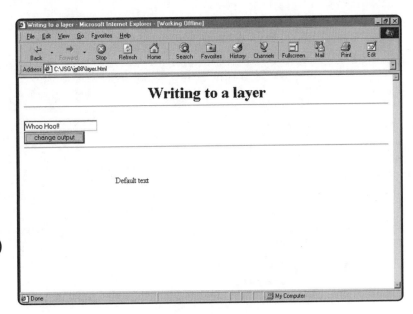

FIGURE 8.10

The user can type data into the text box.

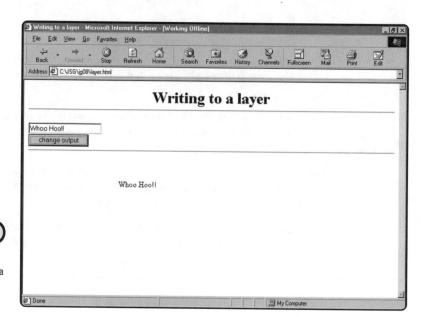

FIGURE 8.11

The program repeats the text in a positionable element.

The program copies the contents of the text box to a positionable element. Unfortunately, the two major browsers have entirely different ways of performing this feat. Still, the HTML is the same, regardless of the browser. Here is the HTML code:

```html
<body>
<center>
<h1>Writing to a layer<hr></h1>
</center>
<span name = "output"
      id = "output"
      class = "output"
      style = "position:absolute;
               left: 200px;
               top: 200px;">
Default text
</span>
<form name = "theForm">
<input type = "text"
       name = "txtInput">
<br>
<input type = "button"
       value = "change output"
       onClick = "changeIt()">
<hr>
</body>
```

Note the existence of the span object with a positionable style. This is the part of the code that will be modified. It has a name attribute and an ID attribute. Netscape generally refers to the span object with the the name attribute, and IE generally prefers the ID attribute, so I simply add them both with the same value.

The code for changing the text in the span object is very browser-dependent. The function starts by checking which browser is active, and then writes to the span object in a manner appropriate to that browser. Here is the changeIt() function:

```
function changeIt(){
  // Writing to a layer
  // Andy Harris

  checkBrowser();

  var theText = document.theForm.txtInput.value;
  if (isNav){
    document.output.document.open();
    document.output.document.write(theText);
    document.output.document.close();
  } else {
    document.all.output.innerHTML = theText;
  } // end if

} // end changeIt
```

The code between the if statement and the else statement will execute only if Netscape navigator is the current browser. The code between the else clause and the end if statement will execute only when Internet Explorer is running.

As you can see, the browsers take a very different approach to this particular problem.

IN THE REAL WORLD

You might use the ability to change an element selectively anywhere that you want to change output directly on the page, without resorting to text areas or frames for output. This approach could be useful in any applications in which you want it to seem as though parts of the page are changing on the fly. You can get a very seamless look with dynamic elements such as these, but the capability comes at the cost of some simplicity.

For example, I once wrote an online catalog, which looked to the user like a database. The user saw a product on the screen with an image and a description. The screen also contained buttons to go to the next or previous product. When the user clicked the buttons, the description and the image changed, apparently in the current page. The description and other text fields were all span objects, and I rewrote the text in the spans each time the user asked for a new element.

Internet Explorer Model

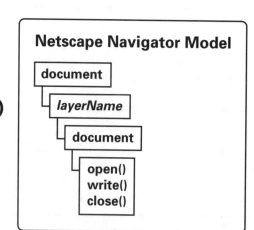

FIGURE 8.12

The positionable element has an `innerHTML` property.

Writing to a span Object in Internet Explorer

The Internet Explorer document model recognizes a span as an object accessible from the `all` group, as you may remember from earlier in the chapter. The span object has an `innerHTML` property. You can change the text of the span object by assigning new HTML to it. You can send plain text to a span object, or send more complex HTML code to the span object if you wish. Figure 8.12 is a diagram of the Microsoft model.

The IE version of the code is very straightforward:

```
document.all.output.innerHTML = theText;
```

Any value that you want to write to the element can be copied to the `innerHTML` property of that element.

Writing to a span Object in Netscape Navigator

The Netscape `document` object model does not recognize the `innerHTML` property. Instead, the positionable element is more like a frame or an external window. It has a document object of its own, with all the characteristics of any other `document` object. Figure 8.13 is a diagram of the Netscape point of view.

Netscape Navigator Model

FIGURE 8.13

The `layerName` has a `document` object. You can open, write to, and close the new document just as if it were a frame.

The Netscape approach is to treat the new element like a frame. It has a document object to which you can write. Of course, before you write to a document object, you should open it; then, after you write to the document object, you should close it. Here's the Netscape version of the code:

```
document.output.document.open();
document.output.document.write(theText);
document.output.document.close();
```

HINT

The document.output.document syntax looks very strange, but it makes sense if you understand how Netscape is viewing the structure. The first reference to document refers to the primary document object. Almost every object reference in JavaScript begins like this. output is the name of a property in the document object, specifically a positionable element. The full name of this element is document.object. Because it has its own document object, you refer to the document object of the output layer as document.object.document. The code is writing to the document object of the layer.

Adding Cross-Platform Sound

Sound effects are an important part of game development. They can add quite a bit to the ambiance of the game and can provide important cues to the user without taking up real estate on the screen.

Both major browsers allow you to play sounds from your JavaScript code. You might not be surprised to find that the technique for storing and playing sounds are totally different for Netscape and Internet Explorer. Figure 8.14 shows a program that demonstrates sound files.

It is not terribly difficult to add sound to a page as a hyperlink, but the browsers have very different techniques for embedding a sound into the page to be played under the control of a program. Here is the HTML code for the sound demo program:

```
<body>

<!-- embedded sound for Nav-->

<embed mayScript
       name = "sndPing"
       src = "ping.wav"
       hidden = "true"
       autostarts = "false">

<!--bgsound for IE -->
```

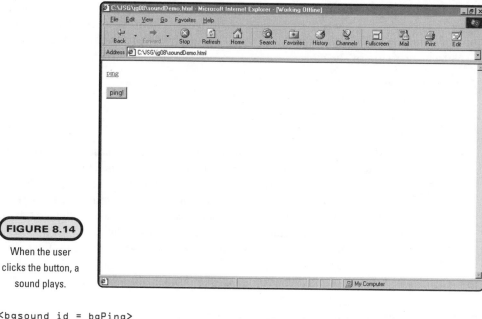

```
<bgsound id = bgPing>

<form>

<input type = button
       value = "ping!"
       onClick = playPing()>

</form>

</body>
```

When it comes to sound manipulation, the browsers don't even agree on the HTML technique. You embed sound in a page via the `embed` tag in Netscape and through the `bgSound` tag in IE.

The Netscape Navigator Approach to Sound

The Netscape view relies on helper applications. If you want to generate a sound in a Netscape document, you use the `embed` tag to indicate that a certain type of file should be embedded into the application (see Figure 8.15). When attempting to render the page, the browser looks at the `src` property of the `embed` tag to determine a plug-in to use. In the case of .wav or .midi files, Netscape uses a default media player. For sounds that a program will control, you should probably set the `hidden` and `autostart` attributes to false. The `mayScript` attribute indicates that the application will access some of the methods or properties of the actual object through a script.

The media player object that Netscape uses to load the sound has a `play()` method. When invoked, this method plays the sound. In addition, you can dynamically change the value of the `src` property to change the sound being played.

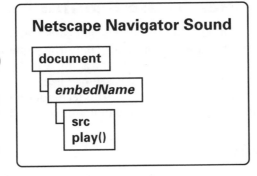

FIGURE 8.15

To play a sound in Netscape, you must have an embed object, which has src property and a play() method.

The Netscape-specific technique for playing the sound is as follows:

```
document.sndPing.src = "ping.wav";
document.sndPing.play();
```

TRAP

Netscape's approach to scriptable sound is notoriously fragile. The user might install some other kinds of helper applications or plug-ins, which would make the browser incapable of playing the sounds. You might want to add a "no sound" option to your programs, so those users who experience problems can simply skip sound but still have a working program.

The Internet Explorer Approach to Sound

Fortunately, the sound model for Internet Explorer is a little more robust. IE supports the bgSound HTML tag. This tag is often used to generate a sound to play in the background. Many people find background sounds that cannot be turned off irritating, so the IE sound model enables you to control the tag through scripts. Figure 8.16 shows how the IE document model sees sounds.

The JavaScript code to play the sound is reasonably simple. It is as follows:

```
document.all.bgPing.src = "ping.wav";
```

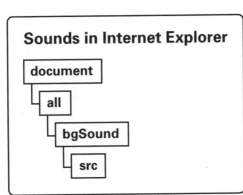

FIGURE 8.16

The bgSound object has a scriptable src property.

Putting It Together in the Stealth Sub Game

The Stealth Sub game takes all the elements in this chapter, plus a few ideas from earlier in the book, to make an interesting action/strategy game. The game's design utilizes positionable elements heavily. It also features sound and a simple lookup table. The main screen is called from another page, just as in the Basketball game in Chapter 7, "Image Swapping and Lookup Tables: The Basketball Game". This technique guarantees that the new browser page will be an appropriate size and will not be resized by the user.

Writing the HTML Code

The design of the main sub page is reasonably simple: The background is drawn in with a grid on it. The page contains three positionable elements. The sub itself is a span object. The scoreboard also is a span object. This element does not move but contains all the scoring results. The score is updated inside the scoreboard dynamically and looks like it's a natural part of the game screen. Finally, the control buttons are also part of a positioned element. This approach offers the easiest way to make sure that the buttons are positioned well.

Here is the HTML code for the Stealth Sub game:

```
<body onLoad = "init()"
      background = "ocean.gif">


<span name = "sub"
      id = "sub"
      style = "position:absolute; left:22px; top:125px">
<img src = "sub.gif"
     height = 30
     width = 30>
</span>


<span id = "output"
      name = "output"
      style = "position:absolute;
               left:330px; top:30px;
               color:white;
               background-color:red;
               border-style:ridge;
               height:60;
               width:60;">
row: 5
col: 0
boats: 0
detected 0 times
</span>


<center>
```

```
<span style = "position:absolute; left:30px; top:325px">
<center>
<form name = "myForm">

<input type = "button"
        value = "/\"
        onClick = "moveSub(NORTH)">

<br>
<input type = "button"
        value = "<--"
        onClick = "moveSub(WEST)">

<input type = "button"
        value = "-->"
        onClick = "moveSub(EAST)">

<br>
<input type = "button"
        value = "\/"
        onClick = "moveSub(SOUTH)">
<br>

</form>
</span>

<!-- Embedded sounds for NS -->

<Embed src = "ping.wav"
        name = "ping"
        hidden = "true"
        mayScript = "true"
        autostart = "false"
        mastersound></embed>

<Embed src = "boat.wav"
        name = "boat"
        hidden = "true"
        mayScript = "true"
        autostart = "false"
        mastersound></embed>

<Embed src = "dive.wav"
        name = "dive"
        hidden = "true"
```

```
        mayScript = "true"
        autostart = "false"
        mastersound></embed>


<Embed src = "torp.wav"
        name = "torp"
        hidden = "true"
        mayScript = "true"
        autostart = "false"
        mastersound></embed>


<!-- bgsound for IE -->
<bgsound id = "soundPlayer">

</center>


</center>


</body>
```

As you can see, the HTML code defines the positionable elements and embeds all the sounds as hidden sounds for Netscape. It also provides a bgSound object for IE. When the body of the page loads, it calls the init() function to do some initializing. All four buttons call the moveSub() function, but with a different value indicating which direction to move the submarine.

Making the Global Variables

When you are examining a new program, one of the best ways to get an overview is to look at the variables that are defined outside the functions. These should give you some idea of the data that is used in the program. Here's the code that generates these variables:

```
var isNav = false;
var isIE = false;
var NORTH = 0;
var EAST = 1;
var SOUTH = 2;
var WEST = 3;

var rows = 10;
var cols = 10;
var currentRow = 5;
var currentCol = 1;
var numHits = 0;

var grid = new Array();
```

The program has variables to determine which browser is active. It also has a series of variables (NORTH, SOUTH, EAST, and WEST) to simplify working with the directions. Since the value of these variables should not change, I capitalized them to remind myself that I consider them constants.

The rows and cols variables specify how many rows and columns are in the grid structure.

HINT

The actual white grid that the user sees is simply a graphic background, and it has no real relationship to the program. I carefully designed the graphic background so that it would have the right number of rows and columns, but all the program needs is the value of the variables. The background could be anything. My first draft of the program didn't have a grid drawn on the screen at all, but my primary beta tester (my wife) said that the game was dumb without a visible grid. Always listen to your beta testers, especially if you are married to them!

The currentRow and currentCol variables are used to determine where the submarine currently is inside the grid structure. The numHits variable tracks how many times the player has been pinged.

The most critical variable in the game is called grid. It is a two-dimensional array that keeps track of where the patrol boats are. Since the player cannot see the boats directly, it is important to have some way of tracking their position. The grid array does this.

The grid variable is the key data structure underlying the program. Everything else in the game somehow relates to this two-dimensional array. Figure 8.17 shows how the grid might actually look.

The playing surface is 10 by 10 cells. The program includes a function that analyzes a cell and counts the values in all its neighbors. It would be very difficult to account for all the variations around the edges, so the easiest solution is to add a border of 0s all around. The only grid spaces that you will allow as positions for the sub are in the 1–10 range; however, other cells containing the value 0 surround this range of cells, so any cell the sub is on is guaranteed to have four neighbor cells.

	0	1	2	3	4	5	6	7	8	9	10	11
0	0	0	0	0	0	0	0	0	0	0	0	0
1	0	0	0	1	0	0	0	0	0	0	0	0
2	0	0	0	1	1	0	1	1	1	0	0	0
3	0	0	0	1	0	1	0	1	0	0	0	0
4	0	0	1	0	0	1	0	1	0	1	0	0
5	0	0	0	0	0	0	0	1	0	0	1	0
6	0	0	0	0	0	0	0	1	0	1	1	0
7	0	1	0	1	0	0	0	1	0	1	1	0
8	0	0	0	0	1	1	1	1	1	0	0	0
9	0	1	0	0	0	0	0	0	0	0	1	0
10	0	1	0	1	0	0	1	1	0	0	0	0
11	0	0	0	0	0	0	0	0	0	0	0	0

FIGURE 8.17

The grid is a 10×10 matrix with a border of 0s around it.

Creating the Functions

In addition to looking at the global variables in a program, it's a great idea to look briefly at the functions provided in a program. This can give you a useful overview of how the program will work. Once you have a wide view, you can look more carefully at the specific functions and see how they work.

checkBrowser()

The checkBrowser() function checks the browser and sets isNav or isIE variables to true or false. This section doesn't repeat the code, because you've seen it several times already.

init()

The init() function initializes key variables in the game, calls the checkBrowser() routine, calls the grid-creation routine, and positions the sub graphic in the appropriate starting position. The function is called in the onLoad event of the body and whenever the user restarts the game. Here's the code for the init() function:

```
function init(){
  checkBrowser();
  makeGrid();
  playSound("dive");
  currentRow = 5;
  currentCol = 1;
  numHits = 0;
  //updateScore();
  //move sub to starting position
  if (isNav){
    document.sub.moveTo(22, 125);
  } else {
    document.all.sub.style.pixelLeft = 22;
    document.all.sub.style.pixelTop = 125;
  } // end if
} // end init
```

makeGrid()

This function turns the grid array into a two-dimensional array to contain the boat data. The resulting grid is actually larger than the number of rows and columns the user will see, to account for the border of 0 cells around the edges. Each element in the grid will contain a 0 (no boat present) or a 1 (there is a boat in this cell). Each square has a 30 percent chance of having a boat in it. The boats are placed randomly. The simplest way to change the difficulty of the game is to change the likelihood that each cell has a boat in it. A value less than .30 makes the game easier, and a value greater than .30 makes the game more difficult. The code for makeGrid() looks like the following:

```
function makeGrid(){
  var row = 0;
```

```
var col = 0;

//clear out borders
for (row = 0; row <= rows+1; row++){
  grid[row] = new Array();
  grid[row][0] = 0;
  grid[row][cols+1] = 0;
} // end row
for (col = 0; col <= cols+1; col++){
  grid[0][col] = 0;
  grid[rows + 1][col] = 0;
} // end col

//randomly populate middle
for (row = 1; row <= rows; row++){
  for (col = 1; col <= cols; col++){
    if (Math.random() < .30){
      grid[row][col] = 1;
    } else {
      grid[row][col] = 0;
    } // end if
  } // end col for
} // end row for

} // end makeGrid
```

getGrid()

The getGrid() function is a utility function that I used for debugging the program. Since there is no visual representation of the grid, I wanted to make sure that it was being created properly, so I wrote a little function to display the grid contents quickly in an alert box. The final program does not need the function, but it's so handy for debugging that I decided not to take it out. However, this section does not repeat the code. If you want to see the code for this function, look on the CD-ROM that accompanies this book.

countBoats()

The countBoats() function looks at the grid cell related to currentRow and currentCol and determines how many of the cell's neighbors contain patrol boats. The function adds up the grid values for the four cells immediately surrounding the current cell. The program returns this value as the sensor's value. Recall that the sensor is the instrument on the player's submarine that returns how many patrol boats are nearby. This procedure would have been much more complicated if it had to act differently on those cells that do not have four neighbors (such as corners and borders). I added a padding of 0-value cells around the edge of the grid to simplify coding of this function.

It is interesting that this function doesn't simply stop when it is finished, but returns the number of boats. Here's how the function looks:

```
function countBoats(){
    //given current row and column, count how many boats are nearby
    var numBoats = 0;
    numBoats += grid[currentRow - 1][currentCol];
    numBoats += grid[currentRow][currentCol - 1];
    numBoats += grid[currentRow][currentCol + 1];
    numBoats += grid[currentRow + 1][currentCol];
    return numBoats;
} //end countBoats
```

updateScore()

The updateScore() function does exactly what it says: It updates the scoreboard. It examines several of the key variables and concatenates them into an HTML string, which the function then prints out to a positionable element.

```
function updateScore(){
    var score = "";
    score += "<font color = white>";
    score += "row: " + currentRow + "<br>";
    score += " col: " + currentCol + "<br>";
    score += " boats: " + countBoats() + "<br>";
    score += " detected: " + numHits + " times ";
    score += "</font>";

    if (isNav){
        document.output.resizeTo(50,50);
        document.output.document.open();
        document.output.document.write(score);
        document.output.document.close();
    } else {
        document.all.output.innerHTML = score;
    } // end if

} // end updateScore
```

Note the way that the program invokes the countBoats() function. Since countBoats() returns a number, the program can assign that value directly to a variable.

playSound()

Given the name of a sound file, the playSound() routine attempts to play that sound in a platform-appropriate manner. Here's the code for playSound():

```
function playSound(soundName){
    if (isNav){
```

```
      var player = eval("document." + soundName);
      player.play();
   } else {
      var soundFile = soundName + ".wav";
      document.all.soundPlayer.src = soundFile;
   } // end if
} // end playSound
```

This particular approach depends on the embedded objects having exactly the same name as the filename of the .wav file.

moveSub()

The sub expects to receive a direction variable (NORTH, SOUTH, EAST, or WEST). The moveSub routine is called by all the button-press events. When the user clicks a button, it calls the moveSub routine with a parameter describing the direction the sub should be moved. The function analyzes that parameter, moves the submarine image appropriately, and checks to see if the sub has been pinged.

```
function moveSub(direction){
   var dx = 0;
   var dy = 0;
   switch (direction){
      case 0:
         dx = 0;
         dy = -30;
         currentRow--;
         break;
      case 1:
         dx = 30;
         dy = 0;
         currentCol++;
         break;
      case 2:
         dx = 0;
         dy = 30;
         currentRow++;
         break;
      case 3 :
         dx = -30;
         dy = 0;
         currentCol--;
         break;
   } // end switch

   if (isNav){
      document.sub.moveBy(dx, dy);
   } else {
```

```
        document.all.sub.style.pixelLeft += dx;
        document.all.sub.style.pixelTop += dy;
      } // end if


      //check for win
      if (currentCol > 10){
        playSound("dive");
        alert("You Win!!!");
        init();
      } // end if


      //check for hit
      if (grid[currentRow][currentCol] == 1){
        playSound("ping");
        numHits++;
        if (numHits >=3){
          playSound("torp");
          alert("You've been sunk!!");
          init();
        } // end sunk if
      } // end  hit if
      updateScore();


    } // end moveSub
```

For each direction, the routine updates the `currentRow` and `currentCol` variables and changes the position of the sub graphic.

The `moveSub()` function then checks whether the sub has reached the open ocean. If so, the player wins, and the program resets the game by calling the `init()` function.

Finally, the `moveSub()` function checks for a boat in the current cell. If there is one, the function plays the ping sound, then checks whether this is the third ping. If so, the game is over, so the program plays the explosion sound and resets the game with a call to `init()`. Table 8.2 details the new syntax I've covered in this chapter.

Summary

This chapter took you through the somewhat frightening world of cross-platform dynamic HTML. You learned how to write code that can determine which browser the user is running. You experimented with cascading style sheet (CSS) syntax as a way to add formatting to your HTML code. You learned how you can use positionable CSS to position your HTML elements more precisely. You built programs that moved an element, changed its text, and played sounds. You have started to grapple with the intricacies of cross-platform design, and have no doubt struggled to make your code work well on either browser. In short, you have earned the right to call yourself a DHTML programmer. In the next chapter, you'll learn an easier way to develop code that works on any modern browser, that allows you to concentrate more on your game and less on how each browser performs each particular task.

TABLE 8.2 SYNTAX SUMMARY

Statement	Description	Example
`navigator.appName`	Returns the browser's name as a string. This statement is used for browser detection.	`var theBrowser = navigator.appName;`
`document.layerName.moveTo(x,y)`	Moves a CSS element to (x, y). This statement applies to Netscape only.	`document.sub.moveTo(30,100);`
`document.all.layerName.style.pixelLeft document.all.layerName.style.pixelTop`	Moves a CSS element to a specified coordinate. This statement applies to IE only.	`document.all.sub.style.pixelLeft = 30;`
`document.all.sub.style.pixelTop = 100; document.layerName.document.open(), document.layerName.document.write(), document.layerName.document.close(),`	Writes new content to a CSS element. This statement applies to Netscape only.	`document.output.document.open();`
`document.output.document.write ("Hello World!"); document.output.document.close(); document.all.layerName.innerHTML`	Writes a new value to the element. This statement applies to IE only.	`document.all.output.innerHTML = "Hello World!";`
`document.embedName.play()`	Plays a sound file previously loaded into the specified `embed` tag. This statement applies to Netscape only.	`document.ping.play();`
`document.all.bgSoundName.src`	Enables you to assign a new URL to play a sound file.	`document.all.soundPlayer.src = "ping.wav";`

EXERCISES

1. Modify the sub program so that it has another theme. (You are escaping from prison, sneaking into enemy headquarters, or searching for some type of treasure.) Consider adding multiple levels of difficulty.

2. Make an enhanced version of the sensor that would still return a number, but with the following difference: a boat to the north is 1 point, one to the west is 2, a boat to the south is 4, and a boat to the east is 8. If the user can figure out the code, he or she can always tell exactly where the boats are. As a bonus, this would be a fun way to teach binary notation, if you happen to be a computer science teacher or something similar.

3. The sound techniques described in this chapter can also be used to play .midi files. Build a jukebox that plays a sound file based on a particular button press. Be sure to check with the owner of a file before using it. Change the output of one of your earlier programs so that it uses a CSS element instead of a frame or text box.

4. Make a home page that the user navigates by moving some object around on the page. For example, if you have a page about turtles, let the user move a turtle around the page. When the turtle is at an appropriate place (for example, over the word "photos"), the appropriate page (a photo gallery) automatically pops up in another frame.

Sprite Animation: The Racer

As your programs have become more powerful, you have spent more effort making them function across browsers. It would be nice to have a trick that would eliminate browser-dependency issues and let you concentrate on writing functional programs. Such a technology exists, and you will learn about it in this chapter. Specifically, you will learn:

- **What an API library is**

- **How to import external JavaScript libraries**

- **What a sprite is and how to make one**

- **How to move sprites**

- **How to deal with frame animation in sprites**

- **How to react to collisions between sprites**

- **How to determine elapsed time for scorekeeping**

The Project: The Racer Program

To illustrate all these points, you will build a program that simulates a top-down view of a racing car. The user will be able to control the car through on-screen controls and will have to drive the car as quickly as possible through a series of tracks. Figures 9.1 through 9.4 show the game's interface.

The game looks interesting enough, but some of its features make the game impressive from a technical point of view. The game is designed to be very easy to customize.

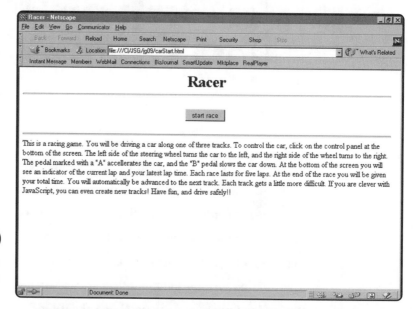

FIGURE 9.1

The instruction form contains a button to launch the game.

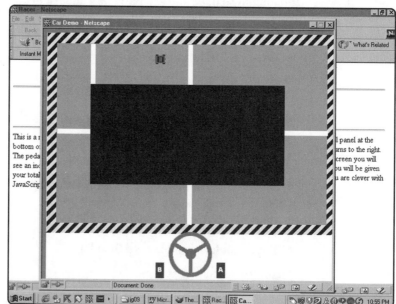

FIGURE 9.2

You control the car with the little dashboard and the mouse.

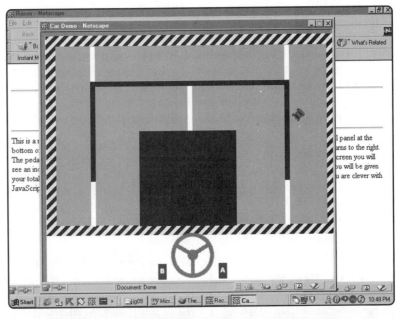

This is a r
bottom o:
The peda
see an inc
your total
JavaScrip l panel at the
rns to the right.
creen you will
u will be given
u are clever with

FIGURE 9.3

Avoid the black
obstacles; the car
stops if you hit one
of them.

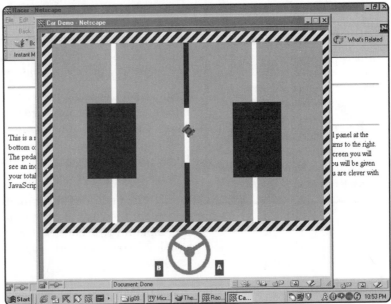

This is a r
bottom o:
The peda
see an inc
your total
JavaScrip l panel at the
rns to the right.
creen you will
u will be given
u are clever with

FIGURE 9.4

The tracks get more
difficult as you
advance in
the game.

It is reasonably simple to build new tracks. As long as you understand the principles, you can easily customize the tracks however you wish. In fact, you could even add a track editor and let the user design new tracks. (That will be one of the exercises at the end of the chapter.) The racing game is reasonably browser-independent; it does not appear to have a single line of browser-checking code, yet it uses positionable elements and dynamic images.

Introducing the Sprite

Game developers have been using graphic objects for a long time. They invented a term for a special kind of graphic used in game programming, called the *sprite*. In theoretical terms, a sprite is an object that can be used in a game environment. The user can move a sprite to a specific position. The sprite should be able to change its image on demand. A sprite also should be able to recognize collisions with other sprites, and it is quite useful if a sprite has some other attributes such as speed and direction.

JavaScript does not directly provide the sprite element, but theoretically you can give an object all the characteristics of the sprite object through the techniques that you learned in the last chapter. It would be great if there was some kind of object you could just magically invoke that would act like a sprite. It would be even better if you could just tell the sprite object to move or change its graphic; then you wouldn't have to worry about what kind of positionable element or layer manipulation was happening behind the scene.

> **IN THE REAL WORLD**
>
> The ability to use APIs is one of the most important skills in modern programming. It is extremely common to have problems that extend beyond the original scope of a language. Programmers working on all kinds of projects can often find or build APIs to help solve such problems. There are APIs for creating graphics, adding special input/output devices, and working with databases and many other kinds of applications.

Fortunately, a number of reusable JavaScript objects have been invented. Several authors have been working on special libraries, called *Application Programming Interfaces* (*APIs*), that simplify the tedium of programming with positionable elements in JavaScript. Using these libraries can spare you the challenges of writing cross-platform dynamic HTML and let you focus on the interesting things, such as writing your games and other programs.

Throughout the rest of this book, I will demonstrate one library that is optimized for game programming. The library, called *gameLib*, was written by Scott Porter. This excellent set of programs makes JavaScript game development much easier than it was just a couple of years ago.

The latest version of the gameLib library and its documentation are provided on the CD-ROM that accompanies this book. Refer to that documentation for instructions on installing the library.

Creating the Sprite Program

You can investigate the gameLib API by examining a very simple program that uses the library to draw a sphere on the screen. Figure 9.5 shows the program's interface. At first the API will not seem to provide much benefit, but you soon will see how powerful sprite objects can be.

Although this page could be produced using standard HTML, it was not. There are a number of interesting things happening in this program.

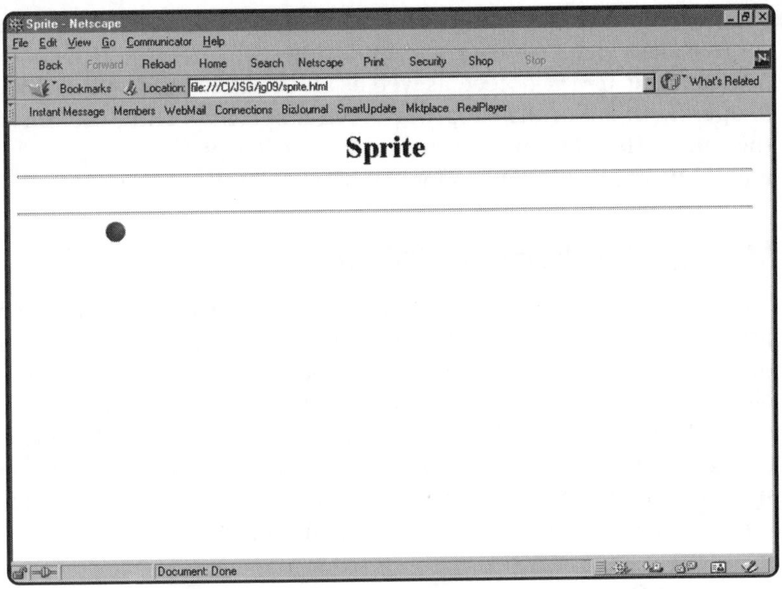

FIGURE 9.5

The page looks
unremarkable from
the user's point
of view.

Importing a Code Library

The programs in this chapter all use modules from the gameLib library. Rather than copying all the code of the library, you can use a variation of the script tag to export text files with JavaScript functions. Following is the code that performs that function in the Sprite program:

```
<html>
<head>
<title>Sprite</title>

<!-- import the basic libraries -->
<script language="Javascript" src="../gamelib196/gamelib/gamelib_core.js">
</script>

<script language="Javascript" src="../gamelib196/gamelib/gamelib_core.js">
</script>
```

The script tag has an src parameter that can be assigned a URL. In this case, the program is loading two modules. The first one is called gamelib_core.js. This module contains a bunch of utility functions and methods that are used by the other modules. As a programmer, you will not need all these features directly, but you may want to look at the documentation to see which ones might be useful. Every program that uses the gameLib library must import the gamelib_core module.

The program also imports the gamelib_sprites module. This is also a text file that contains JavaScript code for manipulating sprite objects. This code contains the definition of the sprite object, as well as all the code that will enable the sprite objects to operate in a platform-appropriate manner. Importing the library in this way has the same effect as copying the entire JavaScript file and pasting it into your program, but you don't have to look at all the details of the code.

Using the Sprite Object

The sprite object defined by the gameLib API is a very powerful object. It uses JavaScript's variation of object-oriented programming, which means that the sprite object has properties and methods. *Properties* are characteristics that describe the object, such as x, y, height, and width. In the gameLib API, most properties are read-only, which means that you use them to get information about the sprite object. To change the sprite's behavior or appearance, you use methods instead. A *method* is a special function that is attached to a particular type of object. Tables 9.1 and 9.2 list the sprite object's primary methods and properties.

HINT

Don't worry if you don't understand these tables on your first glance. You'll get to see most of these properties and methods in action as the chapter progresses. The tables simply give you a bird's-eye view of the sprite object's properties and methods before you actually begin using them.

From a quick look at these tables, you can see that the sprite object is quite powerful. In general, you can use the sprite's methods to control the sprite, and use its properties to inquire about the sprite. The tables might seem a little bit intimidating, but managing sprites is not very difficult at all.

Initializing the Sprite

Here is the code fragment that starts up the sprite for the Sprite program.

```
<script>
var ball;

function init(){
  ball = new Sp_Sprite();
  ball.setImage("redball.gif", 20, 20, 1, 1);
  ball.moveTo(100,100);
  ball.setXlimits(0, 500);
  ball.setYlimits(0, 300);
  ball.setFrame(0);
  ball.switchOn();
} // end init

</script>
```

TABLE 9.1 KEY PROPERTIES OF THE SPRITE OBJECT IN GAMELIB

Property	Description	Example
`on` (read-only)	Describes whether the sprite is visible.	`if (mySprite.on){` `//do something }`
`x, y, height, width` (read-only)	Describes the current size and position of the sprite.	`if (mySprite.x < 0){` `mySprite.x = 0; }`
`Bounces` (read-write)	Determines behavior when the sprite reaches defined limits; if true, the sprite bounces off the border.	`mySprite.bounces = true;`

`Xdir, ydir` (read-only)	Determines the speed of the sprite in x and y	`if (mySprite.xdir == 0)`
		`{ alert ("not going`
		`directions.sideways!"); }`

`Xydegs` (read-only)	Shows the direction that the sprite is moving in degrees.	`if (mySprite.xydegs ==`
		`0){ alert ("going`
		`north!"); } // end if`

`Speed` (read-only)	Shows the speed of the sprite.	`alert (mySprite.speed);`
`Collides` (read-write)	Determines whether the sprite registers collisions.	`mySprite.collides = true;`

The code starts by creating a variable (`ball`) that will contain the sprite. The variable is declared outside any functions, so it can be used anywhere. The code also defines an `init()` function, which the program will call when the body loads. This `init()` function is normal for any type of initialization, and you will usually need something like this function when you work with sprites.

Inside `init()`, I created a new sprite with this line:

```
ball = new Sp_Sprite();
```

Notice the `new` keyword. You have used it before when creating instances of objects. This line generates a new `Sp_Sprite` object called `ball`.

HINT

The `sprite` object in gameLib is technically called a `Sp_Sprite` because that's the name of the class that Porter built. He decided to begin the name of everything defined in his sprite module with `Sp_` so that it would be easier to sort out when debugging the API package. You will almost always refer to your sprite objects by the variable names you assign to them, so the distinction between sprites (a generic term) and Sp_Sprites (the specific term used in gameLib) is not very important.

TABLE 9.2 PRINCIPAL METHODS OF THE SPRITE OBJECT IN GAMELIB

Method	Description	Example
HasHit(object)	Determines whether one sprite has collided with another.	```if (car.hasHit (barrier)){ alert("crash!"); }```
MoveTo(x,y)	Moves the sprite directly to the given x,y coordinates.	`mySprite.moveTo(100, 50);`
SetDir(x,y)	Determines how many pixels in x and y dimensions that the sprite will move at each interval.	```mySprite.setDir(1,3); //moves sprite 1 to left, 3 down```
SetXYdegs(direc)	Sets the direction of the sprite in degrees.	```mySprite.setXYdegs(45); //moves sprite northeast```
SetSpeed(speed)	Determines how many pixels the sprite will move at each interval.	`mySprite.setSpeed(3);`
SetImage(image, width, height, frames, anims)	Determines the image of a sprite; see below for details.	```mySprite.setImage ("car.gif", 20, 20, 1, 1);```
SetFrame(number)	Sets a particular frame of the image.	`mySprite.setFrame(2);`
SwitchOn(), switchOff()	Turns the sprite on or off, controlling its visibility.	`mySprite.switchOn();`
SetXlimits(min, max), setYlimits(min, max)	Determines where the sprite can be placed or moved on the screen.	```mySprite.setXlimits (0,300); //sprite's x will stay between 0 and 300```

Setting the Sprite's Image

A sprite is not very interesting unless it is displaying some sort of image, so you'll almost always want to attach an image to a sprite. When you set up a sprite's image, you need to specify a number of parameters about the object. For the `ball` example, here is the `setImage()` line:

```
ball.setImage("redball.gif", 20, 20, 1, 1);
```

Because `ball` is an instance of the `Sprite` class, you can invoke all of its methods. I set its image to `"redball.gif"`. You can assign any image to a sprite with an absolute or local URL. The next two numbers (20, 20) indicate the size of the sprite. This does not have to be the same as the size of the starting image. The next two parameters (1, 1) refer to the frame and animation levels of the image. You'll learn about frame animation later in this chapter and in the next chapter, but for now, you'll leave these values at 1 to make a simple image with one frame and one animation.

Setting the Ball's Initial Position

The following line moves the ball to the indicated position:

```
ball.moveTo(100,100);
```

When the sprite is displayed, this position is where the ball will appear on the screen. Remember that (0, 0) is in the upper-left corner. The coordinates indicate the location of the top-left corner of the sprite.

The next two lines determine boundaries on the screen. Whenever you create a sprite, you should set its limits using these two methods.

```
ball.setXlimits(0, 500);
ball.setYlimits(0, 300);
```

The playing field thus will extend from (0, 0) to (500, 300). This is a reasonable size for a game, as it will fit inside most commonly used screen resolutions. Of course, the ball isn't moving yet, so specifying boundaries might seem silly at this point. However, you will be modifying this program soon to move the ball.

TRAP

Even if you have sprites that will not move at all, be sure to set limits for them. The default values for the x and y limits seem to be very small, and your sprite might not appear in the right place (or at all) on the screen. Be sure that you have limits broad enough to show the sprite. Also be careful to place the sprite far enough inside these limits so that it is still visible. If you create sprites that are not appearing in the correct places, check whether you have set the limits correctly.

Turning On the Sprite

The last two lines of the `init()` function do some more housekeeping. The following line specifies that the original frame be used:

```
ball.setFrame(0);
```

You'll learn more about frames in the next section. For now, just accept that it is necessary to set the frame to 0.

Then the last line turns the ball on and makes it visible to the user, like this:

```
ball.switchOn();
```

Moving Sprites Around

All of the sprite stuff seems like a lot of work, but it really pays off when you start making the sprites do interesting things, like move around on the screen and crash into things.

Moving Sprite

NW | N | NE
W | | E
SW | S | SE

FIGURE 9.6

When the user clicks a button, the ball moves in the direction indicated by the button.

Creating the Moving Sprite Program

By making a few modifications to the Sprite program, you can make a ball that bounces around on the screen. Figure 9.6 shows just such a program.

Although you can't see it in Figure 9.6, the ball automatically bounces off any of the limits and reverses direction appropriately. The most exciting thing about this program is that most of the new code is HTML for the buttons. The sprite object contains most of the code required to handle the motion of the ball.

Modifying the init() Method

I added two modifications to the init() method.

```
ball.bounces = true;
Gl_start();
```

The ball.bounces line tells the ball sprite that it should use "bouncy" behavior. This means that when it hits a wall, the ball should reverse its direction. Note that this is one of the unusual cases where you control a sprite by a property.

The Gl_start() line contains a subtle but powerful command. It starts up the actual gameLib engine. This in turn starts up a special timer that repeats 20 times per second. This timer activates all the motion in your program.

TRICK

If you want to have this type of behavior in your code without using the gameLib library, you should investigate the setTimeOut() function supplied by both browsers. It is the underlying technology that the gameLib API uses to manage timed behavior.

Writing the HTML for the Moving Sprite Program

The HTML is reasonably straightforward. It is a form with a set of command buttons on it. I used a table for neatness, and placed that table in a span object aligned to the right so it will stay out of the area in which the ball will move. Here's the HTML for one row of the table.

```
<tr>
  <td><input type = "button"
             value = "W  "
             onClick = "moveBall(270)">
  </td>
  <td><input type = "button"
             value = "    "
             onClick = "moveBall(999)">
  </td>
  <td><input type = "button"
             value = "E  "
             onClick = "moveBall(90)">
  </td>
</tr>
```

All the buttons call the moveBall() function, but they pass a different parameter. You might recognize that west is 270 degrees and east is 90 degrees on a standard compass. The center button causes the ball to stop, so I encoded the special value 999, which usually would not be considered a valid direction.

Changing Speed and Direction

The moveBall() function manipulates the ball sprite to make the animation occur. Following is the code for that function:

```
function moveBall(direc){
  if (direc == 999){
    ball.setSpeed(0);
  } else {
    ball.setSpeed(10);
    ball.setXYdegs(direc);
  } // end if
} // end moveBall
```

The direction value is stored in the parameter direc. The first thing that this function does is check whether the user clicked the center button. If so, the function sets the ball's speed to 0, effectively stopping the ball. If the direc value is anything other than 999, the function sets the ball's XYdegs value to that direction and sets the ball's speed to 10. The next time that the timer loop occurs (remember, this

IN THE REAL WORLD

Sprites are clearly useful in game programming, but they can also be handy in any application where you need some kind of flashy movement or image swapping. If, for example, you're building a page for a courier company, you can incorporate vans and aircraft that move across the screen as part of the page's navigation scheme. If you are doing some sort of site for an engineering firm, you might feature a moving parade of some of the parts the company produces.

happens 20 times per second), the function moves the ball approximately 10 pixels in the indicated direction.

The capability to work with direction and speed is one of the most useful features of the `sprite` **object. In game development, the direction and speed of a sprite are probably what you are most concerned about, but all the** `document` **object model gives you is the ability to set an element to a specified x,y coordinate. Without the** `sprite` **object, you would need to do some trigonometric conversions. The** `sprite` **object handles all the math necessary to convert a speed and direction into a pair of coordinates. This is pretty handy if your trig skills are a bit rusty.**

Once the sprite is set up and the gameLib is started, movement is automatic. The ball pretty much moves on its own, bounces when it hits a boundary, and responds to button clicks from the user.

Using Frame Animation in Sprites

If you wish to animate the movement of a ball, you can get away with only one image. However, if the image that you are working with is a car or other vehicle, you have to change the graphic when the direction changes; otherwise, the car will look silly. A vehicle usually goes in the direction of its nose, so it would be great to have some way to point the car in the current direction.

Creating the Moving Sprite Program

The Moving Sprite program faces exactly this dilemma (see Figure 9.7). The sprite is an arrow, and the arrow is always pointing in the direction in which the arrow is traveling.

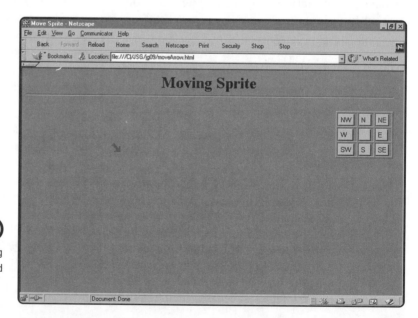

FIGURE 9.7

The arrow is moving to the southeast and pointed in that direction.

Since the arrow is a `sprite` object, it has special methods that make it easy to choose one of a set of images.

Using Clip Graphics

The gameLib library uses a special technique called graphic clipping. The best way to describe how this technique works is to look at the actual image file that is applied to the car sprite (see Figure 9.8).

To create the illusion of an arrow that can go in all directions, you need eight different image files. You then display the appropriate image for the current direction. In Web programming, there is considerable overhead for each image that comes to the page. One large image is transferred more quickly than several smaller images. The clipping technique requires you to build a large composite image with all the component images on it. When you attach an image to a `sprite` object, only a small part of the total image is shown. You can control which part of the image is visible. Although it sounds complicated, it is reasonably simple to use such an image once you have created it.

The image file was specially prepared for use as a sprite image. I designed the car facing north as a 30×30 pixel image. I then made a copy, which I rotated by 45 degrees. I made a larger image that was 40 pixels tall by 320 pixels wide. I carefully placed the first (north) car image so it was centered at (20, 20) in the long skinny image. I then centered the next (northeast) car image at (40, 20) of the longer image. I repeated the process until I had all eight cardinal directions represented in the long image. I saved this image as car.gif. It is important that the smaller images are all the same distance apart, but the exact number of images does not matter.

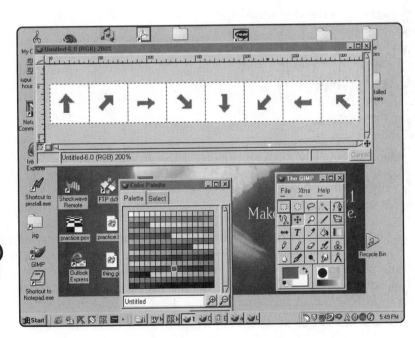

FIGURE 9.8

The arrow image is actually a set of eight images in one file.

Setting Up Direction Variables

This program starts with a set of variables to make things a little easier.

```
var arrow;

var NORTH = 0;
var NORTHEAST = 1;
var EAST = 2;
var SOUTHEAST = 3;
var SOUTH = 4;
var SOUTHWEST = 5;
var WEST = 6;
var NORTHWEST = 7;

var direction = EAST;
```

The `arrow` variable will hold the sprite. The capitalized variables will be used for convenience, to hold the various directions. The directions correlate to the order of the arrow images in the graphic. The variable called `direction` holds the direction that the arrow sprite is currently facing.

Creating a Sprite with Frame Animation

You need to change only one line of code in the initialization to deal with a sprite that uses frame animation.

```
function init(){
  arrow = new Sp_Sprite();
  arrow.setImage("arrow.gif", 30, 30, 8, 1);
  arrow.moveTo(100,100);
  arrow.setXlimits(0, 500);
  arrow.setYlimits(0, 300);
  arrow.setFrame(0);
  arrow.switchOn();
  arrow.setSpeed(0);
  Gl_start();
} // end init
```

The only line that changes is the `setImage()` method of the sprite. In this case, the code specifies that the sprite's image should be set to `"sprite.gif"`. Recall that this image actually is 40×320 pixels, and it actually contains eight different arrow images. The next two parameters (30, 30) indicate the size at which the sprite should be drawn on the screen. The function will draw the sprite as a 30×30 square. The next parameter determines how many frames are in the image. This number is set to 8, which indicates that the original image should be split into eight even pieces. In effect, the sprite will show only one-eighth of the original image at any one time, and it will show that piece of the image as a 30×30 square. You will use the last parameter (1) in the next chapter to add another element of animation. For now, leave the parameter's value set to 1.

HINT   I also turned off the bouncing feature, because I didn't think it made sense for the arrow to bounce off the wall like a ball would.

Why not simply have eight different images? It might seem crazy to force all the small images into one long image, but it actually makes sense. First of all, because the images are all related, it's much easier to keep track of one image than eight. But the most important reason is efficiency. Every time that the browser has to load an image, there is a lot of overhead. The browser contacts the server, sends the image over the Internet, and closes the connection. Eight small images take much longer to download than one larger one. Also, all the image clipping will happen on an image that exists in the computer's memory. This is much faster than swapping between multiple image files. Most browsers have a limited image cache and can keep very few images in memory. This means that if a lot of image swapping is going on, you could have even more network accesses slowing down the system. With the single-image technique, the image is entirely in memory.

Modifying the Direction Parameter

The rest of the Moving Sprite program is also similar to the ball sprite program, with a few significant differences. Here's the new version of the button code. The following HTML code listing shows only the middle row, but you should easily grasp what's going on from this portion of the HTML.

```
<tr>
  <td><input type = "button"
             value = "W  "
             onClick = "moveArrow(WEST)">
  </td>
  <td><input type = "button"
             value = "    "
             onClick = "moveArrow(999)">
  </td>
  <td><input type = "button"
             value = "E  "
             onClick = "moveArrow(EAST)">
  </td>
</tr>
```

This time, rather than specifying the new angle in degrees, I decided to specify the direction through the special constants that I had created. The center button still has the 999 value, because this button is still used to stop the arrow.

The moveCar() function manages the arrow's direction and changes the frame so that the arrow image is pointing in the right direction.

```
function moveArrow(direc){
  if (direc == 999){
    arrow.setSpeed(0);
  } else {
```

```
    arrow.setSpeed(3);
    arrow.setXYdegs(direc * 45);
    arrow.setFrame(direc);
  } // end if
} // end moveArrow
```

The setXYdegs() method changes the sprite's direction based on the value of direc. I noticed that all the directions were multiples of 45 degrees, so I could use some simple math to correlate the 0–7 direction values to compass points. I also used the setFrame() method of the arrow sprite to set the frame to the number associated with the arrow's direction. So, if the user clicks the west button, the value of direc will be WEST, which evaluates to 6. The function would set the arrow's direction to 6 * 45, or 270 degrees. The sprite would load with the sixth frame, which shows the arrow pointing to the west.

Detecting Collision

If sprites are moving around on the screen, they will eventually collide. Collision detection is an important element of game programming, because many of the events in a game are triggered by sprites bumping into each other. The sprite class provided by the gameLib API can detect collisions in a number of ways.

Creating the Collision Program

To practice collision detection, you need to create something for your car sprite to crash into. Figures 9.9 and 9.10 show a variation of the Moving Sprite program, called Checking for Collisions.

I introduced another sprite, which I called barrier. This sprite is simply a big black box.

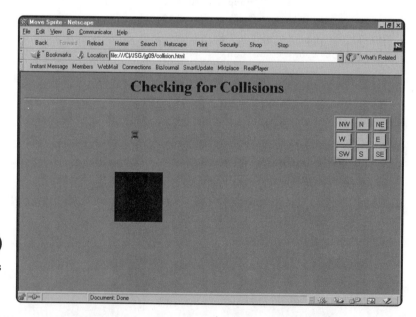

FIGURE 9.9

The car sprite works just as it did in the last program.

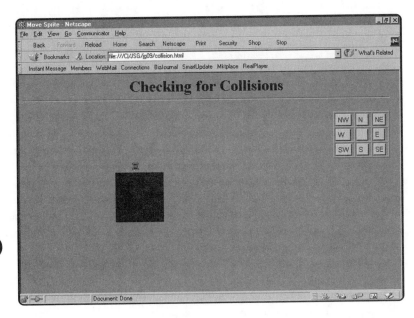

FIGURE 9.10

When it hits
the black box,
the car stops.

Creating the Sprites

The Checking for Collisions program has two sprites. One is the car (almost identical
to the car in the previous program) and the other one is the barrier. Following is the
code that sets up the sprites:

```
function init(){
  car = new Sp_Sprite();
  car.setImage("car.gif", 30, 30, 8, 1);
  car.moveTo(100,100);
  car.setXlimits(0, 500);
  car.setYlimits(0, 300);
  car.setFrame(0);
  car.switchOn();
  car.setSpeed(0);
  car.collides = true;

  barrier = new Sp_Sprite();
  barrier.setImage("black.gif", 100, 100, 1, 1);
  barrier.setXlimits(0, 500);
  barrier.setYlimits(0, 300);
  barrier.moveTo(200, 200);
  barrier.setFrame(0);
  barrier.switchOn();
  barrier.collides = true;

  Gl_hook("checkCollision()");
```

```
Gl_start();
```

```
} // end init
```

Notice the use of the `collides` property in both sprites. I set this property to true in both the sprites so that they would register collisions.

TRICK

The image for the barrier sprite is simply a 10×10 black square. I made a whole series of images of solid colors that are perfect for situations like this. Because the image is a solid color, it will size up very gracefully. It has a very small file size and will transfer quickly across the Internet. These little solid color images are great for normal HTML and game programming purposes, because you can easily use them to make a rectangle of any color. I also have an image that is simply a small transparent gif image. This image is also useful if you want a spacer, such as we used to position the images in the basketball game in the last chapter, or a sprite that responds to collisions but is not visible, such as a ghost or an invisible wall.

Hooking to the Timer Loop

If you look closely, you'll notice one other new line in the `init()` method. That line is as follows:

```
Gl_hook("checkCollision()");
```

Remember that when you call `Gl_start()`, you start a timer loop that occurs 20 times per second. This timer is used to manage sprite movement. The `hook()` method allows you to specify a function to run every time that the timer loop occurs. In this specific case, the method tells the library to run the `checkCollision()` function (which you will see shortly) every time that the timer loop occurs, which will be 20 times per second. Hooking functions to the timer in this way is the principal method for adding logic to your program in gameLib.

HINT

If you have looked carefully at the gameLib documentation, you might have noticed that there is a way to do collision detection without hooking a function to the timer. The approach that this application demonstrates is not always the best choice. However, because the ability to hook up functions is so important, I wanted to demonstrate at least one approach right away. Of course, you can always decide for yourself the best approach for creating your programs.

Creating the checkCollision() Function

After you go through the trouble of hooking up a function, you have an obligation to write the function. Fortunately, the `checkCollision()` function is pretty simple.

```
function checkCollision(){
  if (car.hasHit(barrier)){
    car.setSpeed(0);
```

```
    G1_unhook("checkCollision()");
  } // end if
} // end checkCollision
```

The `hasHit()` method of a sprite determines whether a car has hit whatever sprite is specified. This method always returns a Boolean value. If the car has hit the barrier in this iteration of the function, the value is returned as true. Otherwise, it returns as false.

When the car hits the barrier, you want to stop the car. To do so, you set its speed to 0 with the `setSpeed()` method.

Remember that the program calls the `checkCollision()` function quite often. With the speed set to 0, the car continues hitting the barrier until it has changed direction and the speed has been changed to some other value. I found it best to unhook the `checkCollision()` function temporarily so that the car sprite could be moved. The `G1_unhook()` function is used to stop calling the `checkCollision()` function each time that the timer ticks.

The `moveCar()` function in this program has been modified slightly, to rehook the `checkCollision()` function whenever the car is pointed in a new direction:

```
function moveCar(direc){
  if (direc == 999){
    car.setSpeed(0);
  } else {
    G1_hook("checkCollision()");
    car.setSpeed(3);
    car.setXYdegs(direc * 45);
    car.setFrame(direc);
  } // end if
} // end moveCar
```

Of course, this is just a starting point. You could generate multiple barriers and do more complex collision detection.

Creating a Race Timer

Sprites and collision-detection techniques provide almost all of the functionality needed for the racing program except scorekeeping. It would be nice to have some way to keep track of how long the race lasts. JavaScript provides a Date object that helps with this task.

Writing the Timer Program

Web browsers have ways of querying the system clock of the client machine to figure out the time. JavaScript supplies this information to the programmer via a special object called the Date object. Figure 9.11 shows a program that demonstrates the Date object in action.

The Timer program evaluates the current date, then evaluates each precise time that the user clicked the button. The program does some mathematical manipulations of these values to determine the elapsed time.

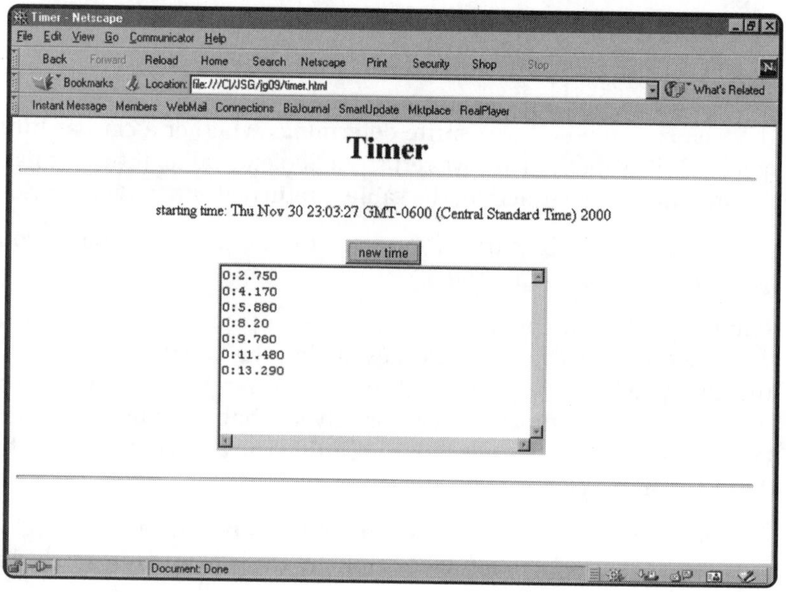

FIGURE 9.11

Each time that the user clicks the button, the Timer program adds to the text area the elapsed time since the browser loaded the page.

Using the Date Object

The key to this program is the timer object built into JavaScript.

Following is the code for the program:

```
var startTime = new Date();
var startInt = startTime.getTime();
var elapsedTime = new Date();
var currentTime = new Date();

function getTime(){
  var output = "";
  currentTime = new Date();
  var currentInt = currentTime.getTime();
  var elapsedInt = currentInt - startInt;
  elapsedTime = new Date(elapsedInt);
  output += elapsedTime.getMinutes() + ":";
  output += elapsedTime.getSeconds() + ".";
  output += elapsedTime.getMilliseconds() + "\n";
  document.myForm.txtOutput.value += output;
} // end getTime
```

You invoke the Date object with new Date(). This function creates a new Date object based on the current time. The Date object has a number of interesting methods and properties, which Table 9.3 lists.

The Date object is usually used simply to get the current date from the system. Here's a simple script, embedded in the HTML code, that uses the Date object in a more typical way.

Method	Description	Example
TABLE 9.3 KEY PROPERTIES AND METHODS OF THE DATE OBJECT		
new Date()	Creates a Date object based on the current date and time.	var myDate = new Date();
new Date(integer)	Creates a new Date object based on the integer passed.	var myDate = new Date(intValue);
getTime()	Returns the number of milliseconds since midnight GMT, as an integer.	var myInt = myDate.getTime;
getDate()	Returns the day of the month.	alert(myDate.getDate());
getMonth()	Returns the month.	alert ("today is the " + myDate.getDate() + " of " + myDate.getMonth());
getYear()	Returns the year that corresponds with this Date object.	alert(myDate.getYear());
getHours()	Returns the hour of the day.	alert(myDate.getHours());
getMinutes()	Returns the minutes.	alert(myDate.getMinutes());
getSeconds()	Returns the seconds.	alert(myDate.getSeconds());
toString()	Returns the entire date as a string value.	alert(myDate.toString());

```
<script>
document.write(new Date());
</script>
```

This code is embedded directly into the HTML code and generates a Date object immediately. The value of that Date object is translated to the Web page as a long string.

IN THE REAL WORLD

The ability to deal with dates and times is very important in many aspects of programming. You might use similar techniques to determine how long it has been since the user last visited your site, or you might want to be able to calculate a person's age in years, months, and days. Of course, it's nice to just be able to display the current date and time in whatever format you wish.

Dealing with Elapsed Time

For the Racer game, you will not need the date or time of day, but the elapsed time between the start and end of a race. This is not difficult to do, but it requires that you understand how the Date object really works.

The date is actually stored as a very long integer that counts how many milliseconds (1,000th of a second) have occurred since midnight Greenwich Mean Time (GMT). The Date object is basically just a series of methods that extract more useful information (such as the month, day, or hour) from that big integer.

The getTime() method returns the actual number that relates to the time. This number wouldn't seem very useful, except that you can subtract the integer value two times. The result gives you an integer that can be translated to a date value. You can count the minutes, seconds, and milliseconds of this new Date object to get an elapsed time. Here's how I got the elapsed time:

Outside the method, I created startTime and elapsedTime as new Date objects.

The program calls the getTime() function each time that the user wants to find a new elapsed time. The first thing that the function does is reinitialize elapsedTime as a new Date object so that it will have a different value than startTime (whose value indicates when the browser loaded the page).

The following two lines get integer values related to the two Date objects:

```
var startInt = startTime.getTime();
var currentInt = currentTime.getTime();
```

The following line creates a new integer by subtracting the millisecond value of startInt from that of currentInt:

```
var elapsedInt = currentInt - startInt;
```

The next line creates a new date based on the difference.

```
elapsedTime = new Date(elapsedInt);
```

Finally, I use a set of date methods to get other useful values from the Date object:

```
output += elapsedTime.getMinutes() + ":";
output += elapsedTime.getSeconds() + ".";
output += elapsedTime.getMilliseconds() + "\n";
document.myForm.txtOutput.value += output;
```

Returning to the Racer Program

The Racer program is primarily a combination of the techniques described throughout this chapter. It relies heavily on sprite technology. The program actually features 11 different sprites, and you can easily customize it to use more if you want more complex tracks. The basic organization of the program relies on a sprite for the car, an array of sprites for barriers, and another array of sprites for time sensors. The barriers are placed on the track to make the different track designs, and the sensors are placed around the track. The program considers a lap complete only when the car has triggered all five time sensors.

Creating the CarStart Page

The initial page for the Racer program uses a now-familiar strategy. This page contains the Help screen and a button that calls up the actual page.

Writing the HTML for Car.html

The HTML for the page is very simple, because most of the work happens with sprites. The body calls the init() function, and all the user interaction is done with an image map.

```
<body bgColor = "gray"
      onload = "init()">
<IMG SRC="track.gif" WIDTH=600 HEIGHT=600 BORDER=0 USEMAP="#map">


<MAP NAME="map">
<!-- #$-:Image Map file created by GIMP Imagemap Plugin -->
<!-- #$-:GIMP Imagemap Plugin by Maurits Rijk -->
<!-- #$-:Please do not edit lines starting with "#$" -->
<!-- #$VERSION:1.3 -->
<!-- #$AUTHOR:Unknown User -->
<AREA SHAPE="RECT" COORDS="351,454,371,489" HREF="javascript:accel()">
<AREA SHAPE="RECT" COORDS="227,455,247,489" HREF="javascript:decel()">
<AREA SHAPE="POLY" COORDS="303,395,325,403,342,424,344,448,335,468,317,482,
307,485,301,485" HREF="javaScript:turnRight()">
<AREA SHAPE="POLY" COORDS="299,396,280,400,261,418,255,440,259,461,270,475,
288,485,299,486" HREF="javascript:turnLeft()">
</MAP>
</body>
```

Creating an Image Map for User Input

An image map is one way to get input from the user without having to use form controls. I wanted the user to interact with a steering wheel and control pedals, so I drew them in an image and created an HTML image map. If you are working with simple regions (such as rectangles), you can build image maps by hand; however, for more complex images, you may want to use an editor. The CD-ROM that accompanies this book includes The GIMP, a powerful, free image editor (see Figure 9.12). I used the image map tool that comes with The GIMP to generate the image map automatically for this program. The image map tool is available by right-clicking an image, then choosing Filters, Web, then Image Map.

Note that instead of specifying a normal URL, I called the turnLeft() function by setting JavaScript:turnLeft() as the URL for this region.

The image map editor creates a text file that you can copy and paste into your page.

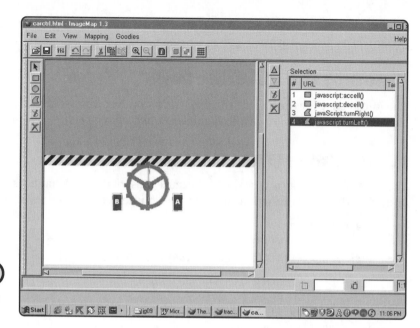

Defining an image map in The GIMP.

Using Libraries and Variables

The car program is reasonably complex, and it has a number of variables. It is also not surprising that it uses the gameLib core and sprite libraries. Here is the code that sets up the program:

```html
<!-- import the basic libraries -->

<script language="Javascript" src="gamelib/gamelib_core.js">
</script>

<script language="Javascript" src="gamelib/gamelib_sprites.js">
</script>

<script>
var car;
var barrier = new Array();
var numSensors = 5;
var timeSensor = new Array(numSensors);
var lapStatus = new Array(numSensors);

var NORTH = 0;
var NORTHEAST = 1;
var EAST = 2;
var SOUTHEAST = 3;
var SOUTH = 4;
```

```
var SOUTHWEST = 5;
var WEST = 6;
var NORTHWEST = 7;

var direction = EAST;
var speed = 3;
var startTime = new Date();
var trackNum = 1;
var lap = 0;
```

The car is a sprite, just like the one used earlier in this chapter. Additionally, the program sets up an array of barriers (which will be sprites) and an array of time sensors (which will also be sprites). Another array is used to keep track of the car's position on the screen. These arrays make the game flexible, because you can place the barriers and time sensors anywhere on the screen and the program will be able to tell whether the car has completed a lap. A set of variables is used to manage the directions, just as in the program earlier in the chapter.

The code initializes the direction to EAST, sets the starting speed to 3, and establishes a new startTime (which is useful for determining the elapsed time later). Finally, the code sets the track number to 1 (so that the user starts with the easiest track) and sets the lap to 0.

Creating the init() Function

The program calls the init() function when the page's body loads. It is chiefly concerned with initializing sprites. Here's the code:

```
function init(){
  car = new Sp_Sprite();
  car.setImage("car.gif", 40, 40, 8, 1);
  car.moveTo(30,40);
  car.setXlimits(20, 600);
  car.setYlimits(30, 400);
  car.setFrame(EAST);
  car.setZ(99);
  car.switchOn();
  car.setSpeed(3);
  car.setXYdegs(EAST * 45);
  car.collides = true;

  //set up barriers
  var barCounter = 0;
  for(barCounter = 0; barCounter < 5; barCounter++){
    barrier[barCounter] = new Sp_Sprite();
    barrier[barCounter].setXlimits(20, 600);
    barrier[barCounter].setYlimits(30, 400);
    barrier[barCounter].setImage("black.gif", 20,20,1,1);
```

```
        barrier[barCounter].moveTo(10,10);
        barrier[barCounter].setFrame(0);
        barrier[barCounter].switchOn();
        barrier[barCounter].collides = true;
    } // end for loop

    //set up time sensors
    for (tsCount = 0; tsCount < numSensors; tsCount++){
        timeSensor[tsCount] = new Sp_Sprite();
        timeSensor[tsCount].setImage("white.gif", 10, 10, 1, 1)
        timeSensor[tsCount].setXlimits(20, 600);
        timeSensor[tsCount].setYlimits(30, 400);
        timeSensor[tsCount].moveTo(10,10);
        timeSensor[tsCount].setFrame(0);
        timeSensor[tsCount].switchOn();
        timeSensor[tsCount].collides = true;
    } // end for loop

    Gl_hook("checkCollision()");
    Gl_start();

    setUpTrack();
} // end init
```

The program sets up the car sprite. This setup should be very familiar now. The only new technique is the setZ() method. Notice that the program sets the z value of the car to 99. This setting tells the system to display the car as if it were on top of everything else. All sprites with lower z values will appear to be underneath the car if they happen to be drawn in the same place.

The array includes five barriers. The program initially sets up each one to be exactly the same, although the program will move them later. For convenience, all the barrier creation is done in a for loop.

The code also includes an array of five time sensors. These are simply sprites that the player is to drive over. You'll place them all over the track later so that the driver can't cheat by driving over the start line, then turning around and driving over the start line again to finish. The program also initializes the time sensors in a for loop for convenience.

I hooked the checkCollision() function to the timer loop so that the program will call the function frequently. I also started up the gameLib engine with Gl_start().

The last line of init() is a call to the setUpTrack() function, which is described next.

Writing the setUpTrack() Function

The setUpTrack() function examines the value of the trackNum variable and sets up the track in one of three configurations. To add or modify tracks, you can simply change this function. Here's the code:

```
function setUpTrack(){

  //preset for a specific track
  switch(trackNum){
    case 1:
      // oval
      barrier[0].resize(400, 200);
      barrier[0].moveTo(100, 110);
      barrier[1].resize(400, 200);
      barrier[1].moveTo(100, 110);
      barrier[2].resize(400, 200);
      barrier[2].moveTo(100, 110);
      barrier[3].resize(400, 200);
      barrier[3].moveTo(100, 110);
      barrier[4].resize(400, 200);
      barrier[4].moveTo(100, 110);

      timeSensor[0].resize(10, 80);
      timeSensor[0].moveTo(100, 30);
      timeSensor[1].resize(10, 80);
      timeSensor[1].moveTo(300, 30);
      timeSensor[2].resize(90, 10);
      timeSensor[2].moveTo(500, 200);
      timeSensor[3].resize(10, 80);
      timeSensor[3].moveTo(300,310);
      timeSensor[4].resize(70, 10);
      timeSensor[4].moveTo(30, 200);
      break;

. . . //other track definitions
} // end switch

  resetStatus();
  alert("ready?");
  lap = 0;
  startTime = new Date();
} // end setUpTrack
```

To save space, I showed only the portion of this code that creates the first track. See the code on the CD-ROM for the other track descriptions.

You create new tracks by changing the size and location of the barrier and time sensor sprites. The first track is very simple, so I put all the barriers in the same place. Notice how the track sensors are placed around the track to ensure that the player has to complete the entire circuit to be credited for a lap. After the track is set up, the resetStatus() function cleans up the lap counter (for details and a description of that function, see the section "Writing the resetStatus() Function"). An alert statement gives the player an opportunity to start the program when he or she is ready. Finally, the setUpTrack() function resets the startTime variable to the current time.

Building the checkCollision() Function

The checkCollision() function checks for collisions with the barriers and the time sensors. If a barrier collision occurs, the function stops the car. The time sensor code calls the lapFinished() function to check whether the car has hit each sensor. If the lap is finished and the sensor that was hit is sensor 0 (the start-finish line), the function calls the showTime() and resetStatus() functions to display the time and reset the sensor counter. Here's the checkCollision() function's code:

```
function checkCollision(){
  var newDir;

  //check for crashes
  for (barCounter = 0; barCounter < 5; barCounter++){
    if (car.hasHit(barrier[barCounter])){
      Gl_unhook("checkCollision()");
      newDir = Math.floor(Math.random() * 7);
      speed = 0;

      //direction = newDir;

      car.setSpeed(speed);
      //car.setXYdegs(direction);
      //car.setFrame(direction);
    } // end if
  } // end for loop

  //check for sensors
  for (tsCount = 0; tsCount < 5; tsCount++){
    if (car.hasHit(timeSensor[tsCount])){
      if(lapFinished()){
        if (car.hasHit(timeSensor[0])){
          showTime();
          resetStatus();
        } // end 'start gate' if
      } //end 'finished' if
      lapStatus[tsCount] = 1;

    } // end ' hit sensor' if
  } // end for loop

} // end checkCollision
```

Creating the lapFinished() Function

The lapFinished() function checks the lapStatus array to see whether all the elements of the array have been turned on, which indicates that the car has hit every sensor at least once. If so, the function returns the value true; otherwise, it returns the value false. The code follows:

```
function lapFinished(){
  var finished = true;

  for (counter=0; counter < numSensors; counter++){
    if (lapStatus[counter] == 0){
      finished = false;

    } // end if
  } // end loop
  return finished;
} // end lapFinished
```

Writing the resetStatus() Function

The resetStatus() function resets the value of the lapStatus array to all 0s. The program calls the function at the beginning of each lap. Here's the code:

```
function resetStatus(){
  for (tsCount = 0; tsCount < numSensors; tsCount++){
    lapStatus[tsCount] = 0;

  } // end for loop
} // end resetStatus
```

Building the showTime() Function

The showTime() function calculates the elapsed time for the current race and displays that time on the screen. It also checks for the lap number; if the car is on the last lap, the function displays the race time. The program then moves on to the next track. The code for the showTime() function is as follows:

```
function showTime(){
  //returns back the time from this lap.
  var currentTime = new Date();
  var currentInt = currentTime.getTime();

  var startInt = startTime.getTime();

  var elapsedInt =  currentInt - startInt;
  var elapsedTime = new Date(elapsedInt);
  lap++;
  var output = "";
```

```
    output += elapsedTime.getMinutes() + ":";
    output += elapsedTime.getSeconds() + ".";
    output += elapsedTime.getMilliseconds();

    window.status = output;

    if (lap==5){

      alert(output);
      trackNum++;
      if (trackNum > 3){
        trackNum = 1;
      } // end if
      setUpTrack();
    } // end if
} // end showTime
```

Creating the turnLeft() and turnRight() Functions

The turnLeft() and turnRight() functions manipulate the direction variable in response to the user's mouse clicks on the steering wheel. The program sets the car's direction and image based on the new value of direction. Here's the code for these functions:

```
function turnLeft(){
  direction--;
  if (direction < NORTH){
    direction = NORTHWEST;
  } // end if
  car.setXYdegs(direction * 45);
  car.setFrame(direction);
} // end turnLeft


function turnRight(){
  direction++;
  if (direction > NORTHWEST){
    direction = NORTH;
  } // end if
  car.setXYdegs(direction * 45);
  car.setFrame(direction);
} // end turnRight
```

Writing the decell() Function

The decell() function decrements the speed of the car, as follows:

```
function decell(){
  speed--;
```

```
  if (speed < 0){
    speed = 0;
  } // end if
  car.setSpeed(speed);
} // end decell
```

the accell() Function

The accell() function rehooks the checkCollision() function (in case the car had crashed into a barrier) and increases the car's speed:

```
function acell(){
  Gl_hook("checkCollision()");
  car.collides = true;

  speed++;
  if (speed > 10){
    speed = 10;
  } // end if
  car.setSpeed(speed);
} // end accell
```

Summary

In this chapter, you learned how you can use an Application Programming Interface (API) to simplify greatly the process of writing cross-browser dynamic HTML. Specifically, you learned how to set up the gameLib core library and the sprite module. You learned how to create and use sprites, add motion, and detect collisions. You also learned how to check elapsed time using the built-in Date object. You then put all these things together in a program that you can easily modify and improve.

EXERCISES

1. Add another track to the Racer program. Modify the setUpTrack() function so it has a fourth track, and set the values of the barriers and time sensors to build a totally new track configuration.

2. Improve the sprite images to make your own car, better-looking barriers and sensors, or an entirely different theme.

3. Write a track editor so the user can edit tracks in the racing game. You might use a form to let the user type in the location and size of each barrier and time sensor, then display how the track will look with these options.

4. Make a simple version of Pacman. Define a path with barriers, and build a sprite to travel on the path.

5. Add ghosts to your version of the Pacman game.

Using Other
gameLib Features:
The Dogfight Game

Sprite graphics are a very powerful tool.
With a few more enhancements, you are
well on your way to building sophisticated 2-D games. In this chapter, you will learn
about some of the other great tools that gameLib
gives you for building better games. Specifically,
you will learn how to do the following:

- Build multiplayer games

- Trap keyboard events

- Manage sound

- Generate layers

- Add missiles

- Improve your animations

The Project: The Dogfight Game

To demonstrate these features, you will build a simple two-player arcade game. The game is simple: Two players sit at the same keyboard and control little biplanes. The players try to blast each other out of the sky. Figures 10.1 and 10.2 show the game's interface.

The game has a number of interesting features that might not all be apparent from the screenshots.

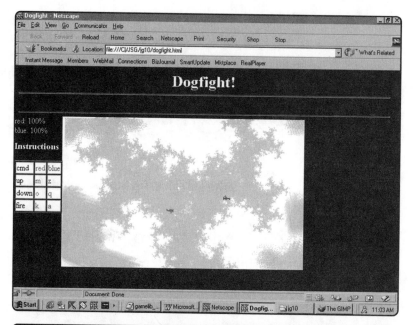

FIGURE 10.1

Two planes enjoying a blissful afternoon.

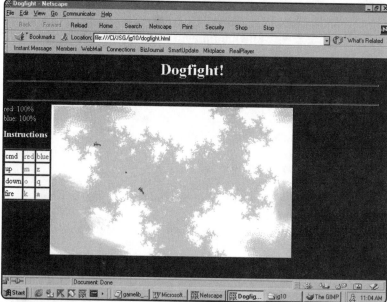

FIGURE 10.2

Take that, Red Baron!

First, this is a two-player game. Although it might seem that writing a game for two players is more difficult than writing one for a single player, this is not always the case. The hardest part of "player versus the computer" style games is developing the artificial intelligence for the computer player. With a two-player game, this is not a problem, as the computer does not need to store any strategies, but simply respond to two sets of input.

The game uses keyboard input. Both versions of the document object model provide techniques to read mouse and keyboard events, but these two models are (surprise) very different in the browser implementations. The gameLib API provides a simpler multibrowser interface, which makes managing keystrokes reasonably straightforward. Keyboard input provides a much smoother type of input for many types of games than the techniques that you have used previously in this book.

HINT Because JavaScript is an Internet technology, you might be tempted to write a two-player game with the players on different computers. Sadly, JavaScript does not have the communication functions to enable you to accomplish this. You would probably need a language like Java to write multicomputer games.

The Dogfight game features sound effects when the players shoot at each other and when they score hits. The gameLib library encapsulates the techniques demonstrated in Chapter 8, "Dynamic HTML: The Stealth Submarine," for generating sound. You might recall from the chapter that generating sound can be quite challenging, but it is reasonably easy using gameLib.

To create the Dogfight game's documentation and scorekeeping parts of the game, I used gameLib layers. A layer is gameLib's way of specifying an object such as a Netscape layer or CSS element. In fact, you will see that with liberal use of layer and sprite objects, you can write the entire program as a series of gameLib objects. The HTML in the program is almost nonexistent.

You will notice some new animation techniques in the Dogfight game. The planes can shoot bullets, and if you look very carefully, you will note that the propellers appear to spin.

Using Layers and the Keyboard

Begin your tour of the new gameLib features by looking at a program that demonstrates keyboard input and gameLib layers. Figure 10.3 shows the program's interface.

The program traps for the *A, B,* and *C* keys. The yellow box is a layer. Its content can be changed dynamically, and it appears to be part of the original page.

Setting Up the Program

As usual, you will begin by importing gameLib modules and setting up some variables.

```
<script language="Javascript" src="../gamelib196/gamelib/gamelib_core.js">
</script>

<script language = "Javascript" src="../gamelib196/gamelib/
gamelib_keyboard.js">
```

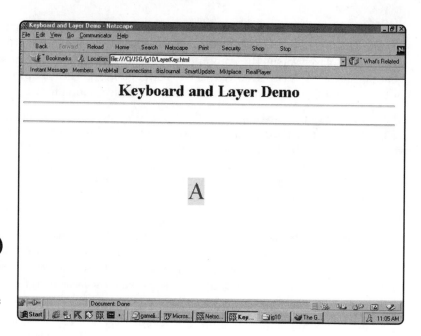

FIGURE 10.3

When the user
presses the *A* key,
the letter *A* appears
in a yellow box.

```
</script>

<script>

var display;
var a;
var b;
var c;
```

I first added the gamelib_core library, and also added the keyboard module. There is not a separate module for layers. Layer handling is done as a part of the core module.

The four variables will all hold various components of the program. The `display` variable will contain a reference to the layer. The `a`, `b`, and `c` variables refer to each keystroke that I intend to trap. (You'll learn more about trapping keystrokes in a moment.)

Creating a Layer

A layer is an object in gameLib, so it is set up like most other objects in JavaScript.

```
function init(){
  // Keyboard and Layer Demo
  // Andy Harris

  //set up display
  display = new Gl_layer(350, 200, 100, "");
  display.setBgcolor("yellow");
  display.show();
```

The new `Gl_layer()` command generates a new layer object. The first two parameters refer to the starting location of the layer. The next parameter (100) refers to the starting width of the layer. The starting height of the layer will be defined when something is added to the layer or when the layer is explicitly resized. The last parameter is the HTML text of the layer. This can be a variable containing an entire HTML page or actual HTML text, or you can leave the variable blank and fill it in later.

HINT

Is this layer a Netscape layer, a gameLib layer, or a CSS element? The short answer is yes; it's a combination of all these things. To simplify coding, Scott Porter (the author of gameLib) defined a new object called a `Gl_layer`, which encapsulates the best features of both the Netscape and IE approaches to positionable elements. It is convenient to call this new element a layer, but keep in mind that it is not exactly like the two types of layering objects defined in the browser Document Object Models. Fortunately, gamLib's layer object seems to be much better behaved than either of the other layer objects, especially when used across browser platforms.

The gamLib layer object is a very intriguing little monster. Table 10.1 lists the most commonly used methods of the layer object.

TABLE 10.1 COMMON METHODS OF THE LAYER OBJECT

Method	Description	Example
`new Gl_layer(x, y, width, startingHTML)`	Creates a new layer at (x, y) that is `width` pixels wide and contains the `startingHTML` as its body.	`var myLayer = new Gl_layer (0, 0, 100, "<H1>Hi there!</H1>");`
`.load (filename, type)`	Loads the specified file into the layer. If `type` is set to true, the file will be always be loaded from the server.	`myLayer.load ("instructions.html", true);`
`.moveTo(x, y)`	Moves the layer's top-left corner to the specified pixels.	`myLayer.moveTo (100, 200);`
`.resizeTo(x, y)`	Resizes the layer to the specified size.	`myLayer.resizeTo (50, 50);`
`.setXlimits(a, b), setYlimits(a, b)`	Sets the boundaries for the layer. This method works as it does in the sprite library.	`myLayer.setXlimits (0, 500); myLayer. setYlimits(0, 300);`
`.write(newHTML)`	Replaces the content of the layer with `newHTML`.	`myLayer.write ("<h3>Whoo Hoo!</h3>");`
`.setBgcolor(color)`	Sets the layer's background to a specified color.	`myLayer.setBgcolor ("red");`
`.show()`	Makes the layer visible.	`myLayer.show();`

IN THE REAL WORLD

The layer object is useful any time you want to have a dynamic part of the screen. I have used layers in a catalog program that displayed parts of a small database. You could use layers in a menu system for your Web page or as an easy way to add dynamic content (such as a message of the day).

In game development, layers are great for text that you want to place precisely on the screen. It is much easier to get a good screen layout with layers than it is using plain HTML formatting. Also, the ability to access the `write()` method of layers makes them great tools for communicating with the user. It's common to use layers for scorekeeping, help screens, or any other place where you might want to place dynamic text.

In the Keyboard and Layer Demo program, I set up `display` as a new layer at position (300, 200) with a starting width of 100 pixels and no beginning text. I then set the background color of the layer to yellow and showed it. The layer object is not automatically shown until you invoke its `show()` method.

Creating Keyboard Handler Objects

The gameLib approach to keyboard handling simplifies the process of getting user input from the keyboard. The key (pun intended) is the `trapkey()` method. Look at the rest of the `init()` function to see how this approach works:

```
//set up keyboard traps
  a = Kb_trapkey("a");
  b = Kb_trapkey("b");
  c = Kb_trapkey("c");

  //start up program:
  Gl_hook("mainLoop()");
  Gl_start();
} // end
```

You probably noticed that the `init()` function initializes the `a`, `b`, and `c` variables by calling the `Kb_trapkey()` function. This function generates an instance of the key handler object. Table 10.2 lists the commands by which you control these objects.

Generally, you initialize keystrokes in some type of initialization function (as I have done in this program) and check whether the user has pressed the key in some type of main loop procedure.

Responding to Keystrokes

If the user presses the `a`, `b`, or `c` key, the program should display the appropriate value in the yellow layer. Here's the code for the main loop:

```
function mainLoop(){

  var letter = "";
```

```
var message = "";

if(a.pressed){
  letter = "A";
} // end if

if(b.pressed){
  letter = "B";
} // end if

if(Kb_lastkey == c){
  letter = "C";
} // end if

message =  "<font color = Blue";

message += "       size = 7>";
message += letter

message += "</font>";
display.write(message);

} // end mainLoop
```

The function starts by setting up two utility variables. `letter` will contain one character denoting the value of a keypress. The `message` variable will contain a simple HTML document that the program will send to the `display` layer.

TABLE 10.2 KEYBOARD HANDLER COMMANDS

Command	Description	Example

`.pressed` (read-only)	Returns true if the user is currently pressing the key.	`if (myKey.pressed)`
		`{   alert("A"); }`
		`// end if`

`Kb_trapkey(keyName)`	Sets up a new key object that responds when the user presses *keyName*.	`myKey = Kb_trapKey("a");`

`Kb_lastkey`	Contains a reference to the last key pressed.	`if (Kb_lastkey ==`
		`myKey){   alert("A"); }`
		`// end if`

The function looks at a and b using the .pressed method. (Remember that this function has been hooked to the timer loop, so it executes 20 times per second.) If the user is currently pressing the *a* or *b* key, the value of letter changes. Just for demonstration purposes, I used the Kb_lastkey technique to determine whether the user had pressed the *c* key.

TRAP

The underlying JavaScript routines can trap only for normal keyboard characters. You cannot (yet) use this technique to trap for arrow keys, function keys, or other special keys on the keyboard. Also, this routine does not distinguish between uppercase and lowercase characters. For most game development purposes, the capabilities of the JavaScript routines are sufficient.

IN THE REAL WORLD

Developers sometimes use keyboard handling as an error-detection scheme. For example, you might want to ensure that a text box contains no numeric characters. Also, you can use keyboard handling as a control technique on certain kinds of applications. For example, I wrote a program that generates presentations with several slides on one long HTML page. I set up the *n* key to move to the next slide, and *p* to go to the previous slide.

After a value has been assigned to the letter variable, the rest of the mainLoop() function involves building an HTML string and writing it to the display layer using the display.write() method.

This is a unique approach to keyboard handling. The keyboard-handling technique used in gameLib is terrific for game development. In this type of programming, developers usually use keystrokes to control a sprite or send other very quick signals from the user to the program. However, if you use other languages (including the JavaScript code on which the gameLib libraries were based), the algorithm used is a little bit different. Most languages have some sort of function or method that looks at the entire keyboard, determines which key has been pressed, then returns some type of integer code relating to the keypress. The programmer then analyzes this code to determine what has happened and writes corresponding code.

Adding Sound

You might recall that sound can be challenging because of the completely different approaches that the major browsers take to embedding sound in Web pages. The gameLib API provides a very easy interface to sound programming in JavaScript.

Creating the Sound Demo Program

Figure 10.4 shows a simple program that demonstrates the basic sound features in gameLib. The program features two sound effects that are controlled by buttons on the Web page. The user can start and stop a music file, or play a sound effect, by clicking the appropriate buttons.

The process of using sounds follows a pattern that you've seen a few times now: You import a special module of the API, create variables that refer to sound objects, then manipulate methods and properties of the sound objects.

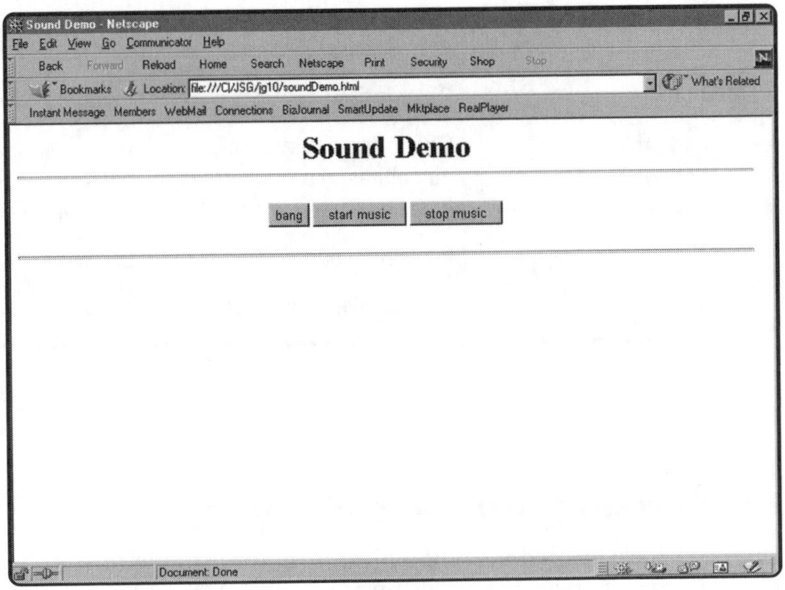

FIGURE 10.4

The Sound Demo program lets the user play a sound effect, as well as start and stop a music file.

Creating a Sound Object

The sound object is created through a function of the sound library. Here's the startup code for the Sound Demo program:

```
<script language="Javascript" src="../gamelib196/gamelib/gamelib_core.js">
</script>

<script language="Javascript" src="../gamelib196/gamelib/gamelib_sound.js">
</script>


<script>
var sndBang;
var sndMusic;

function init(){
  sndBang = new Sd_add_sound("bang.wav");
  sndMusic = new Sd_add_sound("canyon.mid");
} // end init
```

I created variables for two sounds, sndBang and sndMusic. Then I used the Sd_add_sound() method to generate sound objects to assign to the two variables. Table 10.3 lists the key characteristics of the sound object.

The sound object can use either .wav files or .midi files. Generally, .wav files are used for sound effects, and .midi files are used for background music. You can find plenty of sounds on the Internet, although you should get permission of the file's owner before using the sound file in your game.

TABLE 10.3   COMMONLY USED METHODS OF THE SOUND OBJECT

Method	Description	Example
Sd_add_sound (fileName)	Generates a new sound object based on fileName, which is a .wav or .midi file.	var mySound = Sd_add_sound ("bang.wav");
.play()	Plays the sound.	mySound.play();
.stop()	Stops playing the sound.	mySound.stop();

Playing and Stopping Sounds

Once you have created a sound object, it is very simple to start and stop the sound effect. Here's the rest of the code for the Sound Demo program.

```
<body onload = "init()">
<center>
<h1>Sound Demo<hr></h1>
<form>
<input type = button
       value = "bang"
       onclick = "sndBang.play()">
<input type = button
       value = "start music"
       onClick = "sndMusic.play()">
<input type = button
       value = "stop music"
       onClick = "sndMusic.stop()">
</form>

</center>
<hr>
</body>
```

Because the code is so basic, I integrated it directly into the HTML. Of course, you can also use the sound object's play() and stop() methods inside more traditional code.

Improving Sprite Management

Using the keyboard to control a sprite's behavior is one obvious way to spruce up your games. There are some other things that you can do to make your game much more interesting. The Simple Plane Demo program is a simple prototype of the bi-plane game that illustrates how to add keyboard input, as well as a few other new features of sprite objects.

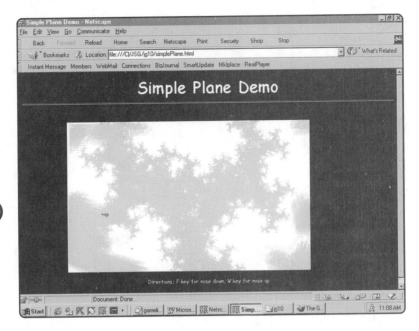

FIGURE 10.5

The program presents a basic airplane with keyboard control and a rotating propeller.

Creating the Simple Plane Program

Figure 10.5 shows this reasonably simple program, which demonstrates a number of new techniques.

Using a Sprite as a Background Image

The background image is actually a sprite with a cloud image set as its only image. There are a number of reasons that you might want to use a sprite as a background:

- If you set the z value of the sprite very low, all other sprites will pass over it.
- It is much easier to position a sprite than it is to position a normal HTML image.
- If you wish, you can have multiple frames of the image to create an animated background, or perhaps a series of different backgrounds (for example, you could add a morning sky with a red background, or a night sky with stars).
- You can use the clipping methods of the sprite object to support scrolling backgrounds. Check the gameLib sprite documentation for information on using clipping.

The beginning code of the Simple Plane Demo program follows. Most of this code is very familiar. Take a look at the cloud sprite code. The program uses this sprite as a background graphic.

TRICK

To get a nice cloud texture, I used a fractal pattern generator in my image program, then tuned it up with a feathered brush. This is a pretty easy way to generate certain natural patterns, such as clouds, waves, and certain types of mountains. Look in the documentation of your image editing software for information about any special effects tools that might be useful for game graphics.

```
var plane;
var clouds;
var upKey;
var downKey;

var NORTH = 0;
var NORTHEAST = 1;
var EAST = 2;
var SOUTHEAST = 3;
var SOUTH = 4;
var SOUTHWEST = 5;
var WEST = 6;
var NORTHWEST = 7;

var direction = EAST;

function init(){

  Sp_xoffset=100;
  Sp_yoffset=100;

  clouds = new Sp_Sprite();
  clouds.setImage("clouds.gif", 500, 300, 1, 1);
  clouds.moveTo(0,0);
  clouds.setXlimits(0, 500);
  clouds.setYlimits(0, 300);
  clouds.setFrame(0);
  clouds.switchOn();
```

The `plane` and `clouds` variables both contain sprites. `upKey` and `downKey` will hold keyboard handlers. The direction constants should be familiar from Chapter 9, "Sprite Animation: The Racer," as should the `direction` variable.

The `Sp_xoffset` and `Sp_yoffset` variables are special variables used in the sprite library. By giving values to these variables, you can specify a new origin for all sprites. This approach can be very useful for centering your game on the screen. All the other code in this segment sets up the clouds as normal sprites.

Creating a More Involved Animation Graphic

If you run the Simple Plane Demo program and look carefully at the biplane, you will notice that the propeller appears to spin. Now there are two versions of each plane picture: one picture of an airplane pointing east with a large propeller, and another picture that is identical, but the airplane has a smaller propeller. The program swaps quickly between these versions of the image to give the illusion of a moving propeller.

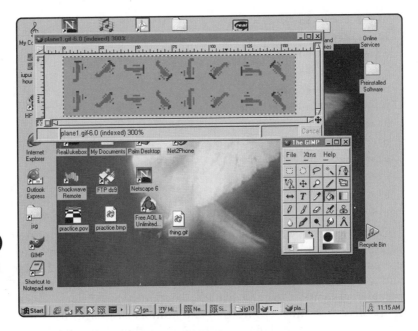

FIGURE 10.6

Now there are two images of the biplane for each direction.

This illusion is accomplished by another trick of the sprite object. Figure 10.6 shows the actual aircraft picture in the graphics editor. (Note that I increased the size of the graphic and added a blue background to make the image easier to see.)

Recall that sprites can have several frames, even though they have only one image. The gameLib API accomplishes this feat by clipping the image into a number of evenly sized frames. In the last chapter, you created an image with eight frames by generating a graphic with eight evenly spaced images in a row. You can also specify another kind of animation by swapping a number of images within a frame. If you arrange your sprite graphic as I did here, you can animate each frame very easily. Just remember that each column represents the animations in a particular frame. Generally your code will explicitly set the frame, but you will automate the animations within the frame.

HINT

Although I chose to have only two animations per frame, you can have as many as you wish. In fact, you are not required to have the same number of animations in each frame. See the gameLib documentation for details on how you control differing lengths of animations.

Incorporating Frame Animation

If you look back at the `init()` function for the Simple Plane Demo program, you will see the plane sprite definition:

```
plane = new Sp_Sprite();
plane.setImage("plane1.gif", 20,20,8,2);
plane.moveTo(0,100);
plane.setSpeed(3);
plane.setXYdegs(90);
plane.setXlimits(0, 500);
plane.setYlimits(0, 300);
plane.bounces=false;
plane.setFrame(direction);
plane.setAnimationSpeed(3, "forward");
plane.collides = true;
plane.switchOn();
```

This code looks very much like the car code from Chapter 9, but there are a couple of subtle differences that involve animation. First, note the difference in the `setImage()` method. The program instructs the sprite to use the plane1.gif image, size it to 20, 20, and use 8×2 frames. If you compare this to the actual image, you will see that these parameters should allow the display of eight different frames with two cells of animation apiece. You must ensure that the number of images used in the graphic is the same as that referenced in the `setImage()` method. If the number of images is not the same as the value in the `setImage()` method call, the program will still work, but it will look very strange.

 To simplify this discussion, I will refer to the row of elements as *frames* (manipulated by the `.setFrame()` method) and the columns as *cells* (manipulated by the `setAnimation()` method).

The other new effect is the `setAnimationSpeed()` method call. This method of the sprite object takes two parameters. The first is the number of cycles to hold a cell on the screen. I set the value to 3, so each piece of the animation is visible for .15 seconds, which means that the propeller image changes about six times a second. If you set a larger value here, the image will animate more slowly. Smaller values cause the sprite to animate more quickly. The second parameter must contain the string `"forward"` or the string `"back"`. This parameter determines whether the animation will run forward or backward.

The library automatically animates all the images that you have set in the column, unless you instruct it to do otherwise.

Table 10.4 describes the sprite animation commands that are available.

Adding Keyboard Input

The remainder of the code in the `init()` function handles creating keyboard handlers and starting up the gameLib engine:

```
//enable keyboard handling
upKey = Kb_trapkey("v");
```

```
    downKey = Kb_trapkey("f");

    Gl_start();
    Gl_hook("mainLoop()");
} // end init
```

Responding to the Keyboard Input

The code in the main loop is reasonably straightforward. All it does is check each key
handler and change the aircraft's position and direction accordingly. The cell animation is completely automatic.

 HINT I chose to model the behavior of an aircraft's joystick. When the pilot pushes the joystick forward, the plane's nose goes down, and when the joystick is pulled back, the
nose goes up. It would be great if you could use the arrow keys, but JavaScript does
not trap for any keys but the normal alphanumeric keys. I decided to go for a set of
keys near the middle of the keyboard and arrange them as if they were the control
yoke of an aircraft. That's why the *v* key pulls the nose up and the *f* key points the nose
down. If you don't like this arrangement, just assign different keys to up and down.

TABLE 10.4 SPRITE ANIMATION COMMANDS

Command	Description	Example
`.setImage(img, x, y, frames, cells)`	Describes the number of animation cells in a specified frame.	`mySprite.setImage ("car.gif", 10, 10, 2, 4); //2 frames, 4 animation cells each.`
`.setAnimation(cell)`	Sets the animation to a specified cell.	`mySprite. setAnimation(2);`
`.setAnimationLoop (min, max)`	Sets up the animation to display cells between `min` and `max`.	`mySprite. setAnimationLoop(1,3); //animate but skip the 0th image.`
`.setAnimationRepeat (times)`	Determines how many times to repeat the animation (−1 specifies an indefinite number of repeats).	`mySprite. setAnimationRepeat(4); //do the animation 4 times, then stop.`
`.setAnimationSpeed (speed, dir)`	Determines the speed and direction in which to run the animation. `speed` determines how many cycles to hold each cell. `dir` can be `"back"` or `"forward"`.	`mySprite. setAnimationSpeed (20, "forward"); // change the cell animation once per second.`

```
function mainLoop(){
  //check for keyboard inputs
  if (upKey.pressed){
    direction--;
    if (direction < NORTH) {
      direction = NORTHWEST;
    } // end boundary check
    plane.setFrame(direction);
    plane.setXYdegs(direction * 45);
  } // end upkey

  if (downKey.pressed){
    direction++;
    if (direction > NORTHWEST) {
      direction = NORTH;
    } // end boundary check
    plane.setFrame(direction);
    plane.setXYdegs(direction * 45);
  } // end downkey

} // end main loop
```

Adding Missiles

Although it can be very pleasant to glide peacefully around the sky, all this pastoral calm is no way to run a video game. It's time to shoot something!

Creating the Balloon Buster Game

Figure 10.7 shows the Balloon Buster game, which is a variation of the plane game that adds a target (a balloon) and the ability to shoot at the target.

This variation of the game has a fire button and a balloon suitable for shooting.

Initializing the Sprites

In addition to providing the cloud and plane sprites, I added two more sprites, the target and the bullet. Here is the code that initializes these two sprites:

```
target = new Sp_Sprite();
  target.setImage("blimp.gif", 50, 50, 1,1);
  target.moveTo(50, 50);
  target.setSpeed(2);
  target.setXYdegs(90);
  target.setXlimits(0, 500);
  target.setYlimits(0, 300);
  target.bounces = true;
```

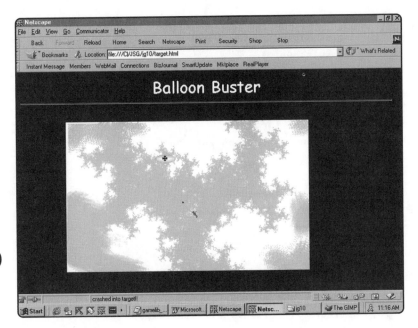

```
target.setFrame(0);
target.switchOn();
target.collides = true;

bullet = new Sp_Sprite();
bullet.setImage("bullet.gif", 10, 10, 1, 1);
bullet.setXlimits(0,500);
bullet.setYlimits(0,300);
bullet.bounces = false;
bullet.setFrame(0);
bullet.collides = true;
```

The target is a slow balloon. I set its speed to 2 and its initial direction to 90 degrees. I turned on the bounces feature, so that the balloon will always simply bounce off the wall and stay in a predictable pattern. The bullet is a tiny sprite, also with only one image. It should not bounce, but stop when it reaches the edge of the boundary area. Both sprites check for collisions.

Writing the Collision-Detection Routines

The plane-movement commands are exactly like those in the Simple Plane Demo program. All the new information has to do with firing the bullets and detecting collisions. Here is the additional code in the mainLoop() function:

```
if (fireKey.pressed){
   bullet.moveTo(plane.x, plane.y);
```

```
    bullet.setSpeed(7);
    bullet.setXYdegs(plane.xydegs);
    bullet.switchOn();
} // end fireKey


//check for collisions
if (plane.hit == target){
  window.status = "crashed into target!!";
} // end if


if (bullet.hit == target){
  window.status = "shot down target!!";
  bullet.switchOff();
  bullet.moveTo (600, 600);
} // end if


//check for bullet bounds
if ((bullet.x >= bullet.xmax - bullet.width) ||
   (bullet.x <= bullet.xmin) ||
   (bullet.y >= bullet.ymax - bullet.width) ||
   (bullet.y <= bullet.ymin) ){
   bullet.switchOff();
   bullet.moveTo(600,600);
} // end if
```

First the program checks the fire-key handler to see whether the player has fired. If so, the bullet's initial direction and position are copied from the plane, and its speed is set to 7. This causes the bullet to fly in the current direction that the plane is going. Then the program checks for various collisions. If the bullet hit the target, something good should happen (good for the player, bad for the balloon). The program also checks for a collision between the balloon and the plane, which would presumably be bad for both.

HINT

Of course, the code for this particular example could be far more robust. It would be nice to add code for some explosions and scorekeeping functionality. Feel free to add those things if you wish. I chose to develop the game in another direction, so I left this code as it is. At a minimum, it's a good idea to include code that says "a collision occurred" so that you can add actual functionality later if you wish. This type of code that serves as a placeholder for future development is sometimes called a *stub*.

Returning to the Dogfight Game

As usual, this chapter has introduced all the required elements to create the game at the beginning of the chapter, so all you have to do to create the Dogfight game is put the pieces together. The only thing that's really new in the Dogfight game is the two-player capability.

Creating the Variables

This program involves four different libraries, so I imported them all. To shorten the code, I decided to make the planes and bullets into arrays. I had variables handle the keystrokes, direction, and damage for each plane. I also created a variable for the instructions and scoreboard (which will be layers) and for the sounds. Here's the code that creates the variables:

```
<script language="Javascript" src="../gamelib196/gamelib/gamelib_core.js">
</script>

<script language="Javascript" src="../gamelib196/gamelib/
gamelib_sprites.js">
</script>

<script language = "Javascript" src="../gamelib196/gamelib/
gamelib_keyboard.js">
</script>

<script language = "Javascript" src="../gamelib196/gamelib/
gamelib_sound.js">
</script>

<script>
//sprites
var plane = new Array(2);
var bullet = new Array(2);
var cloud;

//keyboard handling variables
var up0;
var dn0;
var fire0;

var up1;
var dn1;
var fire1;

//scorekeeping variables
var damage0 = 100;
var damage1 = 100;

//direction constants
var NORTH = 0;
var NORTHEAST = 1;
var EAST = 2;
var SOUTHEAST = 3;
```

```
var SOUTH = 4;
var SOUTHWEST = 5;
var WEST = 6;
var NORTHWEST = 7;

var direction0 = EAST;
var direction1 = WEST;

var scoreboard;

//sound
var sndBang;
var sndHit;
```

Setting Up the Keyboard and Sounds

The `init()` function has a lot of work to do. First, I set up sprite offsets, which are variables I will use to make the program look more centered in the Web page. I then generated all the keyboard handlers with the `Kb_trapkey()` function. Next, I generated the sound files with the `Sd_add_sound()` function. Here's the code:

```
function init(){
  //set offsets
  Sp_xoffset = 100;
  Sp_yoffset = 100;

  //set up key traps
  up0 = Kb_trapkey("z");
  dn0 = Kb_trapkey("q");
  fire0 = Kb_trapkey("a");

  up1 = Kb_trapkey("m");
  dn1 = Kb_trapkey("o");
  fire1 = Kb_trapkey("k");

  //set up sounds
  sndBang = new Sd_add_sound("bang.wav");
  sndHit = new Sd_add_sound("hit.wav");
```

Setting Up the Sprites

The core elements of this game are the sprites. I chose to make arrays of both planes and bullets to make the code a little shorter and easier to debug. The planes and bullets are nearly identical to those in the earlier plane programs, except that they are elements of arrays. Here's the code:

```
//set up background graphic
  cloud = new Sp_Sprite();
```

```
cloud.setImage("clouds.gif", 500, 300, 1, 1);
cloud.moveTo(0, 0);
cloud.setXlimits(0, 500);
cloud.setYlimits(0, 300);
cloud.setFrame(0);
cloud.switchOn();

for (i = 0; i < 2; i++){
  plane[i] = new Sp_Sprite();
  plane[i].setSpeed(3);
  plane[i].setXYdegs(90);
  plane[i].setXlimits(0, 500);
  plane[i].setYlimits(0, 300);
  plane[i].bounces = false;

  plane[i].setFrame(0)
  plane[i].setAnimationSpeed(3, "forward");
  plane[i].collides = true;
  plane[i].switchOn();

  bullet[i] = new Sp_Sprite();
  bullet[i].setImage("bullet.gif", 10, 10, 1, 1);
  bullet[i].moveTo(-20, -20);
  bullet[i].setXlimits(-20,520);
  bullet[i].setYlimits(-20, 320);
  bullet[i].bounces = false;
  bullet[i].setFrame(0);
  bullet[i].collides = true;
  bullet[i].switchOn();
} // end for loop

  plane[0].setImage("plane0.gif", 20, 20, 8, 2);
  plane[1].setImage("plane1.gif", 20, 20, 8, 2);
```

I set up the initial images of the plane to be different graphics, so they would not be the same color.

Setting Up the Layers

The scoreboard and the instructions are both layers. The scoreboard will be dynamically updated with the score. The instruction layer will simply sit there. The code for the instruction layer is long, but very simple, because it simply builds the HTML for the instructions. (I could have put the instructions in a simple HTML page and loaded it up, but I liked having the HTML accessible here in the program for debugging purposes.) Here's the code for the layers:

```
//set up scoreboard layer
  scoreboard = new Gl_layer(0, 100, 100, "");
```

```
scoreboard.write("player 1<br>player 2");
scoreboard.show();
scoreboard.setXlimits(0,300);
scoreboard.setYlimits(0,300);
resetGame();

//set up instruction layer
var instructions = new GL_layer(0, 150, 100, "");
var inText = "";
inText+= "<font color = 'white'><h3>Instructions</h3>";
inText+= "<table border = 1 bgcolor = white>";
inText+= "<tr><td><font color = 'black'>cmd</font></td>";
inText += "<td><font color = 'red'>red</font></td>";
inText += "<td><font color = 'blue'>blue</blue></td></tr>";

inText+= "<tr><td><font color = 'black'>up</font></td>";
inText += "<td><font color = 'red'>m</font></td>";
inText += "<td><font color = 'blue'>z</blue></td></tr>";

inText+= "<tr><td><font color = 'black'>down</font></td>";
inText += "<td><font color = 'red'>o</font></td>";
inText += "<td><font color = 'blue'>q</blue></td></tr>";

inText+= "<tr><td><font color = 'black'>fire</font></td>";
inText += "<td><font color = 'red'>k</font></td>";
inText += "<td><font color = 'blue'>a</blue></td></tr>";

inText+= "</table>";
inText+= "</font>";
inText+= "";
instructions.write(inText);
instructions.show();

GL_hook("mainLoop()");
GL_start();
} // end init
```

The init() function closes with the expected hook() and start() functions.

Writing the resetGame() Function

The program calls the resetGame() function when the game starts or restarts. It is responsible for resetting the score variables and placing the planes in the appropriate starting positions. Here's the function's code:

```
function resetGame(){
  //starts up the main game variables
```

```
  direction0 = EAST;
  direction1 = WEST;


  damage0 = 100;
  damage1 = 100;


  plane[0].moveTo(10, 10);
  plane[0].setXYdegs(direction0 * 45);
  plane[0].setFrame(direction0);


  plane[1].moveTo(380, 10);
  plane[1].setXYdegs(direction1 * 45);
  plane[1].setFrame(direction1);


  writeScore();
} // end resetGame
```

Checking for Direction Changes in the Main Loop

The main loop has a number of jobs that all involve checking for various events in the
game. The first part of the function checks whether either player has chosen to change
the attitude of his or her aircraft:

```
//check for direction key presses

  if (up0.pressed){
    direction0--;
    if (direction0 < NORTH){
      direction0 = NORTHWEST;
    } // end if
  } // end if


  if (dn0.pressed){
    direction0++;
    if (direction0 > NORTHWEST){
      direction0 = NORTH;
    } // end if
  } // end if


  if (up1.pressed){
    direction1--;
    if (direction1 < NORTH){
      direction1 = NORTHWEST;
    } // end if
  } // end if


  if (dn1.pressed){
```

```
    direction1++;
    if (direction1 > NORTHWEST){
      direction1 = NORTH;
    } // end if
  } // end if


  plane[0].setFrame(direction0);
  plane[1].setFrame(direction1);
  plane[0].setXYdegs(direction0 * 45);
  plane[1].setXYdegs(direction1 * 45);
```

After setting up the directions, you set up the planes to use the appropriate frame and direction.

Checking for Gunfire

Now the main loop checks the fire keys to determine whether either player is currently firing:

```
//check for bullet firing
  if (fire0.pressed){
    sndBang.play();
    bullet[0].moveTo(plane[0].x, plane[0].y);
    bullet[0].setXYdegs(plane[0].xydegs);
    bullet[0].setSpeed(10);
  } // end plane 0 fires


  if (fire1.pressed){
    sndBang.play();
    bullet[1].moveTo(plane[1].x, plane[1].y);
    bullet[1].setXYdegs(plane[1].xydegs);
    bullet[1].setSpeed(10);
  } // end plane 0 fires
```

If a player fired, the main loop sets the appropriate bullet into motion and plays an appropriate sound effect.

Checking for Hits

In this program, I decided to check only for hits that involve the bullet striking the plane. The code is reasonably straightforward:

```
//check for hits
  if (bullet[0].hasHit(plane[1])){
    sndHit.play();
    damage0--;
    writeScore();
```

```
} // end if

if (bullet[1].hasHit(plane[0])){
    sndHit.play();
    damage1--;
    writeScore();
} // end if

} // end mainLoop
```

When a hit occurs, the function plays a sound and decrements the damage amount of the victim. It then calls the `writeScore()` function so that the players can tell what occurred. Each plane starts out at 100 percent functional. When the damage value falls below 0, the plane is destroyed.

Creating the writeScore() Function

The `writeScore()` function writes a new score into the scoreboard layer. It also checks whether either player's plane has been destroyed and sends appropriate messages. Here's the function's code.

```
function writeScore(){
    var scoreText = "";
    scoreText += "<font color = white>";
    scoreText += "red:   " + damage0 + "%<br>";
    scoreText += "blue: " + damage1 + "%";
    scoreText += "</font>";
    scoreboard.write(scoreText);

    //check for a win
    if (damage0 < 1){
        alert("blue wins!!");
        resetGame();
    } //end if

    if (damage1 < 1){
        alert("red wins!!");
        resetGame();
    } // end if
} // end writeScore
```

Summary

In this chapter, you have seen how you can improve sprites to handle cell animation. You have also learned how to respond to keyboard input and add sound to your programs. You also learned how to use layers to add dynamic content to your program, and how to use sprites as background graphics.

EXERCISES

1. Improve the Balloon Buster game by adding explosion animations.

2. Add a scorekeeping function (or two) to the Balloon Buster game.

3. Add keyboard handling to the Racer game from the last chapter.

4. Write a version of *Space Invaders* in which the player controls a spaceship that moves along the bottom of the screen. The aliens can be an array of sprites. Start with just one alien, then add more once the first is working correctly.

Cookies and the Mouse: The Jigsaw Puzzle

I n this chapter, you will add sophisticated mouse-handling techniques to your repertoire, and you will learn how to add a measure of permanence to your programs through the use of cookies. Here are the things that you will learn in this chapter:

- How gameLib allows you to react to the mouse

- How to make sprites and layers draggable

- How to respond to a button press on any sprite or layer

- How to make sprites follow the mouse or other sprites

- How to create cookies for data storage

- How to store and retrieve information from a cookie

The Project: The Jigsaw Puzzle Program

To illustrate all these techniques, you will create a jigsaw puzzle program. This program allows you to make a puzzle out of any image on the Internet. You can scramble the image, then use your mouse to piece the picture back together.

Scrambling the Pieces

Initially, the program shows the image totally scrambled (see Figure 11.1). The image is broken into 25 equal squares (although you'll be able to make as many pieces as you want, once you understand the code).

You can rescramble the picture by clicking the Scramble button.

The buttons are interesting because they are not standard HTML buttons, yet they still respond to mouse clicks and even look "pushed in" when the user clicks them.

Using the Solve Button

When the user clicks the Solve button, the program draws the image with all the pieces in the right order, but not quite touching (see Figure 11.2).

Using the Hint Button

If the user wants a hint, he or she can press the Hint button. The program then displays a small version of the image, which can also be moved around on the screen (see Figure 11.3).

Clicking the Hint button again causes the image to disappear.

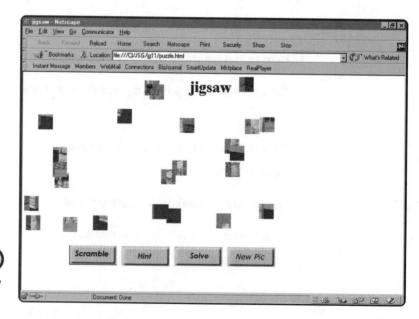

FIGURE 11.1

The image is totally scrambled.

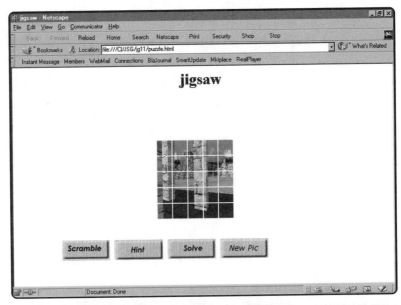

FIGURE 11.2

The program can automatically solve the puzzle (but what fun is that?).

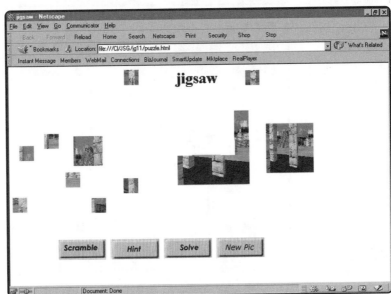

FIGURE 11.3

The Hint button shows what the puzzle will look like when finished.

Changing the Puzzle Image

If the user clicks the New Pic button, a dialog box appears asking the user to supply the address of an image on the Internet. The program then uses that image for the puzzle (see Figures 11.4 and 11.5).

As an added feature, the next time that the user plays the jigsaw game on the same browser, the program will automatically call up the newly selected image.

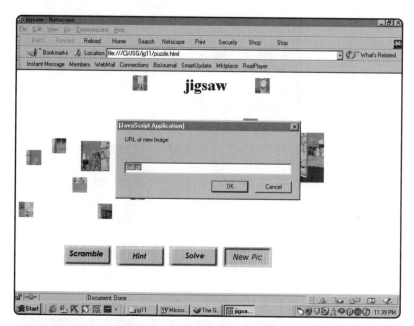

FIGURE 11.4

The user can request a new image for the puzzle.

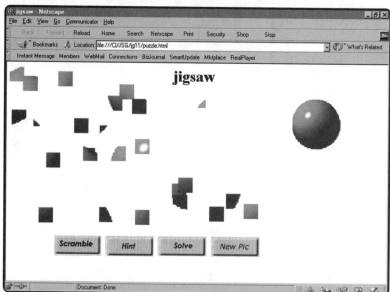

FIGURE 11.5

The new image shows up as a scrambled puzzle.

Using the Mouse to Drag and Drop

The most obvious new element in the puzzle game is the enhanced input from the mouse. To understand how this element works, you'll start by looking at a simpler program that illustrates how you can use the mouse to move a sprite around.

Creating the Dragger Program

The Dragger program features a sprite that the user can move anywhere on the screen by dragging it with the mouse (see Figures 11.6 and 11.7).

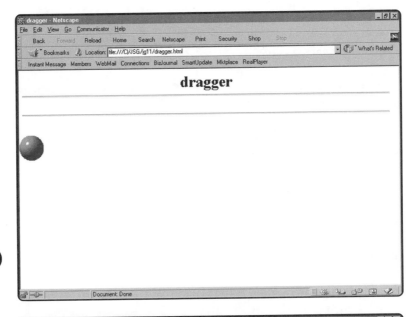

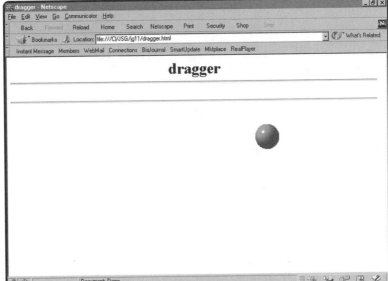

FIGURE 11.6

The ball is in the upper-left corner.

FIGURE 11.7

The user can move the ball by dragging it around the screen.

Both of the major browsers have techniques for reading and responding to the mouse events, but (you guessed it) these techniques are not the same in the two browsers. Fortunately, gameLib simplifies the process of reading the mouse object considerably.

Creating a Mouse Object

The secret to mouse manipulation in gameLib is the mouse object. It is no surprise that you will incorporate a new module and build a mouse object. Here's the script inclusion and variable creation code for the Dragger program:

```
<html>
<head>
<title>dragger</title>

<script language="Javascript" src="../gamelib196/gamelib/gamelib_core.js">
</script>

<script language="Javascript" src="../gamelib196/gamelib/
gamelib_sprites.js">
</script>

<script language="Javascript" src="../gamelib196/gamelib/gamelib_mouse.js">
</script>

<script>

var thePic;
var theMouse;
```

The only major new element is the `gamelib_mouse.js` code module. This module encapsulates a series of objects and functions for using the mouse.

I created variables for the `sprite` and `mouse` objects. As usual, I will give the objects values in an `init()` function.

Making a Sprite Draggable

Inside the `init()` function, I created a `mouse` object with the `Ms_initmouse()` function. I also created a sprite called `theImage`. All it takes to make `theImage` draggable is to set its `draggable` property to true. Here's the code for the `init()` function:

```
function init(){
  // dragger
  // Andy Harris

  theMouse = Ms_initmouse();
  thePic = new Sp_Sprite();
  thePic.setImage("ball.gif", 50, 50, 1, 1);
  thePic.setXlimits(0, 500);
  thePic.setYlimits(0, 300);
  thePic.setFrame(0);
  thePic.setAnimation(0);
  thePic.draggable = true;
  thePic.switchOn();
  thePic.moveTo(200, 200);
} // end init
```

TRAP

Be sure that you have generated a `mouse` object before you set the `draggable` property of a sprite to true. If there is no `mouse` object, the sprite will not drag.

Layers also have a `draggable` property that works in exactly the same way.

HINT

The `mouse` object has very few properties and methods of its own. In gameLib, making an instance of the `mouse` object allows you to activate features of other elements (such as the `draggable` property). Mouse manipulation is usually done differently in other languages. (In many languages, you have to look at the x and y values of the mouse to figure out whether it is over a particular object.) The gameLib technique is a very easy approach to using the mouse as it is needed in game programming.

IN THE REAL WORLD

Dragging and dropping objects is useful in a number of other more serious applications as well as in games.

If you are writing an anatomy tutorial, for example, you could make sprites for each of the major organs and allow the user to drag them around and fit them together in an abdomen image.

Likewise, if you were writing a promotional page for a cruise line, you might let the user drag a ship icon around on a map and pop up relevant information whenever the user drops the ship over a specific port.

Table 11.1 describes the members of the mouse object, and Table 11.2 describes the draggable elements.

TABLE 11.1 PRIMARY MEMBERS OF THE MOUSE OBJECT

Member	Description	Example
`Ms_initmouse();`	Creates a reference to the `mouse` object.	`var myMouse = Ms_initmouse();`
`.x, .y`	Specifies the current x and y coordinates of the mouse.	`alert(myMouse.x + ", " myMouse.y);`
`.mousedown`	Returns whether the user is currently clicking the mouse button.	`if(myMouse.mousedown){`
`alert("ouch!"); }` `// end if .over`	Returns the `sprite` object that the mouse is currently over.	`if (myMouse.over == ball) { score++; }` `// end if`

TABLE 11.2   DRAGGABLE ELEMENTS

Object and Member	Description	Example
sprite.draggable	If set to true, enables the user to drag and drop the sprite.	mySprite.draggable = true;
layer.draggable	If set to true, enables the user to drag and drop the layer.	myLayer.draggable = true;

Responding to Button Presses

In addition to knowing when the user is dragging and dropping a sprite, you might be interested in knowing when the user has passed over or clicked on a particular sprite. These are reasonably easy things to check with gameLib's mouse module.

Writing the Button Program

Figures 11.8 through 11.10 show the Button program, which is a form that includes a sprite that looks like a button. When the user places the mouse cursor over the button, the sprite changes appearance, and when he or she clicks the mouse button over the sprite, the program displays a message.

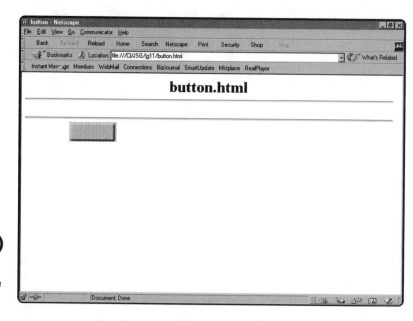

FIGURE 11.8

This form has a sprite that looks like a button.

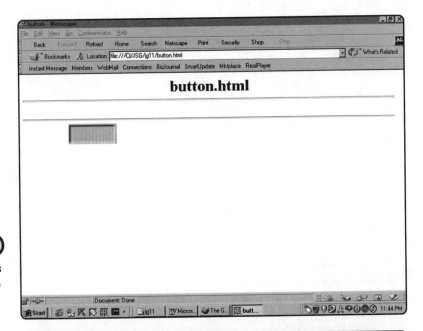

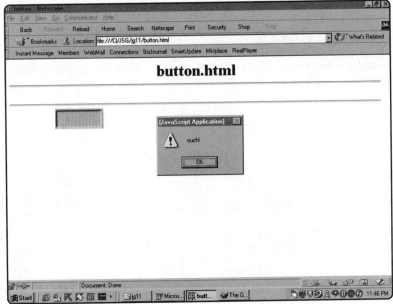

Initializing a Sprite for Mouse Input

This program again uses the mouse object, but it also relies on some properties of the sprite object to do the real work. Take a look at the initialization of the Button program:

```
<script>
var theButton;
```

```
var theMouse;

function init(){
  // button
  // Andy Harris

  theMouse = Ms_initmouse();

  theButton = new Sp_Sprite();
  theButton.setImage("button.gif", 100, 40, 1, 2);
  theButton.setXlimits(0, 400);
  theButton.setYlimits(0, 300);
  theButton.setFrame(0);
  theButton.setAnimation(0);
  theButton.moveTo(100,100);
  theButton.switchOn();
  theButton.onclickdown = "click()";
  theButton.onmouseout = "out()";
  theButton.onclickup = "sayOuch()";
} // end init
```

Table 11.3 lists the mouse event handlers of the sprite and layer objects.

I imported the core, sprite, and mouse objects, then created objects for the button itself and the mouse. The button is a basic two-frame sprite (see Figure 11.11).

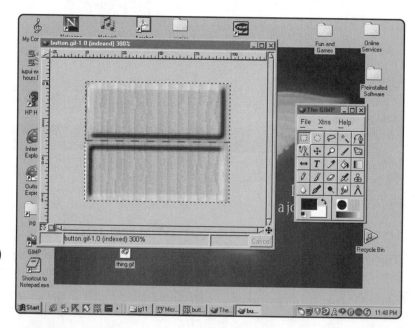

FIGURE 11.11

This is the image used in the button sprite.

Property	Description	Example
,onclickdown	Binds a function to call when the user presses the mouse button while the cursor is over the element.	mySprite.onclickdown = "click()";
,onclickup	Binds a function to call when the user releases the mouse button while the cursor is over the element.	mySprite.onclickup = "released()";
.onmouseover	Binds a function to call when the mouse cursor is over an element (regardless of button status).	mySprite.onmouseover = "over()";
.onmouseout	Binds a function to call when the mouse cursor leaves an element (regardless of button status).	mySprite.onmouseout = "out()";

TABLE 11.3 MOUSE EVENT HANDLERS OF THE SPRITE AND LAYER OBJECTS

These are properties of both the sprite and the layer objects. All are read and write properties. They work just like the event handlers in traditional HTML/DHTML.

I set up the sprite in all the typical ways, but added a few more lines. The onclickdown, onmouseover, onmouseout, and onclickup properties are used much like the event handlers in typical JavaScript. You can assign a JavaScript command or function call to each of these properties, and the sprite will automatically call the appropriate method when the corresponding mouse action occurs. For these special sprite properties to work, you must define a mouse object.

onclickdown occurs when the user presses the mouse button while the mouse cursor is within the boundaries of the sprite. onclickup executes when the user releases the mouse button while the mouse cursor is within the sprite object. onmouseover occurs when the mouse cursor moves over the sprite (whether the button is pressed or not). onmouseout occurs when the mouse cursor leaves the sprite's boundaries (again, regardless of the button's condition).

Responding to the Mouse Events

Of course, when you respond to mouse events, you usually must write a function to handle each of the appropriate events. Here's the rest of the code for the Button program:

```
function click(){
  theButton.setAnimation(1);
```

```
} // end over

function out(){
  theButton.setAnimation(0);
} //end out

function sayOuch(){
  alert("ouch!");
  theButton.setAnimation(0);
```

The `click()` function is associated with `onmousedown`. This function executes when the user clicks the mouse button while the mouse cursor is over the button sprite. The function sets the animation to frame 1, which makes the image look as though it is pressed down.

The `out()` function is set up to run whenever the mouse leaves the sprite. It sets the animation back to frame 0, which makes the button look like it's sticking up again.

The `sayOuch()` function displays an alert message to the user. It is set to the `onclickup` event of the sprite.

TRICK

You might find it surprising, but it is more common to put code in the mouse-up procedure than in the mouse-down procedure. Users typically don't expect the critical action to happen until they release the mouse button. If you place your code in the mouse-up procedure, you give users a chance to move the mouse cursor off of the sprite before releasing the mouse button if they made a mistake.

Following the Mouse and Sprites

Although not used in the jigsaw puzzle program, the `sprite` object works with the mouse in another interesting way. Sprites in the latest version of gameLib have the ability to follow and target the mouse or other sprites. This allows for some very interesting effects.

The Follower Program

In the Follower program (see Figure 11.12), as the user moves the mouse around the screen, a series of balls follow the mouse around.

You'll probably have to run the program to get the full effect, but it is captivating and reasonably easy to create.

The Follow Method

Sprites have a follow method, which allows you to specify a particular sprite (or the mouse) to follow, and an X and Y offset to follow the sprite or mouse.

FIGURE 11.12

My three-year-old calls this a "choo-choo train of dots."

When told to follow another sprite or the mouse, a sprite will stay with that object as if the sprite and the object were one object.

The Target Method

The target method of the sprite object works much like the follow method. However, instead of causing the sprite to follow the targeted object immediately, the method ensures that the sprite will move toward the targeted object according to the speed setting of the sprite.

> **TRICK**
>
> Targeting an object is a great way to add some "artificial intelligence" to sprites on the screen. You can have enemy sprites target the player sprite, and they will head straight for the player. You can also target your bullets at an enemy to simulate "smart missiles" that are guaranteed to hit the enemy.

How the Follower Works

The Follower program is simply a set of sprite objects that follow each other and ultimately follow the mouse. I've added code for the first three sprites; all the others work pretty much the same way.

```
<script>
var biggest;
var bigger;
var big;
var medium;
```

```
var small;
var smaller;
var smallest;

var theMouse;

function init(){
  theMouse = Ms_initmouse();

  biggest = new Sp_Sprite();
  biggest.setImage("ball.gif", 20, 20, 1, 1);
  biggest.moveTo(100,100);
  biggest.setXlimits(0, 500);
  biggest.setYlimits(0, 300);
  biggest.setFrame(0);
  biggest.switchOn();
  biggest.setSpeed(8);
  biggest.target(theMouse, 5, 15);

  bigger = new Sp_Sprite();
  bigger.setImage("ball.gif", 19, 19, 1, 1);
  bigger.moveTo(100,200);
  bigger.setXlimits(0, 500);
  bigger.setYlimits(0, 300);
  bigger.setFrame(0);
  bigger.switchOn();
  bigger.setSpeed(7);
  bigger.target(biggest, 0, 5);

  big = new Sp_Sprite();
  big.setImage("ball.gif", 18, 18, 1, 1);
  big.moveTo(100,200);
  big.setXlimits(0, 500);
  big.setYlimits(0, 300);
  big.setFrame(0);
  big.switchOn();
  big.setSpeed(6);
  big.target(bigger, 0, 5);
```

As you can see, the biggest sprite targets the mouse and has a speed setting of 8. Each succeeding sprite is smaller and slower and targets the previous sprite.

Table 11.4 describes the following and targeting commands of sprite objects.

TABLE 11.4 FOLLOWING AND TARGETING COMMANDS OF THE SPRITE OBJECT

Command	Description	Example
.follow(ob, x, y)	Causes the sprite to follow ob (a sprite or the mouse object) at a distance of (x, y) pixels.	mySprite.follow (theMouse, 0, 10);
.target(ob, x, y)	Causes the sprite to move toward ob at the current speed, aiming toward an offset of (x, y) pixels from ob.	mySprite.target (theMouse, 0, 10);
.stopFollowing(ob)	Tells the sprite to stop following ob.	mySprite.stopFollowing (theMouse);
.stopTargeting(ob)	Tells the sprite to stop targeting ob.	mySprite.stopTargeting (theMouse)

Storing Information in Cookies

Although JavaScript and dynamic HTML are terrific environments for basic game development, the security restrictions of client-side programming make developing certain common game elements very difficult. It would be great if your games could have some type of persistence. You might want to be able to keep track of high scores or custom configurations. Generally, you would use file-handling techniques for these kinds of problems, but JavaScript does not allow you to manipulate files on the user's computer. (This restriction is actually a good thing, because it prevents malicious programmers from writing viruses that are embedded in the JavaScript of innocent-looking Web pages.) JavaScript does support one feature that provides a limited yet capable way of storing a small amount of information on the user's computer. This technology is called a *cookie*.

Creating the Cookie Demo Program

The Cookie Demo program (see Figures 11.13 through 11.15) illustrates the gameLib approach to manipulating a cookie. The program illustrates how cookies can be used to preserve information even after a client has left your site and returned to it.

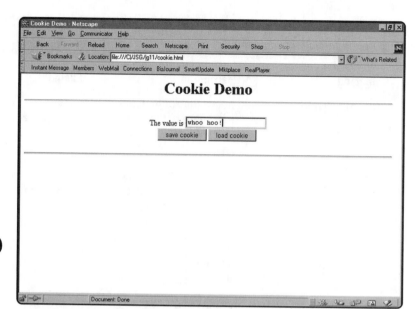

The user types some value into the text box.

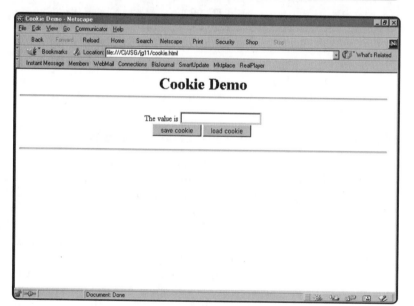

The user has shut off the computer, then later returned to the Web site.

FIGURE 11.15

The stored value
comes back!

Creating a Cookie

Cookie information is part of the gameLib core library. You do not have to import any other modules to use cookies. Here's the initialization code to the Cookie Demo program:

```
<script language="Javascript" src="../gamelib196/gamelib/gamelib_core.js">
</script>

<script>

var myCookie;

function init(){
  // Cookie Demo
  // Andy Harris
  myCookie = new Gl_cookie("cookieDemo");
} // end init
```

Cookies are created like many other gameLib objects. I created a variable called myCookie and then created an instance of the cookie object by calling the new Gl_cookie() function. The string parameter is the name of the cookie.

HINT

Generally, cookies have names and expiration dates, but the gameLib library automates the expiration process for you. The cookie data is stored in a text file on the client's hard drive. Each cookie is normally restricted to 255 characters, and a limited number of cookies are allowed from any one site. Cookies contain only text data, which prevents them from being used as viruses.

Table 11.5 describes gameLib's cookie-handling commands.

TABLE 11.5 COOKIE-HANDLING COMMANDS

Command	Description	Example
`new G1_cookie (cookieName)`	Creates a new cookie object with `cookieName` as its name.	`var myCookie = new G1_cookie("test");`
`.setValue(value)`	Sets the cookie's value to `value`.	`myCookie.setValue("Hi");`
`.value`	Returns the cookie's value.	`alert(myCookie.value);`

Writing the HTML in the Cookie Demo Program

This program uses a basic HTML form, so it will help you to understand the JavaScript if you can see how I named the form elements:

```
<body onload = "init()">
<center>
<h1>Cookie Demo<hr></h1>
<form name = "myForm">
The value is
<input type = "text"
      name = "txtIO"><br>
<input type = "button"
      value = "save cookie"
      onClick = "saveCookie()">
<input type = "button"
      value = "load cookie"
      onClick = "loadCookie()">
</form>

</center>
<hr>
</body>
```

This is pretty standard HTML with a text box and two buttons on it. One button will call the load cookie function, and the other will store the cookie.

Storing to the Cookie

Once you have created a cookie object, the process of sending a value to the cookie is very straightforward. Here's the `saveCookie()` function:

```
function saveCookie(){
  myCookie.setvalue(document.myForm.txtIO.value);
} // end saveCookie
```

The cookie object's `setvalue()` method is used to send a text value to the cookie. Since the cookie is actually part of a text file, the value will be retained even if the user turns off the browser.

TRAP

Don't become too reliant on cookies as a major part of your program, because they have some limitations. First, the user can always turn cookies off, which means your data will not be stored or retrieved. Second, the data in the cookie is specific to the particular browser and computer that the user is currently using. If a user stores data on a Web page at work, then visits the same page at home, the cookie will not be available. Even if the user switches browsers on the same computer, the cookie will not be available, because each browser uses a different cookie file.

Retrieving Data from the Cookie

It's just as easy to get data from a cookie, because the cookie object has a `value` property that contains the text stored in the cookie. Here's the `loadCookie()` function from the Cookie Demo program:

```
function loadCookie(){
  document.myForm.txtIO.value = myCookie.value;
} // end if
```

I simply copied the `value` property of the cookie object back to the text box on the form.

Creating the Jigsaw Puzzle Program

Most of the components in this chapter come together in the Jigsaw Puzzle program. The program doesn't introduce much that is new, but it can look a little bit overwhelming when you see all the pieces working on the same program. This section takes you through the program one chunk at a time.

Modules and Variable Creation

The puzzle requires the core, sprite, and mouse modules, and it involves a number of game-level variables. Here's the startup code:

```
<script language="Javascript" src="../gamelib196/gamelib/gamelib_core.js">
</script>

<script language="Javascript" src="../gamelib196/gamelib/
gamelib_sprites.js">
</script>

<script language="Javascript" src="../gamelib196/gamelib/gamelib_mouse.js">
</script>

<script>

//puzzle piece variables
```

```
var numRows = 5;
var numCols = 5;
var puzzle = new Array(numRows);

//button variables
var btnSolve;
var btnScramble;
var btnHint;
var btnNewImg;

//variables for the hint, the cookie, and the mouse
var lyrHint;
var imgCookie;
var theMouse;

//The image that the puzzle is based on
var theImage = "balls.gif";
var hintShowing = false;
```

The most important variable in the game is the `puzzle` array. It will become a two-dimensional array of sprite objects. Each element of the array contains the entire image, but shows just a small part of it, by assigning a frame and animation value based on the row and column of the puzzle piece. The buttons are all sprites. The program uses a layer for the hint screen, a cookie to store the current image, and a variable to handle the mouse. All the variables for these elements are created outside a function, but they will be initialized within the `init()` function.

The init() Function

This game has a *lot* of initialization. The player does most of the work after the whole thing is set up. The puzzle game's logic is almost entirely devoted to setting up the environment so that the user can play. The program must initialize nearly every object, so I decided to break the initialization into several other functions, then call those functions from `init()`. Here's the `init()` code:

```
function init(){
  // jigsaw
  // Andy Harris

  //get the previous image from the cookie if you can
  imgCookie = new Gl_cookie("puzzle_image");
  if (imgCookie.value == null){
    //if you cannot get an image, go with the default
    theImage = "balls.gif";
  } else {
    theImage = imgCookie.value;
```

```
} // end if

//get a reference to the mouse
theMouse=Ms_initmouse();

//run functions to manage all the other setup tasks
setUpButtons();
setUpPuzzle();
scramble();
setUpLayer();

//start the game loop
Gl_start();
} // end init
```

The first order of business is to look for an image file stored in a cookie. If the user has played this game on this browser on this machine and has chosen an image file, the cookie will store that file (see the section "The newImg() Function" for details on how this is done). The init() function looks for the existence of such a cookie. If the cookie exists, the function uses the image referenced in the cookie. If not, init() uses a default image.

The init() function creates a reference to the mouse object and calls a bunch of other functions to set up the various other screen elements. When these functions are done, the init() function starts up the gameLib engine.

The setUpButtons() Function

The setUpButtons() function is responsible for setting up the buttons. I wanted a custom feel, so each button is a sprite. To simplify things, the buttons all use the same graphic (see Figure 11.16).

I simply copied and pasted the original button image from the Button program earlier in the chapter, then added text for the appropriate buttons.

Here's the code for the setUpButtons() function:

```
function setUpButtons(){
  //initialize the button sprites

  //scramble button
  btnScramble = new Sp_Sprite();
  btnScramble.setImage("pzlBtns.gif", 100, 40, 4, 2);
  btnScramble.setFrame(0);
  btnScramble.setAnimation(0);
  btnScramble.setXlimits(0, 500);
  btnScramble.setYlimits(0, 400);
  btnScramble.moveTo(100, 350);
```

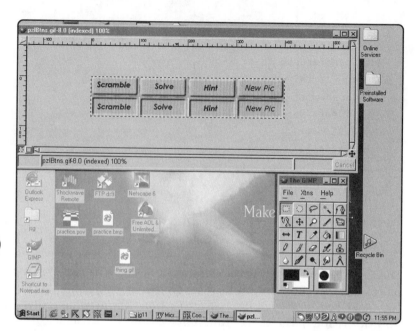

This graphic
contains all the
button images
needed.

```
btnScramble.onmouseover = "over(btnScramble)";
btnScramble.onclickup = "scramble()";
btnScramble.onmouseout = "out(btnScramble)";
btnScramble.switchOn();

//hint button
btnHint = new Sp_Sprite();
btnHint.setImage("pzlBtns.gif", 100, 40, 4, 2);
btnHint.setFrame(2);
btnHint.setAnimation(0);
btnHint.setXlimits(0, 500);
btnHint.setYlimits(0, 400);
btnHint.moveTo(210, 350);
btnHint.onmouseover = "over(btnHint)";
btnHint.onclickup = "hint()";
btnHint.onmouseout = "out(btnHint)";
btnHint.switchOn();

//solve button
btnSolve = new Sp_Sprite();
btnSolve.setImage("pzlBtns.gif", 100, 40, 4, 2);
btnSolve.setFrame(1);
btnSolve.setAnimation(0);
btnSolve.setXlimits(0, 500);
```

```
btnSolve.setYlimits(0, 400);
btnSolve.moveTo(320, 350);
btnSolve.onmouseover = "over(btnSolve)";
btnSolve.onclickup = "solve()";
btnSolve.onmouseout = "out(btnSolve)";
btnSolve.switchOn();

//new Image button
btnNewImg = new Sp_Sprite();
btnNewImg.setImage("pzlBtns.gif", 100, 40, 4, 2);
btnNewImg.setFrame(3);
btnNewImg.setAnimation(0);
btnNewImg.setXlimits(0, 500);
btnNewImg.setYlimits(0, 400);
btnNewImg.moveTo(430, 350);
btnNewImg.onmouseover = "over(btnNewImg)";
btnNewImg.onclickup = "newImg()";
btnNewImg.onmouseout = "out(btnNewImg)";
btnNewImg.switchOn();

} // end setUpButtons;
```

The code sets up each button in basically the same way. The buttons are all typical sprites. The code sets each to a different frame, so that the program's interface displays the appropriate words. All the buttons call the over() function when the mouse cursor is over the button and the out() function when the mouse cursor leaves. The event handlers pass a reference to the current button to these functions. The onclickup event of each button calls a function specific to that event (for example, btnNewImg calls the newImg() function, and btnSolve calls the solve() function).

The setUpPuzzle() Function

The setUpPuzzle() function sets up the puzzle array:

```
function setUpPuzzle(){
  //initialize the puzzle sprites
  var row = 0;
  var col = 0;
  //clear out any puzzle currently in memory
  //if we just came from the new image command, for example
  puzzle = null;
  puzzle = new Array();

  //step through each row
  for (row = 0; row < numRows; row++){

    //make each row a new array
```

```
    puzzle[row] = new Array(numCols);

    //for each object in the row...
    for (col = 0; col < numCols; col++){
      //create a sprite
      puzzle[row][col] = new Sp_Sprite();
      puzzle[row][col].setImage(theImage, 30, 30, numRows, numCols);
      puzzle[row][col].setFrame(col);
      puzzle[row][col].setAnimation(row);
      puzzle[row][col].setXlimits(0, 500);
      puzzle[row][col].setYlimits(0, 300);
      puzzle[row][col].draggable = true;
      puzzle[row][col].switchOn();
    } // end col loop
  } // end row loop
} // end setUpPuzzle
```

If there is a puzzle already in memory, the function clears it out and moves all the pieces out of the way. It then makes a new array for each row, then steps through the row making a new sprite.

HINT

Just as for loops and normal arrays are a natural combination, if you have two-dimensional arrays (as in the puzzle program), you will frequently find yourself writing a pair of nested for loops to step through every element of the array. In this case, the puzzle program has one loop that steps through the rows, and every time that loop executes, it runs another loop that steps through the columns. As a whole, the nested loops work together to ensure that every element in the two-dimensional array is manipulated.

The puzzle sprites are all identical in almost every respect. They all contain the *entire* image of the finished graphic. They all are the same size, and they all have all the same initial characteristics. However, I set the frame to map the current column, and set the animation cell to map the current row. Since these settings reflect how the original image was designed, this technique breaks the image into 25 pieces that fit together perfectly. I played sort of a dirty trick with the clip animation technique used by gameLib, but the results speak for themselves. Note that I did not worry about the placement of the pieces, because the scramble() function takes care of that.

The setUpLayer() Function

The setUpLayer() function manages the layer that holds the hint graphic. The layer setup is reasonably straightforward:

```
function setUpLayer(){

  //initialize the hint layer
```

```
lyrHint = new Gl_layer(600, 10, 200, "");
lyrHint.write("<img src = " + theImage + " height = 100 width = 100>");

//let the user move the layer outside the puzzle boundaries
lyrHint.setXlimits (0, 800);
lyrHint.setYlimits (0, 600);
lyrHint.setZ(0);
lyrHint.draggable = true;

//make the layer invisible until the user asks for it
lyrHint.hide();

} // end setUpLayer()
```

The layer contains nothing but an HTML tag referencing the image. I decided to force the image to 100×100 pixels, so that it did not take over the entire screen. If the original image is not square, you will have some distortion, but the hint image will be exactly proportional to the finished puzzle.

The hint layer is draggable, so the user can choose to move it around.

The over() and out() Functions

over() and out() are utility functions that enable each of the buttons to be pushed down when the mouse is over the button, and to push back up when the mouse leaves the button. I added a parameter so that all four buttons can use the same function. When the program calls these functions, they must include a reference to the button that the program is activating. Here is the code for the functions:

```
function over(theButton){
  //respond when mouse is over a button
  theButton.setAnimation(1);
} // end over

function out(theButton){
  //respond when the mouse leaves a button
  theButton.setAnimation(0);
} // end out
```

The variable theButton stores the button that the mouse cursor is currently over. I then set the animation of theButton so that the button appears to be up or down.

TRICK

Whenever possible, it makes a lot of sense to build functions such as these that you can use for multiple purposes. It would have been very tedious to write separate over() and out() functions for each button in the program.

The scramble() Function

Both the `init()` method and the Scramble button call the `scramble()` function. The function steps through the `puzzle` array. For each piece of the puzzle, `scramble()` generates random x and y values within the appropriate ranges. The piece is then sent to these coordinates. Here is the function's code:

```
function scramble(){
  //put all the puzzle pieces in a random order
  var row = 0;
  var col = 0;
  var x = 0;
  var y = 0;

  for (row = 0; row < numRows; row++){
    for (col = 0; col < numCols; col++){
      //choose random x and y values for the current piece
      x = Math.floor(Math.random() * 500) + 1;
      y = Math.floor(Math.random() * 300) + 1;
      puzzle[row][col].moveTo(x, y);
    } // end col for
  } // end row for
} // end scramble
```

The solve() Function

The `solve()` function generates a solution to the puzzle. It basically re-creates the original picture, although the function deliberately leaves a small gap between the pieces, so that the user still has to do a little work to see the complete picture. Here's the code for the `solve()` function:

```
function solve(){
  //puts all the pieces in order, but not quite touching
  var row = 0;
  var col = 0;
  var x = 0;
  var y = 0;

  for (row = 0; row < numRows; row++){
    for (col = 0; col < numCols; col++){
      //offset the puzzle by (300, 150)
      //put a two pixel gap between pieces
      x = (col * 32) + 300;
      y = row * 32 + 150;
      puzzle[row][col].moveTo(x, y);
    } // end col for
  } // end row for
} // end solve
```

The hint() Function

The `hint()` function displays and hides the hint layer:

```
function hint(){
  //displays or hides the hint layer
  if(hintShowing){
    lyrHint.hide();
  } else {
    lyrHint.write("<img src = " + theImage + " height = 100 width = 100>");
    lyrHint.show();
  } // end if

  //reverse the value of the hintShowing variable
  hintShowing = !hintShowing;
}// end hint
```

The function checks the value of the `hintShowing` variable. `hint()` initializes this variable to false, indicating that the hint is not initially showing. If the hint is currently showing, the function hides it. If the hint is not currently showing, the function displays it. I rewrote the HTML of the image just in case the user changed the image since the last time that the program showed the hint layer. Finally, the `!` (not) operator reverses the value of the `hintShowing` variable. If the value is true, it becomes false, and if it is false, it becomes true.

The newImg() Function

The `newImg()` function lets the user choose a new image for the puzzle:

```
function newImg(){
  //prompts user for a new image URL
  theImage = prompt("URL of new Image:", "ball.gif");

  //clean up old puzzle
  for (row = 0; row < numRows; row++){
    for (col = 0; col < numCols; col++){
      puzzle[row][col].setImage("blank.gif", 30, 30, numRows, numCols);
      puzzle[row][col].moveto(-100, -100);
    } // end col for
  } // end row for

  //reset hint
  lyrHint.write("<img src = " + theImage + " height = 100 width = 100>");

  //store URL in cookie
  imgCookie.setvalue(theImage);

  //reset the puzzle with the new image
```

```
setUpPuzzle();
scramble();

//reset the button so it is sticking up again
out(btnNewImg);
} // end newImg
```

First, the program uses an ordinary prompt to request the URL of the new image. This can be any valid image file (.gif or .jpg) anywhere on the Internet or on the local machine.

The program then clears out the existing puzzle pieces, to ensure that they did not stay on the screen. The function uses a pair of nested `for` loops for this, setting each element to a blank image and moving it off the screen.

The program then resets the hint layer so that it reflects the new image. Then the function stores the URL into the cookie, so that the next time that the browser loads the page, the program will display the new image.

The program calls the `setUpPuzzle()` and `scramble()` functions to initialize the new puzzle. Then finally the program pops up the button, because often the user will move the mouse off of the button without activating the `mouseout` event.

Summary

In this chapter, you have seen how the `mouse` object interacts with sprites and layers. You have learned how to drag and drop elements around the screen, and how to set up event handlers for them. You also have learned how to use cookies to store small amounts of data. Finally, you have put all these things together to make an interesting and configurable puzzle game.

EXERCISES

1. Use a graphic image with words to make a "refrigerator poetry" game. The page will have a series of words on it that can be dragged around with the mouse to generate poems.

2. Add a scorekeeping function to the puzzle game. It will need the capability to surmise that each piece is in the appropriate position. You might do this by looking at the position of the upper-left image and calculating what the position of each other piece should be in relationship to this image.

3. Add a timer to the puzzle game. Let the user time how long it takes to solve a puzzle. Use cookies to add a high-score list.

The Game Creation Process: The Brick Game

Throughout this book, you have built a number of interesting programs by learning simple, isolated concepts, then putting them together to form the games at the end of each chapter. In this last chapter, you will put together many of the skills that you learned throughout the book to make the basis of an arcade game. Specifically, here are the things you will see in this chapter:

- What a design sketch for a game might look like

- Where to start programming

- How to get the ball rolling

- How to add various sprites

- How to create and then improve data structures so that they are more flexible

- What to do if you find that you must change your program design when certain functions become unwieldy

With all that you know by now, you should have all the skills you need to put together interesting games on your Web sites. The thing that usually holds programmers back, however, isn't lack of programming techniques. The real problem is figuring out the process of building a program. Earlier in the book, you saw what programs looked like after I finished them—which might have given you the mistaken impression that I wrote them correctly the first time. Game development never happens that way. In this chapter, you see how to design a game from the beginning of the process until the middle. (The end of the process is up to you; a computer program is never fully complete, but the program presented here is stable enough for you to build on and experiment with your own ideas.) Rather than showing you the finished game at the beginning of this chapter, as I have in the previous chapters, I'll start with an idea, as all good programs do. I'll show you the same program in several incarnations, so you can see one way to design a game.

> **IN THE REAL WORLD**
>
> So far, the game is nothing but an idea. In much of programming, you will have to start with nothing but words (and sketches, which you will learn about next). Make sure that you can describe your program completely, or you will have troubles with the later steps.

The Project: The Brick Game

It occurred to me that this book ought to pay homage to at least one of the classics of the golden age of arcade games. I decided to try a version of *Breakout*. You might recall the game. Basically, the player has a paddle that he or she can move across the bottom of the screen. There is a series of bricks arranged at the top of the screen, and a small ball that can bounce off the walls, the bricks, and the paddle. Each time that the ball hits a brick, that brick disappears. If the ball moves below the paddle, it is lost. The goal is to eliminate all the bricks before losing all three balls. Such programs have many variations, but this is the basic idea behind each of them.

Coming up with game ideas can be one of the most fun parts of game design. Here are a few ways to get started:

- Go with a variation on an existing theme (*Breakout* with a goalie played by the user, or *Pacman* with the user playing the ghost).
- Simulate some part of a real-life game or a dramatic situation (such as landing an airplane using only instruments or playing a soccer shootout).
- Modify the graphics and behavior of an existing game (for example, switch the Basketball game in Chapter 7, "Image Swapping and Lookup Tables: The Basketball Game," of this book to hockey or volleyball).

The game's idea doesn't really matter, as long as the game is fun. Be careful, though, that you begin with only modestly ambitious games, because you've already seen how complex even the very simple designs in this book have been to implement.

Creating the Game Design

The first part of the process is to think thoroughly about the game's design. You can do part of this by writing down a summary of the game's play and goals.

TRICK

Yes, you really should write down a summary of your idea. Even though you will probably remember it anyway, it is amazing how often experienced programmers lose sight of the main goals of their program. Write down your program's goals, then paste them on your monitor or somewhere else that draws your attention regularly to help keep yourself focused.

Sketch of Game

Games tend to be very visual. In addition to writing down your goals, you should sketch out any of the major screens that you will use. On this sketch, you should write all the most critical elements of game play, even if you aren't sure that you will implement them. Figure 12.1 shows my example for the Brick game.

Note that I usually do sketches on plain paper, napkins, or whatever is handy when inspiration strikes (I haven't yet resorted to lipstick on a mirror, but it's an idea). I duplicated the sketch with my drawing program, just so you could see what it looks like (and so you will be able to read the handwriting). If you have a friend or two who program, you might want to show them your sketches and ask for some ideas on implementation.

> **IN THE REAL WORLD**
>
> An entire career path exists for those who design and manage software projects. Although techniques for planning physical constructions such as bridges and buildings have been around for a long time, the field of software engineering is relatively new. This endeavor is dedicated to learning and implementing the best techniques for managing and designing software projects.

TRAP

Don't get too caught up at this phase in exactly how you will do things. I made some mention of images and cookies, but that was all. The main thing here is to understand clearly the programming problems that you will be facing. You will have plenty of time later in the process to look more closely at the specific details.

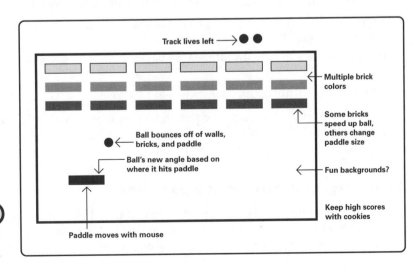

FIGURE 12.1

Here's a sketch of the Brick program.

Feature List

Somewhere, either in your written description or on your sketches, you should have some sort of a feature list. Figure out what your program should do. It is really easy to get carried away with adding features before you've done any real programming, so be sure to prioritize your features. You can add "bells and whistles" (animations, fancy sound effects, and so on) later, but the basic game play must be in place before you release the game. However, getting the game to work once isn't the only goal either. You should conceive your initial design with extensibility in mind. (Think of the multiple tracks in the Racer game, the ability to switch images in the jigsaw puzzle, or the multiple board design that you are about to see implemented in the Brick game.) It takes a little more planning to design a program that you can easily modify, but it almost always turns out to be worth the effort.

Features of the Brick Game

Before writing a single line of code, you should set up some reasonable expectations. You will never be completely satisfied with any program that you've written, but you should still have some sort of goal in mind, so that you'll eventually be willing to release the game. Here are the basic objectives that I hope to meet in this version of the Brick game:

- The ball should move around the screen bouncing off of walls.
- There should be a paddle under user control (using the mouse). User control should be intuitive.
- A bunch of bricks should be at the top of the screen.
- When the ball hits a brick, the brick should disappear and the score should increment. The ball should appear to bounce off the brick.
- When the ball hits the paddle, it should bounce. The direction in which the ball bounces should be based on where it hits the paddle.
- If the ball gets past the paddle, the game should reduce the number of lives that the player has left.
- It would be nice to have different types of bricks. Some might speed up the ball, change the size of the paddle, or change the game's behavior in other ways.
- There should be a number of different initial settings of the bricks, so that the player won't get bored too easily.
- It would be nice to have an interesting background and good graphics for the ball and bricks.
- A high-score feature using cookies would be nice.

This type of prioritized list, and the accompanying diagram, should give you plenty to start with. If you have such a list of prioritized goals, you should never end up staring at a blank screen, wondering, "What do I do next?"

Setting Up the Playground

Once you have some sort of plan in place, you still might wonder what to do first. There are a number of strategies, but the technique that I'll describe in this chapter is pretty good for moderate-size programs written by one programmer. The technique is a form

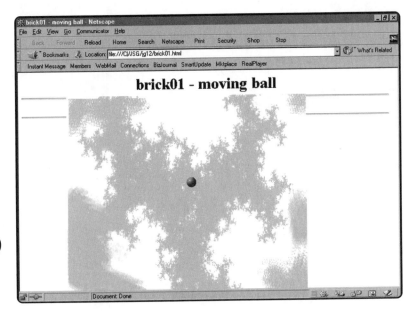

FIGURE 12.2

The ball is moving,
and it bounces off
the screens.

of *stepwise refinement*. The basic idea is to get something small working, save it, then add a little at a time. You never move ahead on the next part until you have the last part working, so you always have something working that you can fall back on.

The Brick01 Program

For my first attempt, I decided simply to get a background screen and a ball on the Web page, with the ball bouncing around. Figure 12.2 shows what I created.

This modest start is admittedly not very glamorous, but it provides a good foundation. It's nice to start with something simple and make sure that it works well before moving on. Here's the code:

```javascript
<script language="Javascript" src="../gamelib196/gamelib/gamelib_core.js">
</script>

<script language="Javascript" src="../gamelib196/gamelib/
gamelib_sprites.js">
</script>

<script>
//The moving ball
var ball;
var bg;

function init(){

  //set offsets
```

```
Sp_xoffset = 100;
Sp_yoffset = 50;

//set up background
bg = new Sp_Sprite();
bg.setImage("clouds.gif", 500, 400, 1, 1);
bg.setXlimits(0, 500);
bg.setYlimits(0, 400);
bg.setFrame(0);
bg.setAnimation(0);
bg.moveto(0, 0);
bg.switchOn();
bg.setZ(0);

//set up ball
ball = new Sp_Sprite();
ball.setImage("ball.gif", 20, 20, 1, 1);
ball.setXlimits(0, 500);
ball.setYlimits(0, 350);
ball.setFrame(0);
ball.setAnimation(0);
ball.collides = true;
ball.bounces = true;
ball.moveto(250, 250);
ball.setXYdegs(0);
ball.setSpeed(6);
ball.switchOn();
ball.setZ(99);

//start up library
Gl_start();

} // end init
</script>
```

I started by including the libraries for the gameLib core and the sprite library. I also set up variables for the ball background. I added an init() function, which is (as usual) tied to the onload event of the body tag.

In the init() function, I set up the sprite offset variables so that the sprites will all appear to be more centered on the page. I also created the background and ball sprites. The ball is set to an initial speed and direction, and its bounces property is set to true. I set the z order of both sprites to ensure that the ball is always visible in front of the background.

Finally, I invoked the Gl_start() function to ensure that the library starts up and that the ball starts to move.

TRICK

Although everything in this version of the program is reasonably basic, be sure to test it as soon as you can. Make sure that it's working before you move on, because things *will* break down later, and you'll want to be sure that you know the last point at which everything was working correctly.

Adding the Paddle

Once you're sure that you have a solid foundation, you can add elements one or two at a time. I chose next to add the mouse handler, because it would involve some other gameLib elements and because it's a pretty important part of the game.

Creating the Brick02 Program

I imported the mouse library, then created a mouse object. I then made a sprite for the paddle and had the sprite follow the mouse. Figure 12.3 shows these additions.

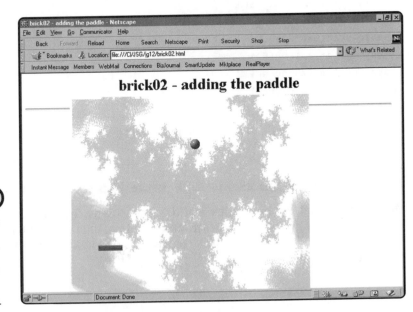

FIGURE 12.3

The paddle moves under mouse control, but the program does not yet have any collision detection.

Note that I'm only concerned that the paddle is moving correctly. I actually had to manipulate the X limits and Y limits of the paddle sprite a little bit to get the behavior that I wanted. I'll deal with the ball bouncing off the paddle or moving past the paddle later.

TRICK

Deciding which tasks you're going to save for later is one of the hardest parts of actual programming. Have a plan and stick with it. In the case of this particular version of the program, for example, it's okay to ignore collision detection until the paddle is moving correctly.

Adding the mouse handler was simply a matter of importing the mouse library, like this:

```
<script language="Javascript" src="../gamelib196/gamelib/gamelib_mouse.js">
</script>
```

I also had to create a variable for the mouse handler outside the functions.

```
var theMouse;
```

Finally, I initialized the `mouse` object in the `init()` function, as follows:

```
theMouse = Ms_initmouse();
```

Adding the Paddle Sprite

Creating the paddle sprite is reasonably straightforward. I created a suitable image in my paint program, then created a reasonably typical `sprite` object:

```
//set up paddle
paddle = new Sp_Sprite();
paddle.setImage("paddle.gif", 50, 10, 1, 1);
paddle.setXlimits(0, 450);
paddle.setYlimits(300, 300);
paddle.setFrame(0);
paddle.setAnimation(0);
paddle.follow(theMouse, 0, 0);
paddle.collides = true;
paddle.switchOn();
```

Note that I set the paddle to follow the mouse. This was the only programming necessary to get the paddle working.

Bouncing the Ball off the Paddle

Once the ball and the paddle are working independently, it is time to make them interact with each other. Remember from the original plan that the ball should bounce off the paddle, but the location of the ball on the paddle should determine the angle at which it bounces.

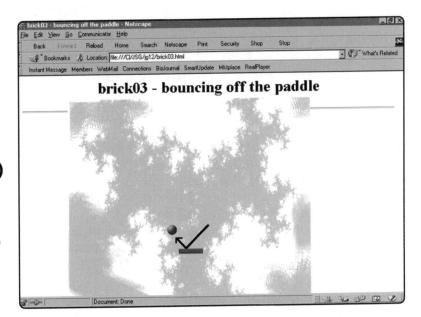

FIGURE 12.4

The ball now bounces off the paddle correctly. I added the arrow so you can see how the ball has bounced off the paddle.

Creating the Brick03 Program

In this version of the program, the ball bounces off the paddle. Hitting the ball near the center of the paddle causes the ball to go straight up. Hitting near the ends of the paddle causes the ball to go in a steep angle to the side. Figure 12.4 shows the ball bouncing at an appropriate angle.

Hooking Up the Main Loop

The next order of business is to ensure that the game library calls a main loop function every time that the timer goes off (recall from Chapter 9, "Sprite Animation: The Racer," that this will be 20 times per second in an ideal situation). This is done by adding the following code to the `init()` function.

```
Gl_hook("mainLoop()");
```

Determining the Ball's New Angle

The code inside the main loop (at least for now) is dedicated to checking whether the ball is touching the paddle. Here's the function:

```
function mainLoop(){

//check ball hits paddle
if (ball.hasHit(paddle)){
  var ballLoc = ball.x - paddle.x;
```

```
    var ballPerc = ballLoc/paddle.width;
    var newX = (5 * ballPerc);
    newX = Math.floor(newX -1);
    ball.setDir(newX, 0 - ball.ydir);
  } // end if

} // end mainLoop
```

The function starts by checking whether the ball has hit the paddle. If so, the function does some work to set the ball's new direction. There are a number of ways to do this, but here's how I did it. I recalled that you can set a sprite's direction directly in terms of x and y values to add each time that the timer occurs. To make the ball bounce back up, all I have to do is set the ball's y direction to its negative value. (The ball will be moving down, so its `ydir` value will be positive. 0 minus the `ydir` value will make the ball move at exactly the same speed in the opposite direction.)

Setting the x direction proved to be a little trickier. I decided to get the ball's location on the paddle by subtracting the paddle's x from the ball's x. I placed the resulting value in the `ballLoc` variable. I then divided that value by the length of the paddle to get a percentage value. A value of 0 means that the ball was touching the absolute farthest left pixel of the paddle, and a value of 1 indicates the farthest right pixel. I then multiplied this value by 5 to get a value between 0 and 4. I next eliminated the decimal value and subtracted 1, to get values between –2 and 2. I then set the `Xdir` of the ball to the appropriate value.

 HINT Although this algorithm might appear to be completely new, if you look at it a little more closely, you might see that it resembles the strategy used for generating dice introduced in Chapter 6, "Petals around the Rose: Dynamic Output."

Adding Bricks

Getting the paddle and ball to work together is nice, but the name of the game is Bricks, so there should be some bricks somewhere in the game.

Creating the Brick04 Program

Bricks aren't terribly tricky taken one at a time. After all, they are simply sprites. The tricky part is to determine how a group of bricks will work together. It might be easiest to start with just one brick, but I decided to make a bunch of them (see Figure 12.5). I determined to go with a simple array of bricks for now, but I suspect that I'll need to make the data structure managing the bricks a little more complex later.

Creating the Simple Brick Array

The bricks themselves are an array of sprites. I created the array outside the functions, as follows:

```
var brick = new Array(8);
var numVisible = 8;
```

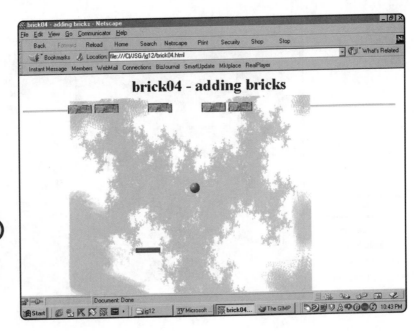

This version features one row of bricks. The ball can hit and destroy them.

In addition to the array of bricks, I created another variable, which will be used to keep track of how many bricks are currently showing on the screen.

Creating the Brick Sprites

As usual, an array of sprites is easiest to initialize and work with inside a `for` loop. Here's the code added to the `init()` function for creating the array of bricks:

```
//set up bricks
 for (i = 0; i < 8; i++){
  brick[i] = new Sp_Sprite();
  brick[i].setImage("brick.gif", 50, 20, 1, 4);
  brick[i].setXlimits(0, 500);
  brick[i].setYlimits(0, 200);
  brick[i].setFrame(0);
  brick[i].setAnimation(1);
  brick[i].collides = true;
  brick[i].bounces = false;
  brick[i].moveto(i * 55, 10);
  brick[i].switchOn();
 } // end for loop
```

The brick is a sprite based on a reasonably simple image. I decided to create an image that would be useful in the later stages of game development, when I had multiple bricks. Figure 12.6 shows the image that I created.

For this version of the program, I set all the bricks to the brown animation frame (1). I used the `moveto()` method to place the bricks. Each brick is 50 pixels wide, so by mul-

FIGURE 12.6

The brick image includes a transparent version as well as three colors of traditional bricks.

tiplying i (the for loop counter) by 55, the computer will place the bricks five pixels apart. All other settings of the brick sprites are straightforward.

Checking for Brick Collisions

The ball should bounce off the brick as well as the paddle, so I had to add some code to the mainloop() function to provide this behavior:

```
//check ball hits brick
 for(i = 0; i < 8; i++){
  if(ball.hasHit(brick[i])){
   ball.setDir(ball.xdir, 0 - ball.ydir);
   brick[i].switchOff();
   brick[i].moveTo(-100, -100);
   brick[i].collides = false;
   brick[i].setAnimation(0);

   //check for win
   numVisible--;
   if (numVisible <= 0){
    alert("You win!!");
   } // end if
  } // end 'ball hit brick' if
 } // end for loop
```

I used a `for` loop to simplify the process of check-ing all eight bricks. Inside the loop, I looked to see whether the ball had hit the current brick. If so, I reversed the ball's y direction, but left the x direction alone. I turned the brick off, but I have found that this does not always make the sprite disappear, so I also moved it off the playing field, set its collision property to false, then set the sprite to a blank image.

Checking whether All Bricks Are Gone

The "ball hit a brick" code is a good place to check for a winning condition, so every time that a brick is hit, I decrement the `numVisible` variable. (Remem-ber, the `init()` function set this variable to be equal to the number of bricks visible on the screen.) If `numVisible` is less than or equal to 0, I'll tell the user but do nothing else at the moment.

Checking whether the Ball Is Past the Paddle

It also makes sense to check for a losing condition. If the ball has gotten past the paddle, you will need to do something as well. This code, in the `mainLoop()` function, does exactly that:

```
//check ball past paddle
 if(ball.y > 300){
  alert("you lost the ball!");
  ball.moveTo(200, 250);
  ball.setXYdegs(0);
 } // end if
```

The code is reasonably self-explanatory. If the ball moves past a certain y coordinate, the program informs the user that this has happened. Then the code resets the posi-tion and direction of the ball to put it back into play.

Adding More Bricks and Sound

The Brick game is really coming into focus now. All the essential pieces are in place, so you can start adding some of the embellishments. The most important thing to figure out is how to make rows and columns of bricks. As you probably guessed, this involves making the `brick` array two-dimensional rather than the single dimension that it was in the last iteration. Also, I decided to put the sounds in at this point. (Actually, I handled the two-dimensional array and sound as two separate steps, but combined them in this explanation because they are both fairly straightforward processes.)

> **IN THE REAL WORLD**
> In the spirit of testing one thing at a time, it's entirely appropri-ate not to worry yet about exactly what happens when the bricks are all gone. You have described what should happen in your plan, so you don't need to imple-ment it yet. In fact, you shouldn't, until you know that the basic brick behavior is work-ing correctly (that is, you need to be sure that the bricks appear, that they respond to collisions with the ball, and that they go away appropriately). You should, however, do something (such as presenting the alert, in this case) that will tell you that the condition is working cor-rectly. Later on, you can replace that statement with some more robust code.

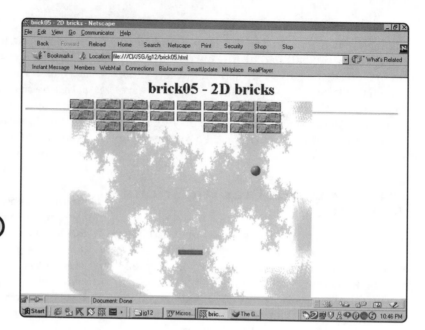

FIGURE 12.7

The program
has rows and
columns of bricks.
It also features
sound effects.

Creating the Brick05 Program

This version of the program has a more complex structure of bricks in rows and columns. Figure 12.7 shows the structure.

Although you cannot tell from Figure 12.7, the program now has sound effects: When the ball hits a brick, it makes a "tick" sound. When the ball hits the paddle, you hear a "boing" noise, and the game makes a "honk" when the ball moves past the paddle.

Preparing for Two Dimensions of Bricks

Converting the brick array from one- to two-dimensional was pretty easy. First, I added a few global variables to make things a little bit easier to follow:

```
var ROWS = 3;
var COLS = 8;
var NUMBRICKS = ROWS * COLS;

var brick = new Array(ROWS);
var numVisible = NUMBRICKS;
```

I assigned constants to keep track of the number of rows, columns, and bricks, and changed the `brick` and `numVisible` variables to reflect these constants.

TRICK

Using constants in this way makes your code much easier to change later. If you want to make a different size grid of bricks, you can just change the value of ROWS and COLS, and everything else is done for you.

Creating a Two-Dimensional Array of Bricks

You need to update the brick initialization section of the init() function to reflect the two-dimensional array:

```
//set up bricks
 for (row = 0; row < ROWS; row++){
  brick[row] = new Array(COLS);
  for (col = 0; col < COLS; col++){
   brick[row][col] = new Sp_Sprite();
   brick[row][col].setImage("brick.gif", 50, 20, 1, 4);
   brick[row][col].setXlimits(0, 500);
   brick[row][col].setYlimits(0, 200);
   brick[row][col].setFrame(0);
   brick[row][col].setAnimation(1);
   brick[row][col].collides = true;
   brick[row][col].bounces = false;
   brick[row][col].moveto(col * 55, row * 22);
   brick[row][col].switchOn();
  } // end 'col' for loop
 } // end 'row' for loop
```

The Brick05 program replaces the single for loop used in Brick04 with a pair of nested loops. The outside loop steps through the rows. The first thing that the loop does is to create an array for the row. It then steps through each element of this new array, creating a sprite. Since brick is now a two-dimensional array, you must use two indices to refer to any element in the data structure. All the actual properties and settings of each brick sprite remain exactly the same as in Brick04. The only change to this version is in the way that the bricks are addressed.

Checking whether the Ball Hits a Brick

Because the brick data structure is now two-dimensional, you must be careful that all references to it reflect this fact. The program checks every brick in the mainloop() function, so you must also update the code in that function:

```
//check ball hits brick
 for (row = 0; row < ROWS; row++){
  for (col = 0; col < COLS; col++){

   if(ball.hasHit(brick[row][col])){
    ball.setDir(ball.xdir, 0 - ball.ydir);
    brick[row][col].switchOff();
    brick[row][col].moveTo(-100, -100);
    brick[row][col].collides = false;
    brick[row][col].setAnimation(0);
    sndTick.play();

    //check for win
```

```
numVisible--;
if (numVisible <= 0){
 alert("You win!!");
} // end if


} // end 'ball hit brick' if
} // end col loop
} // end row loop
```

This revision is just like the code for Brick04, except that the program now uses two loops and two indices to check for each `brick` object.

Adding Sound

Adding the sound is reasonably simple with gameLib. First I imported the sound library:

```
<script language="Javascript" src="../gamelib196/gamelib/gamelib_sound.js">
</script>
```

Then I created a number of variables to refer to the various sound effects in the game:

```
//sound variables
var sndTick;
var sndHonk;
var sndBoing;
```

I then initialized all the sounds in the `init()` function:

```
//set up sounds
sndTick = new Sd_add_sound("tick.wav");
sndHonk = new Sd_add_sound("honk.wav");
sndBoing = new Sd_add_sound("boing.wav");
```

Finally, I just invoked the appropriate sound's `play()` method when I wanted the sound to occur. For example, I added `sndTick.play()` to the code that occurs whenever the ball hits a brick.

Adding Multiple Game Boards

The capability to add multiple-board setups would greatly increase the game's capability to keep the player interested, because then it would not always be exactly the same. To perform this feat, I created a new three-dimensional array called `board`. The board array consists of game boards, and each game board is a two-dimensional array of integers. The program uses the integers to determine how to set up each board.

Creating the Brick06 Program

I set up the game with three boards to start with, as shown in Figures 12.8 through 12.10. The game boards will feature different combinations of colored bricks. Later on I'll set a specific behavior for each brick color. Also, a brick can start out already blank, providing to us the capability to have game boards that start with some bricks missing.

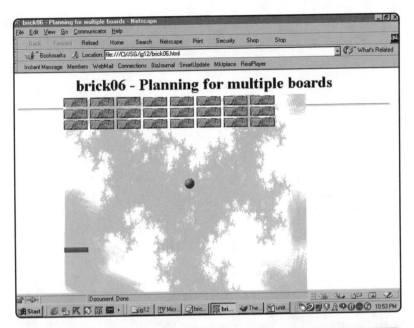

FIGURE 12.8

This is the first (default) board. All bricks are the same color.

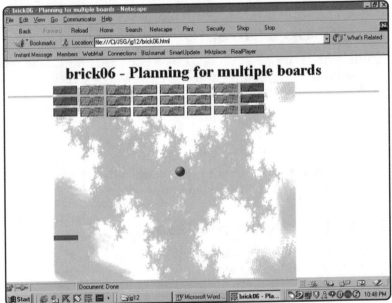

FIGURE 12.9

Here is the second board. It features bricks of different colors.

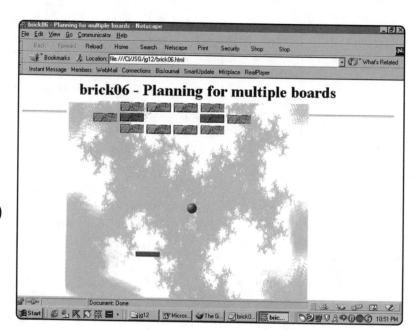

FIGURE 12.10

This is the third board. It has different types of bricks and begins with some bricks already gone.

Setting Up a Three-Dimensional Array

First it is necessary to set up board as a basic array. I made it three elements long, because I will start with three different game boards. Of course, you can change this in your own version of the game.

```
var boardNum = 0;
```

```
var board = new Array(3);
```

The boardNum variable is used to specify which board is currently being played. The board variable is used to hold the playing-board data.

Setting Up Multiple Boards

Because I know before the game begins what data I want in the board array, I'll use a special trick for filling in the data.

```
//set up boards
board[0] = new Array(
  new Array(1, 1, 1, 1, 1, 1, 1, 1),
  new Array(1, 1, 1, 1, 1, 1, 1, 1),
  new Array(1, 1, 1, 1, 1, 1, 1, 1)
);


board[1] = new Array(
  new Array(3, 2, 1, 1, 1, 1, 2, 3),
  new Array(3, 2, 1, 1, 1, 1, 2, 3),
```

```
  new Array(3, 2, 1, 1, 1, 1, 2, 3)
);


board[2] = new Array(
  new Array(0, 0, 2, 1, 1, 2, 0, 0),
  new Array(0, 2, 3, 0, 0, 3, 2, 0),
  new Array(0, 0, 2, 1, 1, 2, 0, 0)
);
```

Each element of the board array is itself an array of three arrays. The board array elements are in effect two-dimensional arrays. When you call the new Array() command with more than one parameter, JavaScript makes an array with the given values as its initial contents. The numbers represent which brick should be displayed in a given position. Board 2, row 0, column 0, for example, will have no brick, so I put a 0 at that position. I specially set up the brick image so that the 0 image would be transparent and not visible to the user. If there is a 1 in the array, that specifies that the first animation (a tan brick) should be displayed.

Drawing the Board

Once the board array is in place, it is easy to copy the values to the bricks themselves as they are being drawn. This line is all that is needed in init():

```
brick[row][col].setAnimation(board[boardNum][row][col]);
```

This line means the following: "Take the value of brick for board number boardNum, row row, and column col, and set the animation of the brick at row and col to that value." At this point, the appearance of the brick will change, but the brick's behavior will not.

Changing the Bricks' Behavior

Now that you can make different types of bricks appear on the screen, you will need to change the behavior of the various bricks.

The Brick07 Program

In this latest incarnation of the program, the different types of bricks have different behavior, as shown in Figure 12.11.

A switch statement in the mainloop() function affects all the behavior. After determining that the ball has hit a brick, the program determines what type of brick was hit by examining the animpos property of the current brick sprite.

```
//deal with special bricks
    switch(brick[row][col].animpos){
    case 1:
      //brown: normal ball speed, paddle size
      paddle.resize(50, 10);
      ball.setSpeed(6);
      break;
```

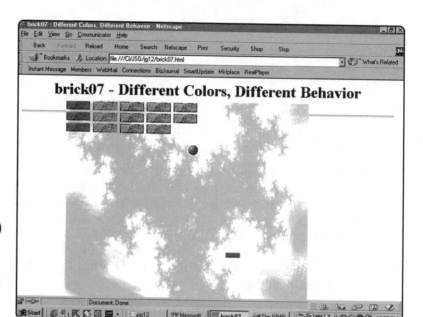

FIGURE 12.11

After hitting a red brick, the ball gets faster. After hitting a silver brick, the paddle gets smaller.

```
  case 2:
   //blue: smaller paddle
   paddle.resize(30, 10);
   break;
  case 3:
   //red: faster ball
   ball.setSpeed(8);
   break;
} // end switch

brick[row][col].setAnimation(0);
sndTick.play();
```

The actions associated with each type of brick are not too complicated. It would be an easy matter to add new brick types with all kinds of strange behavior, such as a brick that reverses gravity or that causes the paddle to move backward.

Adding Scorekeeping Functionality

The game is getting close to completion. It is time to add the ability to keep score. The actual scorekeeping functionality is not tricky, but displaying the score in a way that is informative and not distracting is a little more challenging. I chose to use a layer for scorekeeping, because it allows a lot of flexibility without a lot of work.

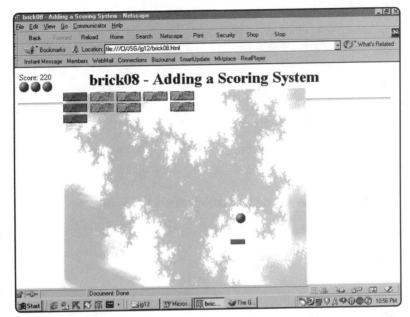

FIGURE 12.12

In this game, the
player has scored
some points and has
three lives left.

The Brick08 Program

This version of the Brick program sports the classic icon-based life indicator (three
balls in the corner means that the player has three lives left) and a scoreboard indicating the player's numeric score (see Figure 12.12).

Adding Some Scorekeeping Variables

Like many variables, the variables for scorekeeping are set up outside the functions:

```
//utility variables
var lyrScore;
var score = 0;
var ballsLeft = 3;
```

The `lyrScore` variable is a reference to a layer object that displays the score. The `score`
variable contains the actual score, and the `ballsLeft` variable keeps track of how many
lives the player has remaining. The program changes these variables when the appropriate events occur. The game increments `score` whenever a brick is hit and decrements `ballsLeft` whenever the ball moves past the paddle.

Setting Up the Scoreboard Layer

The program communicates the score to the player by updating the `lyrScore` layer.
Here's the code that creates the layer:

```
//set up scoreboard
 lyrScore = new Gl_layer(10, 10, 100, "Hi there!");
```

```
lyrScore.setXlimits(0,500);
lyrScore.setYlimits(0, 200);
lyrScore.show();

updateScore();
```

The code sets up the layer in the usual way, at coordinates (10, 10), width 100, and with the initial value "Hi there!"

The actual HTML text of the scoreboard is created in the updateScore() function, which the program calls whenever the score needs to be updated.

Writing the updateScore() Function

The updateScore() function does the actual work of updating the score layer:

```
function updateScore(){
 var scoreText = "";
 scoreText += "<html>";
 scoreText += "Score: ";
 scoreText += score;

 scoreText += "<br> ";
 for (i = 0; i < ballsLeft; i++){
  scoreText += "<img src = ball.gif height = 20 width = 20>";
  scoreText += " ";
 } // end for loop
 scoreText += "</html>";
 lyrScore.write(scoreText);
} // end updateScore
```

The scoreText variable contains all the HTML for the scoreboard. The function concatenates the numeric score into the HTML right after the text "Score: ". To get the appropriate number of ball icons to appear, I made a for loop that executes as many times as the ballsLeft variable indicates. For each ball remaining, the function adds another <img> tag of a ball to the scoreText variable.

At the end of the function, I simply wrote the value of the scoreText variable to lyrScore using the layer's write() method.

Reorganizing and Cleaning Up

The Brick program is really coming along, but it is starting to become unwieldy. The program is heavily concentrated in two functions, and each function is becoming several pages of code long.

Managing the game will become difficult if it gets any longer, so it is probably a good time to reorganize a little bit. Figure 12.13 shows what I did to reorganize the program's internal design. I did not add much code or new functionality to this version, but I did rearrange things and add comments. Taking the time to reorganize the game provides

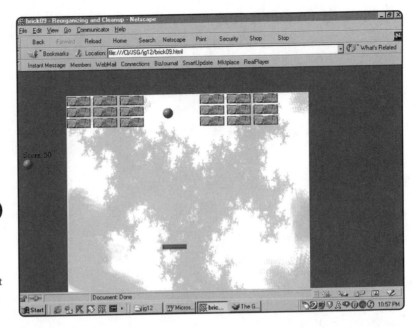

FIGURE 12.13

I changed the background color and some other cosmetics, but most of the new work is behind the scenes.

a good opportunity to check the game's progress, because it requires that you discover and evaluate what your program is doing and how well it is doing it.

TRICK

The technique described in this section is called *encapsulation*. The basic idea is to take a function that has become large and unwieldy and break it into a number of smaller, self-contained segments. The advantage of this approach is that your code will presumably be in smaller segments that are easier to read, understand, and debug.

Note that I have already explained most of the code, so in the following section I will comment only on the things that I did to improve the program.

Library Calls

The Brick program now relies on four gameLib libraries:

```
<script language="Javascript" src="../gamelib196/gamelib/gamelib_core.js">
</script>

<script language="Javascript" src="../gamelib196/gamelib/
gamelib_sprites.js">
</script>

<script language="Javascript" src="../gamelib196/gamelib/gamelib_mouse.js">
</script>

<script language="Javascript" src="../gamelib196/gamelib/gamelib_sound.js">
</script>
```

Variable Creation

I moved around some of the variables and put them in commented groups based on their functions:

```
//constants
var ROWS = 3;
var COLS = 8;
var NUMBRICKS = ROWS * COLS;

//basic sprites
var ball;
var bg;
var paddle;
var brick = new Array(ROWS);

//utility variables
var numVisible = NUMBRICKS;
var lyrScore;
var score = 0;
var ballsLeft = 3;

//the gameboard
var board = new Array(3);
var boardNum = 0;

//sound variables
var sndTick;
var sndHonk;
var sndBoing;
```

The init() Function

One of my goals was to break down the init() and mainloop() functions so that they contain only essential statements and calls to other functions. Here's how I broke up init():

```
function init(){

  //set offsets
  Sp_xoffset = 100;
  Sp_yoffset = 50;

  //initialize mouse
  theMouse = Ms_initmouse();

  setupSprites();
```

```
setupBoards();
setupBricks();
updateBricks();

//set up sounds
sndTick = new Sd_add_sound("tick.wav");
sndHonk = new Sd_add_sound("honk.wav");
sndBoing = new Sd_add_sound("boing.wav");

//set up scoreboard
lyrScore = new Gl_layer(10, 200, 100, "Hi there!");
lyrScore.setXlimits(0,500);
lyrScore.setYlimits(0, 200);
lyrScore.show();

updateScore();

//start up library
Gl_hook("mainLoop()");
Gl_start();

} // end init
```

I still used init() to set up the simpler elements, such as the scoreboard layer and the sound variables, but I delegated all the more complex setup tasks to their own functions.

The setupSprites() Function

The setupSprites() function has the sole purpose of setting up most of the sprites (except the brick sprites, which have their own setup function):

```
function setupSprites(){
 //set up background
 bg = new Sp_Sprite();
 bg.setImage("clouds.gif", 500, 400, 1, 1);
 bg.setXlimits(0, 500);
 bg.setYlimits(0, 400);
 bg.setFrame(0);
 bg.setAnimation(0);
 bg.moveto(0, 0);
 bg.switchOn();
 bg.setZ(0);

 //set up ball
 ball = new Sp_Sprite();
 ball.setImage("ball.gif", 20, 20, 1, 1);
```

```
ball.setXlimits(0, 500);
ball.setYlimits(0, 350);
ball.setFrame(0);
ball.setAnimation(0);
ball.collides = true;
ball.bounces = true;
ball.moveto(250, 250);
ball.setXYdegs(0);
ball.setSpeed(6);
ball.switchOn();
ball.setZ(99);

//set up paddle
paddle = new Sp_Sprite();
paddle.setImage("paddle.gif", 50, 10, 1, 1);
paddle.setXlimits(0, 450);
paddle.setYlimits(300, 300);
paddle.setFrame(0);
paddle.setAnimation(0);
paddle.follow(theMouse, 0, 0);
paddle.collides = true;
paddle.switchOn();

} //end setupSprites
```

The setupBoards() Function

The setupBoards() function manages all of the board setup, which is the creation of that three-dimensional array of bricks:

```
function setupBoards(){

//set up boards
board[0] = new Array(
  new Array(1, 1, 1, 1, 1, 1, 1, 1),
  new Array(1, 1, 1, 1, 1, 1, 1, 1),
  new Array(1, 1, 1, 1, 1, 1, 1, 1)
);

board[1] = new Array(
  new Array(3, 2, 1, 1, 1, 1, 2, 3),
  new Array(3, 2, 1, 1, 1, 1, 2, 3),
  new Array(3, 2, 1, 1, 1, 1, 2, 3)
);

board[2] = new Array(
```

```
   new Array(0, 0, 2, 1, 1, 2, 0, 0),
   new Array(0, 2, 3, 0, 0, 3, 2, 0),
   new Array(0, 0, 2, 1, 1, 2, 0, 0)
 );
} // end setupBoards
```

The setupBricks() Function

The setupBricks() function initializes the brick sprites:

```
function setupBricks(){
 //set up bricks
 for (row = 0; row < ROWS; row++){
  brick[row] = new Array(COLS);
 } // end 'row' for loop
} // end setupBricks
```

The updateBricks() Function

The updateBricks() function sets up the bricks according to the current board variable by looking at the board array.

```
function updateBricks(){
 //set up bricks

 //destroy old bricks
 brick = null;
 brick = new Array(COLS);

 numVisible = NUMBRICKS;
 for (row = 0; row < ROWS; row++){
  brick[row] = null;
  brick[row] = new Array(COLS);
  for (col = 0; col < COLS; col++){
   brick[row][col] = new Sp_Sprite();
   brick[row][col].setImage("brick.gif", 50, 20, 1, 4);
   brick[row][col].setXlimits(0, 500);
   brick[row][col].setYlimits(0, 200);
   brick[row][col].setFrame(0);
   brick[row][col].setAnimation(board[boardNum][row][col]);
   if (brick[row][col].animpos == 0){
    numVisible--;
    brick[row][col].switchOff();
    brick[row][col].moveTo(-100, -100);
    brick[row][col].collides = false;
   } // end if
   brick[row][col].collides = true;
```

```
    brick[row][col].bounces = false;
    brick[row][col].moveto(col * 55, row * 22);
    brick[row][col].switchOn();
  } // end 'col' for loop
 } // end 'row' for loop
} // end setupBricks
```

HINT

Note that I did some memory management tricks. I attempted to destroy each old row and sprite before re-creating them by assigning null to the appropriate variables. The game appears to get more sluggish as it goes on. I suspect that this is because JavaScript does not have sophisticated techniques for reclaiming memory when a program finishes with a particular array, and it is making multiple copies of the `brick` array. Assigning null to the values seems to help, but it does not completely alleviate the problem.

The updateScore() Function

You've already seen the `updateScore()` function, but I made some minor modifications to the HTML that it generates:

```
function updateScore(){
 var scoreText = "";
 scoreText += "<html>";
 scoreText += "Score: ";
 scoreText += score;
 scoreText += "<br> ";
 for (i = 0; i < ballsLeft; i++){
  scoreText += "<img src = ball.gif height = 20 width = 20>";
  scoreText += " ";
 } // end for loop
 scoreText += "</html>";
 lyrScore.write(scoreText);
} // end updateScore
```

The mainLoop() Function

Again, the `mainLoop()` function was getting a little long and complex, so I broke it down into a few major tasks and put each of them into its own function:

```
function mainLoop(){
 ballHitPaddle();
 ballHitBrick();
 ballPastPaddle();
} // end mainLoop
```

The ballHitPaddle() Function

The `ballHitPaddle()` function encapsulates all the action required to check for the ball hitting the paddle:

```
function ballHitPaddle(){
 //check ball hits paddle
 if (ball.hasHit(paddle)){
  sndBoing.play();
  var ballLoc = ball.x - paddle.x;
  var ballPerc = ballLoc/paddle.width;
  var newX = (5 * ballPerc);
  newX = Math.floor(newX -1);
  ball.setDir(newX, 0 - ball.ydir);
 } // end if
} // end ballHitPaddle
```

The ballHitBrick() Function

The code for the `ballHitBrick()` function checks whether the ball hit a brick. It also calls a function that checks for a winning condition (that is, that all the bricks are gone):

```
function ballHitBrick(){
 //check ball hits brick
 for (row = 0; row < ROWS; row++){
  for (col = 0; col < COLS; col++){

   if(ball.hasHit(brick[row][col])){
    updateScore();
    ball.setDir(ball.xdir, 0 - ball.ydir);
    brick[row][col].switchOff();
    brick[row][col].moveTo(-100, -100);
    brick[row][col].collides = false;

    //deal with special bricks
    switch(brick[row][col].animpos){
     case 1:
      //brown: normal ball speed, paddle size
      paddle.resize(50, 10);
      ball.setSpeed(6);
      score += 10;
      break;
     case 2:
      //blue: smaller paddle
      paddle.resize(30, 10);
      score += 20;
      break;
     case 3:
```

```
      //red: faster ball
      ball.setSpeed(8);
      score += 30;
      break;
   } // end switch

   brick[row][col].setAnimation(0);
   sndTick.play();
   checkWin();


  } // end 'ball hit brick' if
 } // end col loop
 } // end row loop
} // end ballHitBrick
```

The ballPastPaddle() Function

The ballPastPaddle() function checks whether the ball has gone past the paddle:

```
function ballPastPaddle(){
 //check ball past paddle
 if(ball.y > 300){
  sndHonk.play();
  ball.moveTo(200, 250);
  ball.setXYdegs(0);
  ballsLeft--;
  updateScore();
 } // end if
```

Using a Cookie to Track the High Score

At this point, I was pretty satisfied with the game. However, after returning to the sketch that I drew at the beginning of the project, I decided the game needed one more feature to be complete. The only feature not in place was the ability to add a high score using a cookie (see Figure 12.14). Fortunately, the reorganization of the program that I did in the last step made modification much simpler.

Initializing the Cookie

The process for using a cookie is just like the one used in Chapter 11. I added a cookie variable:

```
//high score stuff
var scoreCookie;
var highScore = 0;
```

The scoreCookie variable will contain a reference to a cookie object. The highScore variable will contain (you guessed it) the high score.

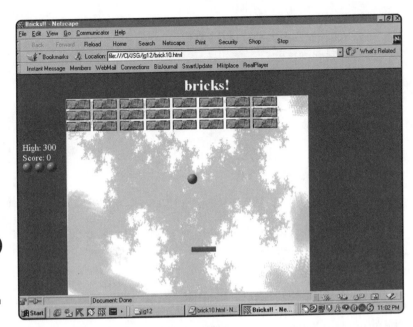

FIGURE 12.14

Now the program
keeps track of the
high score between
visits to the game.

Getting the High Score

I added some code to the `init()` function that checks the cookie for a previous high-score value and loads it into the `highScore` variable.

```
//get high score
 scoreCookie = new Gl_cookie("brick score");
 if (scoreCookie.value == null){
  highScore = 0;
 } else {
  highScore = parseInt(scoreCookie.value);
 } // end if
 updateScore();
```

If the cookie has no previous value, the function returns null. So I trapped for that value, then instead sent the value 0 to `highScore`.

Improving the Code Used at the End of Game

The code that handled the end of the game was pretty weak, so I spruced it up a little bit:

```
//check for end of game
  if (ballsLeft <=0){
   alert("Game Over!");
   if (score > highScore){
    highScore = score;
```

```
    alert("New High Score!!");
    scoreCookie.setvalue(score);
    updateScore();
} // end 'high score' if
score = 0;
ballsLeft = 3;
boardNum = 1;
updateScore();
updateBricks();
} // end 'game over' if
```

Once the game is over, the program informs the user of his or her bad luck, then checks the current score against the high score. If the player achieved a new high score, the function stores the new high score in the cookie.

Summary

Although this chapter didn't introduce much code syntax that was new, you still managed to cover a lot of ground. You looked at the design and creation of a program from the ground up. You looked at the stepwise refinement technique for building programs. You learned a bit about refinement techniques and encapsulation. You saw a program grow from a simple idea to a workable, if not completely polished, game. You have come a very long way in a short time. You should be extremely proud of yourself.

EXERCISES

1. Add new boards to the Brick game.

2. Create new types of bricks with different behaviors. (Make the paddle go backward, change gravity, scramble the bricks, give the player a bomb, and so on.)

3. Design a two-player variant of the game (perhaps one in which one player uses a keyboard, the other the mouse).

4. Write a version of one of the other 1980s classics, such as *Space Invaders* or *Missile Command*.

5. Design an adventure game with a hero figure who climbs ladders, jumps, and shoots villains.

6. Use your imagination and come up with something that I can't even dream of! Have a great time!

Syntax Reference

The following tables document the syntax elements featured in this book. Please note that this is not a complete reference to JavaScript or gameLib. Instead, I have tried to focus on the syntax elements that are proven to work across browsers. There are more complete references available on the Web that feature platform-dependent or newer commands. You might also wish to investigate the gameLib documentation that comes on the CD-ROM for the original documentation of that library. You will find some features there that I did not have room to mention in this introductory book.

JavaScript and Dynamic HTML Reference

BASIC VARIABLES AND IO

Expression	Description	Example
`var varName`	Create a variable called `varName`.	`var userName;`
`var varName = value`	Create a variable called `varName` with a starting value of `value`.	`var userName = "";`
`alert(msg)`	Send the string `msg` to the user in a dialog box.	`alert("Hi there");`
`varName = prompt (question)`	Send a dialog box with the string `question` and a text box. Then return the value to `varName`.	`userName = prompt("What is your name");`
`eval(string)`	Evaluate the string expression. If it's a number, return the number.	`number = eval("3");`
`stringVar. toUpperCase()`	Convert `stringVar` to all uppercase letters.	`bigName = userName. toUpperCase()`
`Math.random()`	Generates a random number between 0 and 1.	`MyVar=Math.random();`
`Math.floor(varName)`	Lops off trailing decimal values, converting a real number to its next lowest integer.	`newVar = Math.floor (oldVar);`

DOCUMENT OBJECT PROPERTIES

Property	Description
`bgColor`	The background color assigned to the page's body
`taglastModified`	The date that the document was last changed
`title`	The title of the document
`url`	The address of the document
`domain`	The domain name of the document's host
`referrer`	If the user got to this page via a hyperlink, this property shows the address of the page that referred to the current one.

BRANCHING COMMANDS

Expression	Description	Example
`if (condition)` `{    expression }`	Branches program logic based on the value of a condition.	`if (score > 50) {` `alert("Winner!");`
`} else {`	Denotes code within an if structure to execute when the condition is false.	`} else {    alert` `("Loser"); } //end if`
`switch(varName){`	Sets up one variable to check against multiple values.	`switch (year){`
`case value:`	Denotes a value for a variable within a switch structure.	`case 1964:       alert` `("Correct");`
`break;`	Moves execution directly to the end of the current structure. The break statement is used most frequently with switch statements.	`break;`
`default:`	Catches any case clauses not caught by case statements within a switch structure.	`default:      alert` `("Incorrect");`

LOOPING EXPRESSIONS

Expression	Description	Example

`for (init; condition;`
`increment)`
`{    repeated code }`
`// end for`
	Sets up a loop that executes a set number of times.	`for(i=1; i<10; i++){ }`
		`// end for`

`Init`	Sets the starting value of a counting variable.	`i++`
`Condition`	Specifies a condition that evaluates to true or false. The loop continues executing as long as condition is true.	`i < 10`
`Increment`	Changes the value of the counter.	`i++`

`while (condition)`
`{    code body }`
`// end while`
	Creates a loop that continues as long as condition is true.	`While (finished ==`
		`false){ }`

FORM COMPONENT FEATURES

Expression	Description	Example
`function funcName () { }`	Creates a new function.	`function doIt() { alert("I did it"); } // end function`
`Checkbox.value`	Returns the value associated with a specific checkbox object (defined in HTML).	`TheVar = myCheck.value;`
`Checkbox.checked`	Returns true or false depending on whether the box is currently checked.	`if (myCheck.checked) { theVar = myCheck. value; } // end if`
`Radio[i].value`	Returns the value associated with a specific radio button object (defined in HTML). Radio buttons are usually defined in an array.	`for(i=0; i <5; i++) { theVar = myRadio [i].value; } // end for loop`
`Radio[i].checked`	Returns true or false depending on whether the radio button is currently checked. Radio buttons are usually defined in an array.	`for(i=0; i <5; i++) { if (radio[i]. checked){ theVar = myRadio[i].value; } // end if } // end for loop`
`Selection. selectedIndex`	Returns the index of whichever option is currently selected.	`alert ("you chose option # " + mySelect. selectedIndex);`
`Selection[i]`	Returns the ith option in the array.	`myOption = mySelect[3];`
`Option.value`	Returns the value of a specified option (usually called as part of an array.	`alert (myOption.value);`
`window.parent. framename.document`	Refers to the `document` object of the `frameName` frame.	`window.parent. frameOutput.document. write("I'm a frame");`
`document.open()`	Opens up a document for writing.	`window.parent. frameOutput.document. open();`
`document.close()`	Signals that nothing else will be written to the document and that the browser can render the document.	`window.parent. frameOutput.document. close();`

FORM COMPONENT FEATURES (CONTINUED)

Expression	Description	Example
`window.open (url, targetName, properties)`	Opens a new window. The starting address `url`. `targetName` refers to the name of the window if you are using the window as an HTML target. You describe window characteristics in `properties`.	`myWindow = window. open("", "goofyWin", "height=400,width= 400,resize");`
`windowName.close()`	Destroys the window called `windowName`.	`myWindow.close();`
`windowName.focus()`	Pulls the window called `windowName` in front of all other windows.	`myWindow.focus();`
`navigator.appName`	Returns the browser's name as a string. This statement is used for browser detection.	`var theBrowser = navigator.appName;`

KEY EVENT HANDLERS OF THE ANCHOR OBJECT

Event	Description
`onClick`	The user clicks the anchor.
`onDblClick`	The user double-clicks the anchor.
`onMouseOver`	The mouse moves over the anchor.
`onMouseOut`	The mouse moves off of the anchor.

DYNAMIC HTML TECHNIQUES

Expression	Description	Example
`document.layerName.moveTo(x,y)`	Moves a CSS element to (x, y). This statement applies to Netscape only.	`document.sub.moveTo(30,100);`
`document.all.layerName.style.pixelLeft document.all.layerName.style.pixelTop`	Moves a CSS element to a specified coordinate. This statement applies to IE only.	`document.all.sub.style.pixelLeft = 30;`
`document.all.sub.style.pixelTop = 100;` `document.layerName.document.open(),` `document.layerName.document.write(),` `document.layerName.document.close(),`	Writes new content to a CSS element. This statement applies to Netscape only.	`document.output.document.open();`
`document.output.document.write ("Hello World!");` `document.output.document.close();` `document.all.layerName.innerHTML`	Writes a new value to the element. This statement applies to IE only.	`document.all.output.innerHTML = "Hello World!";`
`document.embedName.play()`	Plays a sound file previously loaded into the specified `embed` tag. This statement applies to Netscape only.	`document.ping.play();`
`document.all.bgSoundName.src`	Enables you to assign a new URL to play a sound file.	`document.all.soundPlayer.src = "ping.wav";`

Element	Description	Example
background-color	Sets the color of whatever element is being described.	background-color:blue
background-image	Adds a background image to the element.	background-image:bg.gif
border-color	Sets a border of the specified color around the element.	border-color:blue
border-style	Sets the type of border. Both browsers support double, groove, inset, outset, ridge, and solid borders, or you can specify the none variable if you don't want any border.	border-style: double
border-width	Describes the width of border in pixels (px), inches (in), or centimeters (cm).	border-width: 3px
color	Defines the foreground color of the element.	color:red
font-family	Sets the font of the element to the first font in the list that is found on the browser's system.	font-family:'Arial', 'Times New Roman'
font-size	Determines the size of the font in points.	font-size: 20pt
height	Defines the minimum height of the element in inches(in), centimeters(cm), or pixels (px).	height: 2in
width	Defines the minimum width of the element in percent (%), inches (in), centimeters (cm), or pixels (px).	width:2%
left	Determines where the element is placed horizontally.	left:2.5cm
top	Determines where the element is placed vertically.	top: 4in
position	Makes the element positionable. Legal values are absolute and relative.	position:absolute

KEY PROPERTIES AND METHODS OF THE DATE OBJECT

Member	Description	Example
new Date()	Creates a Date object based on the current date and time.	var myDate = new Date();
new Date(integer)	Creates a new Date object based on the integer passed.	var myDate = new Date(intValue);
getTime()	Returns the number of milliseconds since midnight GMT, as an integer.	var myInt = myDate.getTime;
getDate()	Returns the day of the month.	alert(myDate.getDate());
getMonth()	Returns the month.	alert ("today is the " + myDate.getDate() + " of " + myDate.getMonth());
getYear()	Returns the year that corresponds with this Date object.	alert(myDate.getYear());
getHours()	Returns the hour of the day.	alert(myDate.getHours());
GetMinutes()	Returns the minutes.	alert(myDate.getMinutes());
getSeconds()	Returns the seconds.	alert(myDate.getMinutes());
toString()	Returns the entire date as a string value.	alert(myDate.toString());

USEFUL METHODS AND PROPERTIES OF THE MATH OBJECT

Method	Description	Example	Result
abs()	Calculates the absolute value.	Math.abs(-3)	3
ceil()	Returns the next higher integer.	Math.ceil(3.5)	4
cos()	Returns the cosine of an angle (in radians).	cos(Math.PI/2)	0
floor()	Returns the lower integer.	Math.ceil(3.5)	3
max()	Returns the larger of two values.	Math.max(3,5)	5
min()	Returns the smaller of two values.	Math.min(3,5)	3
pow()	Returns the first number raised to power.	Math.pow(2,3)	8
random()	Returns a random value between 0 and 1.	Math.random()	0.348557233 (the result varies)
round()	Rounds to the nearest integer.	Math.round(3.2)	3
sin()	Returns the sin of an angle (in radians).	Math.sin (Math.PI/2)	1
sqrt()	Returns the square root of a number.	Math.sqrt(16)	4
tan()	Returns the tangent of an angle (in radians).	Math.tan (Math.PI/4)	1

GameLib Reference

KEY PROPERTIES OF THE SPRITE OBJECT IN GAMELIB

Property	Description	Example
on (read-only)	Describes whether the sprite is visible.	`if (mySprite.on){` `//do something }`
x, y, height, width (read-only)	Describes the current size and position of the sprite.	`if (mySprite.x < 0)` `{ mySprite.x = 0; }`
Bounces (read-write)	Determines behavior when the sprite reaches defined limits; if true, the sprite bounces off the border.	`mySprite.bounces = true;`
Xdir, ydir (read-only)	Determines the speed of the sprite in x and y directions.	`if (mySprite.xdir == 0)` `{ alert ("not going` `sideways!"); }`
Xydegs (read-only)	Shows the direction that the sprite is moving in degrees.	`if (mySprite.xydegs ==` `0){ alert ("going` `north!"); } // end if`
Speed (read-only)	Shows the speed of the sprite.	`alert (mySprite.speed);`
Collides (read-write)	Determines whether the sprite registers collisions.	`mySprite.collides =` `true;`

GAMELIB KEYBOARD HANDLER COMMANDS

Command	Description	Example
.pressed (read-only)	Returns true if the user is currently pressing the key.	`if (myKey.pressed)` `{ alert("A"); }` `// end if`
Kb_trapkey(keyName)	Sets up a new key object that responds when the user presses *keyName*.	`myKey = Kb_trapKey` `("a");`
Kb_lastkey	Contains a reference to the last key pressed.	`if (Kb_lastkey ==` `myKey){ alert("A"); }` `// end if`

PRINCIPAL METHODS OF THE SPRITE OBJECT IN GAMELIB

Method	Description	Example
HasHit(object)	Determines whether one sprite has collided with another.	if (car.hasHit (barrier)){ alert ("crash!"); }
MoveTo(x,y)	Moves the sprite directly to the given x,y coordinates.	mySprite.moveTo (100, 50);
SetDir(x,y)	Determines how many pixels in x and y dimensions that the sprite will move at each interval.	mySprite.setDir(1,3); //moves sprite 1 to left, 3 down
SetXYdegs(direc)	Sets the direction of the sprite in degrees.	mySprite.setXYdegs(45); //moves sprite northeast
SetSpeed(speed)	Determines how many pixels the sprite will move at each interval.	mySprite.setSpeed(3);
SetImage(image, width, height, frames, anims)	Determines the image of a sprite; see below for details.	mySprite.setImage ("car.gif", 20, 20, 1, 1);
SetFrame(number)	Sets a particular frame of the image.	mySprite.setFrame(2);
SwitchOn(), switchOff()	Turns the sprite on or off, controlling its visibility.	mySprite.switchOn();
SetXlimits(min, max), setYlimits(min, max)	Determines where the sprite can be placed or moved on the screen.	mySprite.setXlimits (0,300); //sprite's x will stay between zero and 300

COMMONLY USED METHODS OF THE GAMELIB SOUND OBJECT

Method	Description	Example
Sd_add_sound (fileName)	Generates a new sound object based on fileName, which is a .wav or .midi file.	var mySound = Sd_add_sound("bang. wav");
.play()	Plays the sound.	mySound.play();
.stop()	Stops playing the sound.	mySound.stop();

COMMON METHODS OF THE GAMELIB LAYER OBJECT

Method	Description	Example
`new Gl_layer(x, y, width, startingHTML)`	Creates a new layer at (x, y) that is `width` pixels wide and contains the `startingHTML` as its body.	`var myLayer = new Gl_layer (0, 0, 100, "<H1>Hi there!</H1>");`
`.load (filename, type)`	Loads the specified file into the layer. If `type` is set to true, the file will be always be loaded from the server.	`myLayer.load ("instructions.html", true);`
`.moveTo(x, y)`	Moves the layer's top-left corner to the specified pixels.	`myLayer.moveTo (100, 200);`
`.resizeTo(x, y)`	Resizes the layer to the specified size.	`myLayer.resizeTo (50, 50);`
`.setXlimits(a, b), setYlimits(a, b)`	Sets the boundaries for the layer. This method works as it does in the sprite library.	`myLayer.setXlimits (0, 500); myLayer. setYlimits(0, 300);`
`.write(newHTML)`	Replaces the content of the layer with `newHTML`.	`myLayer.write("<h3>Whoo Hoo!</h3>");`
`.setBgcolor(color)`	Sets the layer's background to a specified color.	`myLayer.setBgcolor ("red");`
`.show()`	Makes the layer visible.	`myLayer.show();`

PRIMARY MEMBERS OF THE GAMELIB MOUSE OBJECT

Member	Description	Example
`Ms_initmouse();`	Creates a reference to the mouse object.	`var myMouse = Ms_initmouse();`
`.x, .y`	Specifies the current x and y coordinates of the mouse.	`alert(myMouse.x + ", " myMouse.y);`
`.mousedown`	Returns whether the user is currently clicking the mouse button.	`if(myMouse.mousedown){`
`alert("ouch!"); } // end if .over`	Returns the `sprite` object that the mouse is currently over.	`if (myMouse.over == ball) { score++; } // end if`

GAMELIB SPRITE ANIMATION COMMANDS

Command	Description	Example
`.setImage(img, x, y, frames, cells)`	Describes the number of animation cells in a specified frame.	`mySprite.setImage ("car.gif", 10, 10, 2, 4); //2 frames, 4 animation cells each.`
`.setAnimation(cell)`	Sets the animation to a specified cell.	`mySprite. setAnimation(2);`
`.setAnimationLoop (min, max)`	Sets up the animation to display cells between min and max.	`mySprite. setAnimationRange(1,3); //animate but skip the 0th image.`
`.setAnimationRepeat (times)`	Determines how many times to repeat the animation (–1 specifies an indefinite number of repeats).	`mySprite. setAnimationRepeat(4); //do the animation 4 times, then stop`
`.setAnimationSpeed (speed, dir)`	Determines the speed and direction in which to run the animation. speed determines how many cycles to hold each cell. *dir* can be "back" or "forward".	`mySprite. setAnimationSpeed(20, "forward"); //change the cell animation once per second.`

FOLLOWING AND TARGETING COMMANDS OF THE GAMELIB SPRITE OBJECT

Command	Description	Example
`.follow(ob, x, y)`	Causes the sprite to follow ob (a sprite or the mouse object) at a distance of (x, y) pixels.	`mySprite.follow (theMouse, 0, 10);`
`.target(ob, x, y)`	Causes the sprite to move toward ob at the current speed, aiming toward an offset of (x, y) pixels from ob.	`mySprite.target (theMouse, 0, 10);`
`.stopFollowing(ob)`	Tells the sprite to stop following ob.	`mySprite.stopFollowing (theMouse);`
`.stopTargeting(ob)`	Tells the sprite to stop targeting ob.	`mySprite.stopTargeting (theMouse)`

DRAGGABLE ELEMENTS IN GAMELIB

Object and Member	Description	Example
sprite.draggable	If set to true, enables the user to drag and drop the sprite.	mySprite.draggable = true;
layer.draggable	If set to true, enables the user to drag and drop the layer.	myLayer.draggable = true;

MOUSE EVENT HANDLERS OF THE GAMELIB SPRITE AND LAYER OBJECTS

Property	Description	Example
.onclickdown	Binds a function to call when the user presses the mouse button while the cursor is over the element.	mySprite.onclickdown = "click()";
.onclickup	Binds a function to call when the user releases the mouse button while the cursor is over the element.	mySprite.onclickup = "released()";
.onmouseover	Binds a function to call when the mouse cursor is over an element (regardless of button status).	mySprite.onmouseover = "over()";
.onmouseout	Binds a function to call when the mouse cursor leaves an element (regardless of button status).	mySprite.onmouseout = "out()";

These are properties of both the sprite and the layer objects. All are read and write properties. They work just like the event handlers in traditional HTML/DHTML.

GAMELIB COOKIE HANDLING COMMANDS

Command	Description	Example
new Gl_cookie (cookieName)	Creates a new cookie object with cookieName as its name.	var myCookie = new Gl_cookie("test");
.setValue(value)	Sets the cookie's value to value.	myCookie.setValue ("Hi");
.value	Returns the cookie's value.	alert(myCookie.value);

Index

GAME DEVELOPMENT.
IT'S SERIOUS BUSINESS.

License Agreement/Notice of Limited Warranty

By opening the sealed disc container in this book, you agree to the following terms and conditions. If, upon reading the following license agreement and notice of limited warranty, you cannot agree to the terms and conditions set forth, return the unused book with unopened disc to the place where you purchased it for a refund.

License:

The enclosed software is copyrighted by the copyright holder(s) indicated on the software disc. You are licensed to copy the software onto a single computer for use by a single user and to a backup disc. You may not reproduce, make copies, or distribute copies or rent or lease the software in whole or in part, except with written permission of the copyright holder(s). You may transfer the enclosed disc only together with this license, and only if you destroy all other copies of the software and the transferee agrees to the terms of the license. You may not decompile, reverse assemble, or reverse engineer the software.

Notice of Limited Warranty:

The enclosed disc is warranted by Prima Publishing to be free of physical defects in materials and workmanship for a period of sixty (60) days from end user's purchase of the book/disc combination. During the sixty-day term of the limited warranty, Prima will provide a replacement disc upon the return of a defective disc.

Limited Liability:

THE SOLE REMEDY FOR BREACH OF THIS LIMITED WARRANTY SHALL CONSIST ENTIRELY OF REPLACEMENT OF THE DEFECTIVE DISC. IN NO EVENT SHALL PRIMA OR THE AUTHORS BE LIABLE FOR ANY OTHER DAMAGES, INCLUDING LOSS OR CORRUPTION OF DATA, CHANGES IN THE FUNCTIONAL CHARACTERISTICS OF THE HARDWARE OR OPERATING SYSTEM, DELETERIOUS INTERACTION WITH OTHER SOFTWARE, OR ANY OTHER SPECIAL, INCIDENTAL, OR CONSEQUENTIAL DAMAGES THAT MAY ARISE, EVEN IF PRIMA AND/OR THE AUTHORS HAVE PREVIOUSLY BEEN NOTIFIED THAT THE POSSIBILITY OF SUCH DAMAGES EXISTS.

Disclaimer of Warranties:

PRIMA AND THE AUTHORS SPECIFICALLY DISCLAIM ANY AND ALL OTHER WARRANTIES, EITHER EXPRESS OR IMPLIED, INCLUDING WARRANTIES OF MERCHANTABILITY, SUITABILITY TO A PARTICULAR TASK OR PURPOSE, OR FREEDOM FROM ERRORS. SOME STATES DO NOT ALLOW FOR EXCLUSION OF IMPLIED WARRANTIES OR LIMITATION OF INCIDENTAL OR CONSEQUENTIAL DAMAGES, SO THESE LIMITATIONS MIGHT NOT APPLY TO YOU.

Other:

This Agreement is governed by the laws of the State of California without regard to choice of law principles. The United Convention of Contracts for the International Sale of Goods is specifically disclaimed. This Agreement constitutes the entire agreement between you and Prima Publishing regarding use of the software.